TIME
STOOD
STILL

A Survivor's
Perspective

TIME
STOOD
STILL

A Survivor's
Perspective

By Chad Taylor

TIME STOOD STILL
A Survivor's Perspective

Copyright © 2024 by Chad Taylor
Cover design by Chad Taylor, Copyright © 2024 Chad Taylor
This book is registered with the Library of Congress
Published by Rustic Trail Productions LLC
ISBN: 979-8-2276699-6-4

Mailing address and fan mail:
Rustic Trail Productions LLC
1030 E Hwy 377
Suite 110, #352
Granbury, TX 76048

All rights reserved. Except as permitted by the U.S. Copyright Act of 1976, no portion of this book including the front cover, spine, back cover or interior may be duplicated or reproduced in any form, by mechanical or electronic means, including scanning, photocopy, photograph, screenshot, recording or by any other means, nor can any portion of this book be stored in any type of retrieval system, or transmitted in any form, without the prior written permission of the publisher.

Scripture quotations marked (NIV) are taken from the Holy Bible, New International Version®, NIV®. Copyright © 1973, 1978, 1984, 2011 by Biblica, Inc.™ Used by permission of Zondervan. All rights reserved worldwide. www.zondervan.com The "NIV" and "New International Version" are trademarks registered in the United States Patent and Trademark Office by Biblica, Inc.™

Scripture quotations marked (ESV) are from the ESV® Bible (The Holy Bible, English Standard Version®), copyright © 2001 by Crossway, a publishing ministry of Good News Publishers. Used by permission. All rights reserved.

Scripture quotations marked (NLT) are taken from the Holy Bible, New Living Translation, copyright ©1996, 2004, 2007, 2013, 2015 by Tyndale House Foundation. Used by permission of Tyndale House Publishers, Inc., Carol Stream, Illinois 60188. All rights reserved.

Scripture quotations taken from the Amplified® Bible (AMPC), Copyright © 1954, 1958, 1962, 1964, 1965, 1987 by The Lockman Foundation Used by permission. lockman.org

Scripture quotations from the COMMON ENGLISH BIBLE. © Copyright 2011 COMMON ENGLISH BIBLE. All rights reserved. Used by permission. (www.CommonEnglishBible.com).

The author and publisher assume no responsibility for the use or misuse of the information contained in this book. By opening this book you agree to hold harmless the author, publisher and anyone else associated with this book in any way, including licensors and their respective employees, or any third party content providers. You agree that anyone associated with this book in any way is not liable under any circumstance for any potential outcomes from the content of this book, including any potential results from suggestions, thoughts, pointers, tips or anything else that may be contained, suggested or implied in this book.

Every effort was made in assembling this book to ensure there has been no infringement of the intellectual property of others. If there has been any accidental issue, please email info@rustictrailproductions.com to resolve any potential issue. Many of the bullet point statistics throughout this book are direct quotes or are paraphrased from direct quotes from other sources. Please visit the reference address in the back of the book correlating to each citation number to see the original source for more information.

A special thanks to Dan Brannan for the three outstanding interior drawings.
He does excellent artwork and can be reached at: danbrannan@protonmail.com

DISCLAIMER

The reader should always consult his or her healthcare provider to determine the appropriateness of the information for his or her own situation or if he or she has any questions regarding a medical condition or treatment plan. Reading the information in this book does not constitute a physician-patient relationship. The author and publisher expressly disclaim responsibility for any adverse effects that may result from the use or application of the information contained in this book.

The information provided by Chad Taylor and Rustic Trail Productions ("we," "us," or "our") is for general informational purposes only. All information in this book is provided in good faith, however we make no representation or warranty of any kind, express or implied, regarding the accuracy, adequacy, validity, reliability, availability, or completeness of any information in this book. UNDER NO CIRCUMSTANCE SHALL WE HAVE ANY LIABILITY TO YOU FOR ANY LOSS OR DAMAGE OF ANY KIND INCURRED AS A RESULT OF THE USE OF THIS BOOK OR RELIANCE ON ANY INFORMATION PROVIDED IN THIS BOOK. YOUR USE OF THIS BOOK AND YOUR RELIANCE ON ANY INFORMATION IN THIS BOOK IS SOLELY AT YOUR OWN RISK.

This book may contain links and URL addresses to websites or content belonging to or originating from third parties or links to websites and features in banners or other advertising. Such external links and URL addresses are not investigated, monitored, or checked for accuracy, adequacy, validity, reliability, availability, or completeness by us. WE DO NOT WARRANT, ENDORSE, GUARANTEE, OR ASSUME RESPONSIBILITY FOR THE ACCURACY OR RELIABILITY OF ANY INFORMATION OFFERED BY THIRD-PARTY WEBSITES REFERENCED IN THIS BOOK. WE WILL NOT BE A PARTY TO OR IN ANY WAY BE RESPONSIBLE FOR MONITORING ANY TRANSACTION BETWEEN YOU AND THIRD-PARTY PROVIDERS OF PRODUCTS OR SERVICES. WE DO NOT GUARANTEE ANY URL ADDRESSES REFERENCED IN THIS BOOK WILL REMAIN ACTIVE. EVERY EFFORT HAS BEEN MADE TO REFERENCE INFORMATION AND WEBSITES THE INFORMATION WAS FOUND. SOME OF THE WEB ADDRESSES MAY NOT BE AVAILABLE OVER TIME DUE TO THEM BEING THIRD PARTY WEBSITES.

This book cannot and does not contain medical/health advice. Any and all medical/health information is provided for general informational and educational purposes only and is not a substitute for professional advice. Accordingly, before taking any actions based upon such information, we encourage you to consult with the appropriate professionals. We do not provide any kind of medical/health advice. THE USE OR RELIANCE OF ANY INFORMATION CONTAINED IN THIS BOOK IS SOLELY AT YOUR OWN RISK.

This book may contain links to affiliate websites, and we receive an affiliate commission for any purchases made by you on the affiliate website using such links. We are a participant in the Amazon Services LLC Associates Program, an affiliate advertising program designed to provide a means for us to earn advertising fees by linking to Amazon.com and affiliated websites.

Some names contained in this book have been changed to protect anonymity.

Emergency Suicide Number, call or text 988

**National Suicide Prevention Hotline
1-800-273-8255**

TIME STOOD STILL
A Survivor's Perspective
(The Audio Book)

Copyright © 2024 by Chad Taylor
Published by Rustic Trail Productions LLC
ISBN: 978-0-9993221-6-1

(All legal disclaimers and references still extend and apply from this physical book to the audio book).

Audio Book

Scan this QR code to listen to the audio book.
Or visit **chadtaylor.com/tstaudiobook**

For additional copies of this book,
or to see other work by Chad Taylor,
please visit **chadtaylor.com** or scan this QR Code:

CHADTAYLOR.COM

chadtaylor.com

WHAT OTHERS ARE SAYING:

"...While this might be a hard topic to read about, it will hit home for so many. Whether the struggle resonates close to your heart (as it does with me) or you know someone struggling, find courage and read this book. I will also say if you are a parent, read this book. I firmly believe it will bring healing and hope to you as it has done for me. You will be forever changed."

"...This is a must read for anyone who may be having suicidal thoughts, for anyone who[has] been affected by the suicide of a loved one and most importantly for parents. The parenting strategies gave me a lot to think about in terms of how I raise my own children. Wonderful Read!!"

"...During the time it took me to read this eye opening book, two families I know were utterly devastated by suicide. Chad is sounding the alarm bell and opening the door to conversations that need to be had with our kids, friends and family members. The stats and information presented in this book with teens is beyond alarming- it's a MUST READ for parents today! We cannot remain silent on this topic anymore.......lives are at stake..."

I am grateful you're reading this. From the bottom of my heart I believe there's something valuable for everyone in this book, and at this moment, *I'm talking about you.* My encouragement for you is to finish this book. Too many people give up, right before they're about to receive the good, meaningful gifts in life. I firmly believe there's at least one important message for you in this book. Be like the tortoise, and just...keep...going.

There are QR codes and web addresses in this book for ease of seeing references, etc. At the time of writing this, all of the QR codes and web addresses are active, however at any time they may not work as I have no control over 3rd party websites, including their content.

I am not a doctor, psychiatrist or counselor. This book is for informational purposes only. What you are about to read is my perspective and my understanding. Even though I believe this book will be very beneficial for many people, I have no liability for what you or others do with this information.

- Chad Taylor

This book is dedicated to those who've found themselves somewhere they never imagined, and still CHOOSE to be an overcomer and a warrior. My hope is that this book brings insight, comfort, and clarity to you.

Chad Taylor

Table of Contents:

                                                                                                 Page

Audio Book 𝄞 (Scan QR Code) 6
Introduction 13

Chapter 1: <u>A Difficult Subject</u> 15
        If you, then 16
        The Beginning 17
        Statistics 18
        Taboo? 20

Chapter 2: <u>Testimonies</u> 22
        The Golden Gate 22
        My Friend Dennis 25
        A Sunny Awakening 27
        As a Weapon 29
        A December Day 30
        Two Important Tips 55

Chapter 3: <u>Kids</u> 58
        Acceptance 59
        The Fad 64
        Devices 66
        Bullying 72
        Cyber Bullying 80
        The Younger Me 82
        Used for Good 89
        The Outlet 91

Chapter 4: <u>Life Happens</u> 92
        The Blue Bird 92
        Depression 95
        Finances 97
        Isolation 101
        Veterans 105
        To Hurt and Manipulate 109

Page

Chapter 5: <u>Drugs, Alcohol and Mental Illness</u> ... 112

Chapter 6: <u>Warfare and Temptation</u> 134
- The Snow Man 135
- Spirit/Heart 143
- Broken 146
- The Boxer 156
- The Visitation 162
- Lowered Defenses 168
- A Breach in the Hedge 170
- The Foothold 175
- Planting Seeds 177
- The Moment of Clarity 179

Chapter 7: <u>Getting Personal</u> 182

Chapter 8: <u>What now?</u> 223
- Someday 223
- Forgiveness 224
- Temptation, Shame and Guilt 231
- Grief 233
- The First 1000 Days 239
- Hope and keep on Hoping 251
- Face your Fears 255
- A Common Question 258

In Conclusion 265
More Resources 265
What you can do to help 268
References 269
About The Author 275

Introduction:

It has been 1394 days since the worst day of my life. That's 199 weeks or about 2 million minutes, yet parts of it feel like yesterday. How can I write this book about a subject I really don't want to talk or even think about? How can I take the time to reach in and bring out the pain and memories I just want to forget? I believe I am supposed to. I believe this book is very important and will help those who've gone through the unimaginable pain of losing a loved one so unexpectedly. I also believe this will help those who are struggling with strong temptations.

Over the years, I've been blessed with peace and insights into this dark and misunderstood topic. Who else would God have share a subject, but someone with experience in that subject? I believe what you will find in this book is rarely discussed and will be very helpful insight, bringing peace and understanding to those searching for it.

I want those who have experienced a devastating loss by suicide to know, you are not alone. Even though you may feel like you are screaming in silence, many others, including myself, know the inexpressible pain and tremendous pressure you feel. By the end of this book, I believe sadness and despair will be replaced by something even more powerful....*hope*.

I was the speaker at my Wife's memorial service, and one thing I shared with everyone in attendance was this:

> Godly sadness produces a changed heart and life that leads to salvation and leaves no regrets, but sorrow under the influence of the world produces death.
>
> -2 Corinthians 7:10 (CEB)

Good can truly come from unimaginable pain and torment. What you're going through right now can be used for good and can be used to bring peace, but you have to believe that and choose it. Are you ready to come out of the place you may be in right now? It is possible to be an overcomer. Some people have no intention of getting better and have a morbid enjoyment of the attention they get, while others truly want to drastically improve. Not only for themselves, but for those that depend on them. I know which kind of person I am, which one are you?

I have been on both sides of suicide. I've experienced both the temptations of suicide as well as the unimaginable pain of a sudden loss by suicide. What you are about to read is a survivor's perspective and a survivor's testimony.

> "Heavenly Father, I pray in Jesus' name that those you want to impact with this book will continue all the way through it and receive whatever it is you want them to, and that nothing and no one will stop them from receiving it, amen."
>
> *-Chad*

Chapter 1: A Difficult Subject

The sound woke me. The familiar sound I've heard countless times, but never like this. As I jump and run....terror, panic and helplessness fill and begin to consume me. On an average morning of an average day, four lives are changed forever.

More on this later...

People who commit suicide do so because they're sad. Keep them from being sad and suicide would end....right? Well, many people believe that. Many people believe suicide is black and white and some people just hit a tough point in life and decide to check out. I'm here to tell you, for the most part, this couldn't be further from the truth.

In reality, suicide is like a three dimensional fog filled with torment, confusion, grief, regret, ups and downs. It's a dark, murky and very misunderstood subject that millions of people from all walks of life find themselves in every year. In my opinion, suicide is understood so little that most people just avoid talking about it altogether. It's like having a huge elephant in the room that few people ever talk about, or even look at.

I'm not exaggerating when I say that everyone I've talked to about this topic has known someone that died from suicide. As they shared their experiences with me, I could hear it in their voice...the unanswered questions and the pain that persists. It seems like each of them has a longing in their words, a desire for understanding and a pain that sits there, waiting to be healed.

I recently heard a testimony from a veteran in his eighties. Even though it happened many years prior, he broke down when sharing his story about losing his daughter to suicide. It may have been a long time ago for most people, but for him...it's like being frozen in time. The unanswered questions and hurt are still there. The questions and pain may be less noticeable at times, but for most people that have lost someone to suicide, they usually remain for the rest of their lives, unless insight and healing take place.

If you, then...

If you have the courage to continue through this entire book, then I believe you will begin to receive answers and healing. I believe warm rays of peace will bring clarity and begin to drive the foggy haze away. I believe light can flood the dark and good really can come out of such turmoil.

If you continue on, what you read may challenge you. It may poke hurtful areas. It may cause you to think differently. But what if you don't have the courage to continue on? That's easy, you can stay where you're at. Indecision is a decision and choosing not to choose is your choice to make.

The Beginning

I'm sure I'd heard the word before, but my oldest memory of suicide was from the first week of 8th grade in our small Montana town. I was 13 at the time. Like many kids that age, I lacked confidence, was quiet and a bit timid around so many new kids.

If I went back to that school, I could point out exactly which room I was in, one particular day. After all of us students were at our desks and class had started, two men I'd never seen before entered the room. One of them was there to introduce the other. After a short introduction, the man who was there to speak took center stage. I'm guessing he was in his mid 20's, but when you're 13, he might as well been middle aged. He was there to talk about suicide, and opened with this;

"Look at the kid to your left, now look at the kid to your right, one of the three of you is going to contemplate suicide."

I'm sure the man had good intentions, but you know what? Before he ever set foot in that school, I don't recall EVER thinking about suicide. Yet, after he finished his talk that morning, I looked around at my fellow classmates, and with an undue sense of shame, wondered...

"Am I *the one*? Out of the three of us is it going to be me?"

Seeds were planted that day and whether he meant to or not, they were not all good seeds. I had a strange sense of shame. Like I'd been found out for doing something wrong, even though I'd never even thought about suicide.

Oh, I wonder if my life would've gone differently had I missed school that day. Would blissful ignorance have graced me through High School? Could I have skipped the torment of seeing a knife at my wrist through drunken, tear-filled teenage eyes?

I'll discuss this more as we go, but in my late teens/early twenties I made a decision. *I chose to change.* I chose to never let anyone treat me the way I'd allowed a particular person to treat me. I also chose to use my earlier struggles with suicide to make me better, push me harder and help me accomplish more than I otherwise would have been able to.

More about this later...

Statistics

Now, let's look at some statistics about suicide. Remember, these numbers are sons and daughters. They're husbands, wives, fathers and mothers. They're our friends and loved ones.

> Listed below are the most recent suicide statistics for *The United States* at the time of writing this.

- 45,979 people died by suicide in 2020. That averages to 125 people per day, or roughly one person every eleven minutes.[2]

- 1.2 Million Adults attempted suicide in 2020.[3]

- 629,000 adolescents (12-17 years old) attempted suicide in 2020.[2]

- 12.2 Million Adults seriously thought about suicide in 2020.[3]

- 3.0 Million Youths aged 12 to 17 had serious thoughts of suicide, made suicide plans, or attempted suicide.[4]

- For every suicide death, there were 27 self reported suicide attempts.[3]

- Firearms are the #1 method used by men AND women, and are used in more than 50% of suicides.[3 & 27]

- Suicide is the 2nd leading cause of death for 1-44 year olds, (after accidents)[1] and the 3rd leading cause of death for 15-24 year olds, (after accidents and homicides).[2]

- Suicide is the 12th leading cause of death overall in the U.S.[2]

- There were 3.9 male deaths by suicide for each female death by suicide, however, 3 females attempted suicide for every 1 suicide attempt by a male.[2]

- There was a suicide attempt every 27.5 seconds in 2020.[2]

- 581 10-14 year olds committed suicide in 2020.[2]
  That is 11 young children per week!

- Approximately 40-50% of the population will know someone in their lifetime who died from suicide.[2]

- For every suicide, more than 6 people close to them are estimated to experience devastating effects and major life disruptions.[2] This means that at least 750 people *every day* in this country experience what my kids and I have and what some of you reading this have.

> Listed below are the most recent suicide statistics for *The Entire World* at the time of writing this.

- Roughly 800,000 people die every year from suicide. That's one person every 40 seconds.[5]

- Suicide is one of the leading causes of death in young people.[5]

- 1.4% of all deaths in 2017 were from suicide.[5]

- Suicide rates are typically higher for older individuals.[5]

Taboo?

In my opinion, suicide is treated similar to sex and drugs.
It can be uncomfortable to discuss, so most people don't.

*'That's something other people deal with,
not me or my_____.'*

Fill in the blank with whoever you want, brother, mother, wife, friend, etc. In general, we tend to have a mindset that bad things can't happen to us, and those close to us. Like somehow, we and our loved ones are the exception and by avoiding difficult subjects, things will just go away. Well, what happens to cancer if we ignore it? What about ignoring weeds in a garden or rodents in our house? Does the problem get better or worse by looking the other way?

There's a term called *normalcy bias,* and I believe it applies to suicidal warning signs of ourselves and our loved ones. In a nutshell, the normalcy bias is the mindset that *because it hasn't happened, it can't happen.*

In high stress, potentially life or death situations, many people act as though things are 'normal,' like a potential catastrophe isn't really happening. Imagine a deer in the headlights, staring blankly at the car that's about to hit him. The deer has probably stood on roads countless times with no issues, but this time if he does nothing, he will die. He does not understand that inaction in this moment will get him, (or the deer with him) killed.

Am I implying that we are often like deer in the headlights and choose to pretend everything is 'normal' instead of acknowledging looming peril? Why yes I am! If history shows us anything, it's that most people don't learn from history. The *'this is normal'* mindset gets people hurt or killed in many ways: natural disasters, illness, violent attackers, accidents, emergencies, weather, bad relationships, etc.

Chapter 1: A Difficult Subject

Let's stop treating suicide like it's strange and taboo. It's one of the leading causes of death, so why avoid it? If 125 people died from bear attacks every day in the U.S., would we ignore signs of a bear being in our house or the houses of our loved ones? Of course not. With the state of the World today and the direction it appears to be going, can we assume more or less people are going to be subject to suicide? LET'S TALK ABOUT IT!

Earlier, I mentioned bad seeds being planted when I was in junior high. Like most major topics, I believe there's a right time and place to discuss suicide, *especially with kids.* I was not ready to have this subject pushed on me at 13. If you're seeking insight into suicide, then now's the right time for you to be reading this book. You're likely wanting understanding and peace for yourself and/or a loved one.

Let's bring suicide into the light. Things look scarier in the dark where they're hard to comprehend. Suicide may seem like a scary boogeyman lurking in the closet, but let's turn on the lights, open the door and find out.

Chapter 2: Testimonies

If we look back at the U.S. statistics from earlier, we see that nearly two million people, (ages 12 and up) attempted suicide in 2020, yet "only" 45,979 people actually died from suicide. I put the word ONLY in quotes, because even one person dying from suicide is terrible, let alone tens of thousands.

    45,979 out of 1,829,000 means that roughly 2.5% of the people 12 years old and up that attempted suicide in 2020, actually died. To me, these numbers give us clarity into most people's suicide attempts. In my opinion, these numbers mean that the vast majority of people that attempt suicide, don't actually want to die...*or they would.*

The Golden Gate

In 2006, a documentary came out called *The Bridge*. At the time of writing this, it's available to watch on Amazon. A crew of about a dozen people filmed The Golden Gate Bridge for an entire year. Their purpose was two-fold. They wanted to see how many people they could film committing suicide by jumping off the bridge, as well as try to prevent whoever they could from jumping.

They ended up with roughly 10,000 hours of footage and were able to record 23 of the 24 known 'Jumpers' that year.[9] The crew was able to stop six people from jumping during their time filming. They also captured people being talked off the ledge as well as one person being forcibly pulled off by a passerby. At the time they filmed the documentary, The Golden Gate Bridge was the suicide capital of the world. Approximately 1200 people had already jumped off it since it was opened in May of 1937.[9]

Falling the 245 feet from the bridge yields a 95% chance of death from the roughly 75mph impact with the water. Of the 5% that survive the impact, most of them drown or die from hypothermia.[12] The Golden Gate Bridge has since only been topped in suicide deaths by the Nanjing Yangtze River Bridge in China.[9]

One of the people in the documentary is a man named Kevin Hines. In 2000, at the age of 19, he jumped off The Golden Gate Bridge. He's one of the rare people that survived the jump and lived to talk about it.

> "The second my hands left the bar, (the railing), I said, 'I don't want to die! What am I going to do? This is it, I am dead.'"
>
> - Kevin Hines
> From the documentary; *The Bridge*

This was from the same young man who went to the bridge that day hearing voices in his head telling him to jump. However, the moment he let go, he realized it was a huge mistake, but there was nothing he could do at that point. Even after Kevin miraculously survived the impact with the water, he had drowning and hypothermia to deal with. Amazingly, a seal came along and kept him afloat until the coast guard rescued him.

"It was a seal circling me and apparently it was the only thing keeping me afloat, and you cannot tell me that wasn't God, because that's what I believe and that's what I'll believe 'til the day I die."

- Kevin Hines
From the documentary; *The Bridge*

Kevin has since gone on to speak across the country about suicide prevention. He has spoken at schools, colleges and even major TV networks. He urges people contemplating suicide to get help and hopes they realize suicide is not the answer.

Here's a quote from another rare Golden Gate Bridge survivor:

"I instantly realized that everything in my life that I'd thought was unfixable was totally fixable—except for having just jumped."[9]

- Ken Baldwin

The fall from the bridge takes a person about four seconds to hit the water, with the force of a speeding truck meeting a concrete building.[9] Can you imagine the amount of people who've spent those four long seconds feeling the same intense regret as Kevin and Ken? How many of the jumpers immediately regretted their decision, the moment it was too late for them to change it? For some, I'd imagine those seconds felt like an eternity of torture they could not turn back from. Later in this book I'll share another factor of this regret called *the moment of clarity*.

Eric Steel was inspired to make *The Bridge* after reading a 2003 New Yorker article entitled *Jumpers*.

Here's a quote from that article;

"Dr. Seiden's study, "Where Are They Now?," published in 1978, followed up on five hundred and fifteen people who were prevented from attempting suicide at the bridge between 1937 and 1971.

After, on average, more than twenty-six years, ninety-four per cent of the would-be suicides were either still alive or had died of natural causes. "The findings confirm previous observations that suicidal behavior is crisis-oriented and acute in nature," Seiden concluded; if you can get a suicidal person through his crisis—Seiden put the high-risk period at ninety days—chances are extremely good that he won't kill himself later."[6]

- From the 2003 New Yorker article, *Jumpers*

My Friend Dennis

I have a good friend named Dennis. He had a very interesting marriage. In the 20 years he was married to his first wife Caroline, she tried to commit suicide repeatedly! When he told me that years ago, I was very surprised, as I'd never heard of anything like that before.

He said it originally started in 1969 when he was just 19 years old. He was about to be sent off to fight in the Vietnam war when he got the first red flag. She gave him an ultimatum, "Either marry me before you leave, or I'll not be alive when you get back." At the time he figured, 'What the heck, I probably won't survive the war anyway.' So before boarding a plane, bound for Vietnam, he married her.

But guess what, after many close calls and even being blown up, he survived the war and came back to her. They ended up having kids together and then he started to see more red flags. She was diagnosed with being manic and bipolar, and was put on medications. Caroline swung between highs and lows. Her medications seemed to even her out. Inevitably, that lead to her feeling 'cured,' so she stopped taking them and had huge swings, again.

The method of her first suicide attempt would rarely kill anyone. Dennis took it as a cry for attention. But over the years, every time she attempted suicide, they became more and more serious. Eventually she danced with death long enough and the game turned ...*deadly*.

Dennis came home early one day. After entering his house, he could hear the sound of a car running in the attached garage. In bewilderment, he opened the door to find the garage completely full of exhaust smoke, with his wife's car being the source. Frantically, he rushed and rolled up the garage door. As he did, a plume of smoke billowed out into the air. He ran around to the driver's door to find Caroline's lifeless body slumped over.

"I saw many dead bodies in Vietnam. I know what dead looks like, she was dead. The whites of her eyes were brown and there was no life in them."

He told me the emotion he felt in that moment, *anger*. Their youngest child, an 8 year old boy was usually the first one to arrive home, after being dropped off by a school bus. She wanted her young son to be the one that found her like that? Slumped over dead in her car from exhaust smoke and overdosing?

Dennis pulled her lifeless body out of the car and carried her out to the driveway. In his anger, he threw her onto the hood of his car..... then, the most amazing thing happened. After her impact with the car, she let out a gasp as smoke puffed from her mouth. She then began to breath. He went inside and called for an ambulance. After a short time, both ambulance and police arrived. After years of repeated suicide attempts, Dennis had enough. Knowing sooner or later she'd die for real, he told the police that he'd sign whatever needed signing. He wanted her committed to a place that could help her for as long as possible.

Caroline ended up making a full recovery at the hospital and was transported to an institution that specialized in dealing with mental issues. After she was released, Dennis took a stance like he never had before.

"If you ever kill yourself, I will make sure your tombstone reads, *'Here lies the most selfish woman that ever lived.'* Because that's what you are, selfish. You would take your problems and dump them onto the very people you say you care about most. You'd make them live out their days thinking it was their fault."

They got divorced shortly after that. During that process she asked him a simple question and gave a simple statement.

"Why didn't you talk to me like that before?
Maybe things wouldn't have gotten this bad."

It was at that moment Dennis realized the way he'd dealt with her all those years, was only enabling her to try harder. In hindsight, he wished he'd taken a stronger stance with her many years earlier. Eventually, he was willing to speak the hard truth that may have saved her life. Three decades later, she hasn't attempted suicide since.

> It's worth noting here that ultimatums have their place. Sometimes they're exactly what's needed, while other times an ultimatum is the last thing to do. My advice would be to pray about what words and tone to use (or not use), when dealing with major subjects like this.

A Sunny Awakening

Let me tell you about Steve and Linda. Steve was an abusive husband and had three young children with his wife Linda. Eventually, Linda had enough of Steve and his hurtful ways. She was in the process of divorcing him, when he called and asked her to swing by with the kids. Linda felt God telling her, 'Do not go to Steve with the kids.' Guess what she learned the next day...Steve was planning to kill all of them!

After they didn't show up, Steve followed through on the second part of his plan. He set the house on fire and killed himself. Her decision to listen saved the lives of her children and herself.

Fast forward many years...Linda took a vacation to Florida with her three kids, who had grown up. She also brought her mother along. Imagine that, three generations vacationing on a sunny Florida beach. What a great experience, except one of them had a secret. Linda's daughter Brittany had purposely overdosed on drugs to kill herself, while laying on the sand between her mother and grandmother.

You see, even after her father died, Brittany continued to have a troubled up-bringing. She was rough around the edges, didn't get along with many people and was generally unhappy. In Brittany's state of mind, she felt dying by her family members while on vacation was the solution. The thought of what her family would go through after noticing her dead didn't factor into her equation. *She was consumed with self.*

Brittany didn't die though. Instead, she wound up in a coma. As she lay between life and death on a hospital bed, her brother Terry decided to pick up the phone and call his step-brother, who was also a pastor.

A few thousand miles away in Washington, Terry's step-brother picked up the phone to a burst of frantic words. After hearing everything, Terry's step-brother prayed about what to do. He then instructed Terry to hold the phone to his comatose sister's ear. With a calm voice, these words were spoken into Brittany's ear from clear across the Country;

"God says; 'If you want to die, I will let you go. But I have something more for you. If you want out, I will let you out.'"

Some time later, Terry had this good report for his step brother;

"Well, it's amazing. After you said whatever you said into her ear, I put the phone away. Then a little while later, she came out of the coma a new person. She got her life together and became a productive person for the first time in her adult life."

His step brother said that in her coma, God spoke directly to her spirit and her spirit chose to live. After waking up, her spirit helped the rest of her stay in line and fulfill the life God wanted for her.

One take-away here (and I've heard other testimony of this); a person's spirit inside them likely doesn't sleep and is aware, even though the body is asleep.

More on this subject later...

As a Weapon

I have a good friend named Sarah, she shared a story with me about her teenage daughter Jenny. Mothers and daughters can often butt heads and their relationship was no exception. Despite Sarah's best efforts, Jenny had grown to be a rebellious and angry teenager. During one of their heated disagreements, Jenny told her mom that she would just kill herself. After some questioning, Sarah determined she may actually be serious. Years earlier they'd both lost a close loved one to suicide, and Sarah knew she had to do something.

Sarah made a very difficult decision. One phone call and a short time later, a police officer showed up and took her daughter to a crisis center. After her ride in the police car, Jenny was terrified to enter the building. She pleaded with her mother to have them let her go. Sarah was determined to help her struggling daughter and felt this was the only option.

Once inside, they stripped Jenny of her belongings, gave her a gown to put on and placed her in a padded room. After what seemed like hours, she was evaluated by doctors and put back in her room to wait.

After she was evaluated, Sarah got the call to come in and talk with the doctors. They informed her they believed Jenny did not want to harm herself, but was actually trying to harm her mother with her words. Deep down Jenny knew her mother loved her and saying she wanted to kill herself was a way to verbally hurt her as much as possible.

After being released from her short stay in the crisis center, Jenny swore to her mother she didn't mean those words, but was just angry. Since that unforgettable day, she has never said anything like that again. Jenny is now grown with children of her own.

A December Day
Losing Joy

I woke to the sound of a gun shot. Having grown up in Montana around guns and hunting, I knew exactly what I heard. It was the small sudden explosion of gunpowder igniting in a small brass case, inside of a cylindrical chamber, resulting in a copper coated piece of lead to travel quickly through, and out the barrel of a pistol...*and it came from inside my house!*

In Washington State in 2019, 1263 people died from suicide[13] ...my wife was one of them.

For those of you who've experienced something like this, I know...the sudden extreme and helpless panic. I know what it's like in that moment. The longing to jump back in time 30 seconds and prevent whatever just happened. When tunnel vision quickly sets in as your pulse races; *this can't be happening!*

It was around 6 a.m. on a Tuesday in December. Normally my wife Joy would be setting a hot cup of coffee on the headboard of our bed at any moment. This particular morning would be an extreme exception...I didn't calmly wake to the smell of coffee, or the gentle sound of ceramic touching wood. Instead, I exploded out of bed

Chapter 2: Testimonies

within a fraction of a second, completely terrified of what I feared just happened. The weeks leading up to that moment had been like a roller coaster ride, but I absolutely didn't see it ending with a gunshot. I truly believed we were just going through a rough patch and we'd come through it even stronger than before.

Joy and I had been together for nearly ten years at that point. It was almost Christmas and eleven days later would've been our 6th wedding anniversary. Right now, there's a very popular TV show called *Yellowstone*, starring Kevin Costner. The town Joy and I grew up in is near where it's filmed in Montana.

We originally met at a small gym there. We dated for about a year before we moved west to Washington state, for expanding a business and starting another one. Deep down I knew we'd only be in Washington for a finite amount of time. I felt like we were sojourners in a foreign land. We planned to eventually move back to the Rockies. For the most part, those years in Washington were a wonderful time of growth for both of us, as we built a life together.

She was very supportive of me and my endeavors. I have seen many wives tear their husbands down and squash their dreams. She was the opposite. She encouraged me in my passion for music as well as various business ventures.

One Father's Day, it just so happened we found out we had another Taylor on the way. Joy and I always wanted kids, so it was very special for us. We'd unexpectedly lost my dad earlier that year, so this was welcome news and great timing. We even happened to find out we were having a boy on what would have been my dad's birthday.

Our son had complications during birth and spent two weeks in the NICU. After seeing our nearly lifeless baby enter the world, and the two weeks that followed, she remained faithful and calm. Even though our little boy was covered in tubes and wires, she was incredibly grateful and happy to be a mother. You can see it on her face in those pictures at the hospital. It was as if her years of struggle and uneasiness had suddenly passed, and being with her baby she found peace.

You see, Joy had it pretty rough growing up. Both of her parents died within a few months of each other when she was just 11 years old. After that, she was basically raised by her teenage brothers and then eventually couch surfed from place to place as a teenager.

Graciously, a very nice couple took her in when she was 17. They treated her like one of their own. Although her time with them was brief, they made a lasting impact on her. She always spoke highly of them and how much they helped her. God knows what her life would've been like without them. I keep in touch with them to this day.

Early on in our relationship I could tell Joy had deep anger issues. There was an angst about her, she'd react to certain things in an unnecessary way. There were many great qualities that I loved about her and I figured over time, her anger and abandonment issues would slowly go away. I loved her and I was willing to stick by her and help however I could.

As the years passed, I learned when and how to do things with her. What to say or not say. What to do or not do. Much of the time it was simply giving her space, knowing we'll chat after she calms down. I also learned early in our relationship that a few years before I met her, police came and took her to a crisis center. I only got her side of the story at the time. She made it sound like she shouldn't have been there and it was all a misunderstanding.

Joy told me that during her time there, she heard voices on the other side of the walls that sounded like people she knew. She also claimed she found a letter in her dad's handwriting with a message for her...even though her dad died many years earlier.

I wanted a fresh start with her. Even after hearing these things, I didn't want us digging into the past. We've all done things we're not proud of and I didn't want to bring them into our relationship. I figured if she wanted to share details about her past, I'd let her. I did my best to keep things about the present and building a future together.

A couple months after Joy died, I learned more details about her. One of her closest relatives told me she visited Joy in the crisis center, and that her behavior there was the scariest thing she'd ever seen.

I also learned that after she was released, her room mate took everything out of the house that she could potentially hurt herself with. I didn't know either of those details. The way I look at it, if I was supposed to know those things about her past, I would have. Would I have treated her different had I known those things? Would I have stayed with her early on? Would we have still gotten married and had two wonderful kids together? God only knows, but I choose to not live in regret and battle with *'what ifs.'*

After our boy was healthy enough to come home from the hospital, I asked Joy if she wanted to be a stay at home mom. It was important to me to give her that option, even though I'd have to work harder due to losing her income. She absolutely did and I was grateful for it. I watched her shine as she spent every day playing and interacting with our sweet, healthy little guy. It seemed like every day while I was working, she'd text pictures of them playing at a park or having lunch somewhere.

During our years together, we both had a leading to draw closer to Jesus. It seemed to come in seasons. Like being invited to come a little closer, then a little closer, then a little closer. Over time, we progressively gained more peace and understanding for our lives.

In early 2015 I felt a strong leading to start writing my first book. By the end of 2017, it was finished and released. Up to that point in my life, it was the single hardest thing I've ever accomplished. I'd spend all day away from my wife and our little boy working. Then commute an hour home where she'd give me a warm welcome and have dinner ready.

After we ate together, I'd put in nearly another full day of work on the book, getting to bed in the wee hours of the morning. That was the basic schedule, 5-6 days a week for nearly two years. During that time, she didn't complain. She was my biggest supporter and we worked as a team. We both made sacrifices and I know it was hard for her too. Even though we knew it'd be temporary, it was still difficult.

Shortly after the book came out, I began getting invitations to speak across the Country. They were great opportunities, I met many wonderful people who are still friends to this day. This was a very peaceful time for the three of us at home. No longer was I putting in such long days. We started tasting the fruit of our labor, it was great. Getting to spend so much more time with them was such a blessing.

Then, another wonderful thing happened. We found out there was another Taylor on the way! This time, a sweet little girl. We were both so excited. We always wanted at least two kids, and after having one, we had a better idea of what to expect. When Joy was about 8 months pregnant with our daughter, we were notified by our landlord that we had less than two months to move out. We'd lived there for years with no issues, it turns out, they wanted to rent the house to a relative.

Even though it was very inconvenient to move with short notice, especially with a newborn, Joy took the news with complete peace. God had always provided for us and we knew this time would be no different. We then moved into a larger house, double the size, but also double the rent than before. Joy had a lot of fun getting the place just the way she wanted it. She was very frugal and found good deals on furniture and fixtures.

'Nesting' is ingrained in women (especially moms), and it was enjoyable to watch her plan how she wanted our new place to look. The only areas I was particular about was my studio and the garage, so she had a lot of space to work with. She made our new home warm and welcoming.

It was about a year of growing as a family in that new house. Business was going well, which meant I had to spend most days working while she was with the kids. I have hundreds of pictures she texted me while she was with our two little ones, during those final months in that house.

Joy never wanted to have a babysitter. She didn't want to leave the kids, not even for a short time. I can only remember a few times they ever stayed with a relative or close friend while we went out for dinner. Even then, she didn't enjoy being away from them and would text periodically to check on the kids.

This is one of the reasons many people that knew her said there was no way she would commit suicide...they saw the way she was with our kids. They witnessed her longing to always be with them and her reluctancy to be apart from them. I think she had dealt with so much as a kid, that she often acted like one. She had so much fun with our little ones that she would sit and play with them for hours. She loved them both so much.

Joy was also very hard on herself. She wanted to do the absolute best she could as a mother. I always gave her compliments, yet in her eyes, she was never good enough. She could never quite live up to the standard she envisioned a mom should be. It's probably because she never had a full example of a mother herself. She'd often get parenting books from the library. Instead of helping, they only made her feel bad about herself and her abilities. The more she learned about what other moms were doing, the more she felt shame. Joy didn't know what she didn't know. As she learned and grew into motherhood, I wanted her to do so with grace, instead of being so hard on herself.

The last few months in that house was also one of those special seasons of coming closer to Jesus. I watched my wife progressively take more ownership of her faith. I witnessed her dig even more into scripture, pray a lot, meet more with our pastors and participate more in our weekly Bible study...*and that's when I started to notice some things.*

The more on fire she was for Jesus, the more things would get stirred up. Imagine having a cup of coffee with coffee grounds in it. If you let it sit there, the grounds go to the bottom and you don't even notice them. However, if you stir the cup, they become noticeable, even though they only make up a small fraction of what's in there.

Joy was finally at a point of confronting the deep hurt, pain and anger she had within herself since she was a child. She would make such a huge effort to overcome and then obstacles would come up. Some larger than others. Through laying on of hands and prayer after one of our small Church services, she felt The Lord restore her heart. Like He put broken pieces back together. *That's when really good...and really bad things started happening.*

One evening as I was laying in bed, God gave me a quick vision of what was happening inside of her...I saw two fields separated by a fence. The field on the left was sunny, nice, well taken care of and orderly. The field on the right was unkept, dark, foreboding, and gloomy. Suddenly, the fence that separated them dropped. Like dandelion seeds in the wind, weed seeds began drifting from the bad field, into the nicely manicured field. Just like that, the vision was over.

I'm going to discuss *brokenness* later in this book, but it was like suddenly seeing two people in one body. Most of the time I'd see and interact with my loving wife who was on fire for Jesus. However, sometimes I'd catch a glimpse of someone else who was not. She started to have more difficulties but also incredible perseverance. Joy was on a mission to overcome and she was very determined.

There were moments I would look at her and not recognize the face I was seeing. I believe I was witnessing a different person in those brief moments, then suddenly, the normal Joy would be back. One example I remember; I was standing off to the side observing Joy, while she was watching our daughter play. This may be hard for some people to understand, but in Joy's eyes and face was a hurt little girl. I would guess around six or seven years old. This hurt child was watching our daughter's happiness and I had a sense that she wanted to relate, but couldn't. She was in pain, regretful and seemed jealous of our happy and loved little girl. Then, at the first sound I made, that little girl disappeared and Joy was instantly back.

People that have experienced what I have can relate, but most people probably think this sounds strange. In my opinion, this 'phenomenon' is much more common than most people realize. Most people don't see it for what it actually is...*brokenness.*

Aside from the spiritual issues of her heart, Joy was also experiencing hormonal changes. She was not sleeping well, having night sweats and mentioned signs of Peri-menopause (pre-menopause). In hind-sight, I also believe she was experiencing postpartum issues. I didn't connect these dots until recently. Following the birth of our Son, Joy had a very violent outburst that was totally out of character for her. Considering she was still nursing our daughter at the time of her death, postpartum complications could have played a factor in her suicide.

By today's standards, she was an older 'new' mother. I have since learned that dealing with postpartum and pre-menopause at the same time can be very difficult for women. Everything is clearer in 20-20 hindsight. So far we have discussed internal brokenness, pre-menopause symptoms, lack of sleep and likely postpartum issues. If that wasn't a heavy enough burden for her to bear, an unforeseen affliction, outside of most people's understanding surfaced.

When God speaks, listen.

"For we wrestle not against flesh and blood...

The last conference I spoke at was in Ohio, at a beautiful location on the shores of Lake Erie. It was founded and hosted by my friend Chris and his wife Liz. This one was different though. Going into it, I knew that I knew, *this was my last conference.* I can't explain it in words, but God put it in my heart to pause. At the conclusion of the conference, Chris invited me to speak the following year. I told him;

"God wants me to pause from conferences. I don't know for how long, but I know I'm supposed to pause."

Shortly after returning from Ohio, I was invited to speak at another conference. Normally I would've said yes, but I politely declined the invitation. At the time, I thought I was pausing because God wanted me to get back to making music. Oh, how ignorant I was, but God is so good. The next thing stirred up in Joy's 'coffee cup,' was demons.

Too many terrible movies have been made about demons that skew how they really operate, leading us to believe we're not in control. Contrary to those beliefs, you do not need to fear demons. Later in this book, I'll cover more details about spiritual warfare and how to deal with demons. With that said, it all comes down to authority.

One thing going on inside of her became obvious. She had demons and they needed kicked out. Demons do not want to be kicked out of their host. All of the things she had been doing; fasting, reading her Bible, praying, etc. had been pushing them into a corner and they knew their time was short. Our pastor was in deliverance ministry for years, so I scheduled a time for her deliverance.

If I had known what state Joy was in on this particular day, I never would have left her alone. I don't recall exactly why she wanted to stay home, but the kids and I went to the gym. Joy was waiting to meet me at the front door when we returned.

Her hands were trembling when she looked at me and said, "They are terrified." Imagine a dark room filled with cockroaches. They are gross critters, drawn to darkness and fearful of light. When the light is turned on, they scatter to the corners in search of darkness in which to thrive. The demons in Joy were panicking, trying to hide in the remaining shadows within her.

They knew their time was short. The room was being flooded with light. Soon, there wouldn't be enough shadows to hide in. They were forced to leave or perish. But before they left, they wanted to cause as much destruction as possible. (Similar to Mark 9:20-27)

The reason God instructed me to pause from conferences became EXTREMELY clear with what happened next. *(The following may be hard to read or understand, please stick with me).*

Chapter 2: Testimonies

> I would have been thousands of miles away when they tried to get her to *rip her own eyes out, in front of our kids.*

We were going to be leaving for our pastor's office in a few hours for her deliverance when suddenly, the demons started throwing everything they could at her. She was being assaulted from the inside out, right in front of me. Joy started pacing the room in torment, holding her head while making painful groans.

She began saying "I have to rip my eyes out! I can't stand to see what they're showing me!" I had to physically grab her hands and pull them away from her eyes or she would have clawed them out. It was then that she frantically said, "I have to kill myself...I have to kill myself to make it stop!" (Which is exactly what the demons wanted).

"Absolutely not!" I exclaimed as I took charge and started speaking directly to the demons. "In Jesus' name, you will not hurt this woman! You will stop what you're doing, be muzzled and remain quiet!"

Even though we were a few hours early, it was time to get her to the pastor. I noticed one of our sleeping eye patches, putting that over her eyes calmed her down some. Then we made our way out to the car. I held on to her hands with one of mine as I struggled to get our one and four year old into the car with my free hand. Yes, this was difficult. Yes, this was very tense. It took everything I had to make things appear calm and normal in front of the kids.

Once everyone was in the car, I locked the doors and told her to keep the eye patch on. Both her hands remained in my right hand as I drove with my left. During the drive, the demons struggled against my commands. I had to continually remind them of my orders and that they must obey. They were unable to break free.

"Don't talk to mommy like that!" My four year old suddenly states. "I'm not talking to mommy son, mommy is being messed with. I'm talking to the ones who are messing with her."

Jesus has the ultimate authority. As His followers, He's given us His authority, which includes authority over demons. If they had their way, they would have tried to get her to jump out of the car or do anything they could to destroy herself and/or us.

After the most tense drive of my life, we arrived safe and sound. I walked her into the office where our pastors and two others from our fellowship were waiting. She took off her eye patch, then I got the *we'll take it from here* gesture from the pastor. I gratefully walked back to the car, where the three of us waited. I felt a sense of relief that she was exactly where she needed to be.

A little over an hour later, Joy suddenly emerged from the office. In one look I could tell she was back in her right mind. She had a stern and confident look on her face. I jumped out and gave her a big hug. With boldness, she stated; "We need to go home and pray over our house." When we reached home, we walked in and started praying out loud. I don't remember the exact words, but we declared it was our house and the enemy had no place in it. Joy and I knew we still had work to do. At that moment things seemed normal, but we knew we couldn't let our guard down.

I received a text that evening from our pastor. He wanted to meet with me the next morning, and said he had important instructions for me. The next day, I showed up bright and early to hear what God had put on his heart to tell me. He informed me that in Joy's weakened state, the enemy had been busy trying to plant weed seeds. The demons were trying to twist various words in an attempt to get her to doubt her own reality and to doubt Jesus. They were doing what they always do; trying to steal, kill and destroy, much like how the devil twisted God's own words to trick Eve.

Another example would be when the devil tried to twist scripture to get Jesus himself to commit suicide by jumping off the temple. Joy'd been having strange reactions to various sights and sounds that made no logical sense. She'd take lyrics from a random song as a message specifically for her. Almost always in a very negative way.

Random words on a TV commercial, a song title, or comments

about other topics, she'd take as a message just for her. Much like the note she said was from her dad in the crisis center. It's illogical, *but to her it was real.*

It all made sense after the meeting with our pastor. I became more alert to things that could effect her, and I did my absolute best to filter what got to her. No matter how trivial it would be to everyone else, to her, the wrong words at the wrong time could be devastating.

In our meeting that morning, the
instructions God had for me were;

- To remove from our home every single source of doubt or confusion that might cause Joy to question the reality of her life or her relationships with God and man.

and...

- For me to be as attentive and alert as I could be for the next 30 days. He was letting me know not to be sloppy in my walk, but purposeful with her and the kids.

I took my 30 day instruction very seriously and fully embraced it. I was blessed that it was the slower time of year at work. I rescheduled my calendar and spent the majority of those 30 days with her and the kids. We basically had a December family vacation. Day after day, I was as intentional and present as I could have been. We went to the Zoo, the Aquarium, various parks and took many walks. We worked out at the gym regularly and drove to new places we'd never been.

One outing, we took the kids to the theater to watch a children's movie. There were moments during the movie where I could tell Joy was over analyzing phrases, like they were a message for her. I felt like this was all part of her healing process and a strange season that she'd get over. I truly believed that during this special and devoted time together Joy would heal from whatever was going on inside of her.

To ensure she was getting good input, I typed up a few inspirational Bible verses for her and left copies laying around the house. I also read them to her every day, especially when she looked upset. During this time, I also put her favorite uplifting Christian songs on her phone. She'd play them over and over during the day.

One evening she sat up and began singing a song she claimed to be hearing. I could not hear it, but she was singing along to it. No matter how hard I tried, the only thing I could hear was the faint sound of a neighbor's heater, through our open bathroom window.

I went and closed the window. When I did, she said the song suddenly stopped. I tried to explain to her that it wasn't a song, it was just the neighbor's heater making noise. I had only love and empathy for my loving wife. It pained me to see her in such a vulnerable state. Through it all, I firmly believed this was just an abnormal bump in the road and things would get better.

One morning during the 30 days, I woke up to her sitting cross legged beside me. As I lifted my head and said good morning to her, the first thing she said was;

"I was up all night thinking about killing myself."

"What!?!?" I exclaimed.

She then began trying to justify those thoughts.
I interrupted her and said;

"Do you have any idea what that would do to us? I don't even know where to start. I don't even know what we'd do!"

This was such an alarming and unexpected conversation we were suddenly commenced in. I began trying to paint the picture of what we'd be left like;

Chapter 2: Testimonies

"I would not be able to work. The kids and I would probably go broke. We'd likely be forced to move back to Montana and live with relatives. The kids need you and I need you. *That would be completely devastating to all of us!*"

She then started to justify her thoughts again, trying to convince me that her killing herself was a good idea. That's when I did something else I've never done...halfway through her speaking a sentence about killing herself, three fingers from my right hand suddenly contacted her left cheek.

In an utter reaction, I slapped the mouth that was talking about murdering my wife. Neither one of us saw it coming and we were both surprised. I've never laid a hand on a woman in my life, but this was something different. This came from within me and was out of love, desperately wanting the woman I love to come to her senses. There was a moment of silence after that.

"We need you and we love you. We need you here with us.
I don't want to imagine what life would be like without you."

I was extremely surprised and alarmed by those first few minutes of that morning. A little while later, I called my pastor to tell him everything that happened and to get advice and prayers.

I don't know about you, but I remember hearing periodically over the years that it's very rare for women to use guns to commit suicide. In our 'discussion' that morning, Joy never mentioned any methods of suicide. In hindsight, I would have asked her those types of questions, though I still choose to not live with any type of regret.

I support responsible gun ownership and am a big advocate for gun safety, especially keeping guns safely stored away from kids. I always wanted Joy to be able to quickly access a gun (that our kids couldn't), should I be gone and there were a threat to her or the kids. But after that discussion, I took the one nearest our bedroom and tucked it away in a safe place.

After putting it away, I went to the other one on the lower level that was in a very secure lock box. I remember thinking;

"I think she snapped out of those thoughts of suicide. She never said anything about using a gun and I have heard women rarely use guns anyway.* If I put this one somewhere else, then I may as well change the code to the safe, then remove all the knives in the house, then where does it stop? Do I get rid of any type of rope? What about any medicines she could overdose on? Where would it stop?"

So I left that one in the lock box.

*I have since learned that firearms are the #1 method used in suicide deaths by both men AND women in the USA.[27] (More on this later)

Later that day, Joy seemed back to her normal self. She even thanked me for the slap that morning. She said she needed it and it helped her snap out of the thoughts she was having. I let her know it was just a spontaneous reaction to the words coming out of her mouth, and it sprung up from a place of love. She understood and agreed with me. It was very refreshing to see her behaving normally.

After that day, she never said anything about suicide or having suicidal thoughts again. She continued to impress me with her drive for Jesus and I was greatly enjoying our continued family time together.

During the 30 days, our Son was wanting to listen to our pastor's recorded teachings. I thought it was so great that our four year old enjoyed going to bed listening to Biblical teachings. In hindsight, I realized God was preparing that little guy for the sudden incredible loss he was about to experience.

I was as attentive to my family as I could've been during those 30 days, and I'm grateful for that priceless opportunity. Those days were filled with quality time; the four of us laughing, eating and playing together. All while Joy's favorite uplifting music played in the background.

I expected that we would all continue to grow closer as a family and this would've just been a strange but growing time for us. Little did I know what would happen next...*I didn't see it coming.*

Remember how I said Joy hadn't been sleeping well? One evening, well after midnight, I woke to the sounds of her putting cleaning supplies away. She couldn't sleep, so she'd been straightening up the house and told me she'd be back to bed soon. A bit later, I woke to her by me in bed. This time, she said something very strange. It was something about her being the cause of Eve's original sin in the Garden.

"*What?!*"

I then explained that those thoughts made absolutely no sense. I told her that happened thousands of years ago, and that she was in no way responsible, just confused. I remember being puzzled and very alarmed by this. Like so many times before, I believed it was just one more thing we'd get through. She laid down by me and I went back to sleep, (I assume she didn't). Some time after this, I woke to her getting out of bed.

"Whatcha doing?" I asked.

"Just going downstairs for a little bit." She responded.

I don't remember exactly what I said after that, but it was something like; *"OK...Sound mind."* (2 Timothy 1:7 KJV reference). Then I laid my head back down and briefly went back to sleep.

Oh, it's amazing what I'd change in hindsight. I never would have let her leave the room had I understood the state she was in, and what was about to happen. How could I've known that was the last time I'd see her alive, and those would be our last words to each other?

The sound woke me. The familiar sound I've heard countless times, but never like this. As I jumped and ran....terror, panic and helplessness filled and began to consume me. I knew it was the sound of a pistol going off in the house, but I couldn't tell where.

I jumped out of bed in an indescribable panic, the first room I ran into was our daughter's. She was still asleep in her crib and the only one in the room. I turned to run to our son's room, and that's when I heard a second shot go off!

> "She just killed herself! The first
> shot was when she killed our son!!!"

There are no words to describe how I felt in that moment. *"Joy! ... Joy! ... Joy! ... Joy! ..."* All I could do was yell her name as I ran as fast as I could.

Our kid's rooms were only about 15 feet apart on the upper level, but they may as well have been 1000. I could not sprint to his room fast enough. I burst into the room, expecting to find two of the three people I loved most in the world, dead.

THANK GOD! He was alone in his room and had just woken up. Finding my boy unharmed was the most relieving moment of my entire life. I'd thought in whatever state she was in, she'd just killed him and then herself.

I don't remember shutting his door. I don't remember if I told him to stay in bed, or if I said anything to him at all. All I remember was frantically yelling my wife's name as I ran down a dark staircase looking for her.

Being early in the morning, the house was still dark. As I hit the bottom of the stairs, I looked left and saw the only light in the house....the thin yellow glow around the closed door of our kid's play room.

Chapter 2: Testimonies

I ran to it. "Oh God! What am I about to find?!?!" I quickly opened the door and entered. The first thing I noticed was the smell, *Gunpowder!*

'This is really happening!' Then, there on the floor...

The body of the woman I love.

TIME STOOD STILL

Less than a minute earlier she was standing right there, alive. Surrounded by pink and blue...a room full of kid's toys, costumes and finger paintings. A cozy place, normally full of happiness and the sound of children's laughter. But that cheerful room she spent so much love and care putting together, became horrific. I saw the woman I'd made a wonderful life with, in a state I don't want to describe. I saw the mother of our two sweet kids, the woman that couldn't stand being away from them, never able to see them again... in this life anyway. I knew from one look at her there was absolutely nothing any man could do to save her.

After decades of hunting in Montana, I am familiar with the sight of death. After an animal dies, their bodies usually go through a shut down process. Even though they may be obviously dead, their bodies still try to breath, make sounds, twitch and move. It's like their body has been alive and moving for so long that it just wants to keep going, even though the mind has stopped sending it signals and the heart's stopped beating. Inevitably, this phase slows down and eventually stops. Then there's no more sounds or movement.

I understood immediately what was happening in front of me, but I couldn't fully comprehend it was actually happening to my wife. This was the woman I loved and the mother of our kids. There was a traumatic disconnect...*this can't be happening..this can't be happening...!*

I kneeled over her, pleading and yelling as I watched her go through the phase I've seen so many animals go through. Except this was not a big game animal in the Montana woods...it was my wife on the floor of our kid's playroom!

The dull moans that emanated from her mouth were torture to me. Gasps and gurgles pierced my heart. Every movement was pure torment. I just wanted it to stop, but I knew what that would mean. I knew that soon, what I was witnessing would slow down and eventually stop, and the room would go silent. Then, I'd be alone with the lifeless body of the woman I loved.

Chapter 2: Testimonies

I know this will sound strange to many of you. As a Jesus follower, in that moment I knew that if I believed and didn't have any doubt in me, I could've commanded her to rise and walk...and she would have. The problem was, in that moment, my faith was not strong enough to overpower everything else. As I knelt over her, I knew it was possible to command her to come back, yet at the same time I also knew I didn't have that kind of faith in that moment. I know this sounds odd, but I had a sense of guilt for not having the faith to command her back to life.

I believe Jesus when he said these words:

"I tell you the truth, anyone who believes in me will do the same works I have done, and even greater works, because I am going to be with the Father."

-John 14:12 (NLT)

It's only by the grace of God that He kept our little boy in his bed. I'm so incredibly grateful he didn't walk downstairs wondering what all the commotion was and why I'd been yelling.

The first phone call I made was not to 911. It was to our pastor. I knew there was nothing an ambulance could do. In that moment I needed two things, I needed him to come get the kids and I needed Jesus. Even though it was early (a little after 6 am I think), he picked up. It was the most panicked and chaotic moment of my life and somehow in a frantic rush of words, I was able to convey what had happened.

The second call I made was to 911. I understand they have a job to do and ask questions. All I could do was let them know what had happened and there was nothing that could be done. The guy on the other end of the phone understood and stopped asking questions. I'm grateful for people like him, but I would not want his job. I can only imagine the kinds of heartbreaking phone calls he gets.

He wanted me to stay on the line until police arrived. At one point, I set the phone down and walked upstairs to talk to my son. I put myself together enough to open his door and calmly tell that sleepy boy he'd be hearing people downstairs and to stay in bed.

Within a few minutes, two sheriff's deputies knocked on the door. Just like the 911 operator, I understand they have a job to do. They assessed the situation and began a very obvious good cop/bad cop routine on me. One of them was basically interrogating me as the other one seemed compassionate and friendly. I don't hold it against him, I'm sure he's seen people do terrible things and lie about it.

> "Wait, you called 911 second?
> Why wouldn't you call us first?"

> ...Just one of his many questions.

> "Because, after I saw her, I knew I needed Jesus and there was nothing that you or anyone else could do to help her."

The questions kept coming until my pastor and his wife walked through the door. It was all I could do to stand and hug him, then I collapsed in his arms. Here was a 70+ year old man holding up a 220 pound man in his 30s. It was a moment where I felt like Jesus himself was hugging me with immense compassion, because I believe He was, through my pastor.

I collected myself and asked him if we could pray over her body. What I wanted was to nullify and forgive anything she'd done. He was willing to pray over her, but the deputy said we couldn't enter the room. The three of us then took hands and prayed that this would not impact our kids in a negative way and that the enemy would not use this tragedy against our family.

After we finished praying, the deputy that had been interrogating me asked my pastor to talk outside. To this day, I don't know what was said, but the deputy changed the way he treated me after he came back in. He was empathetic and treated me much better the rest of his time there.

I wanted my pastor take the kids so they wouldn't see any of what was happening. I asked the police to stay out of view while I got them both to the car. They obliged. My pastor and his wife took them to some friends of ours, where they played with their kids all day.

For the next few hours, there was a steady flow of uniformed officers in and out of the house. Some would glance over at me as they walked by, but most didn't make eye contact. I can't imagine what they must do to deal with seeing such terrible things. At one point, two detectives pulled me to the side and told me what I already knew, except they informed me of one thing.

> "I heard two shots, was she wounded from the first?
> Was she suffering even briefly from the first one?..."

They let me know sometimes people will fire a 'test' round, before using the second one on themselves. This brought on another flow of tears again. We looked over at the kitchen counter and discussed the kid's water bottles. They were covered in condensation. Joy had filled them with ice water sometime during the night and by this time, the ice had already melted. "Why would she fill their bottles in the middle of the night?" They also told me she didn't leave a note.

Eventually, one by one they slowly left. The last two people there was a lady medical examiner and the sheriff's deputy that had been questioning me a few hours earlier. They let me know they were going to put her body in a bag and carry her out.

"Before you do, can I have a moment alone with her?" I asked.

They said the next step was to take her to have an autopsy and I was not allowed to be alone with her or touch her. They were polite and said they'd bring her out of the room and stop near the front door. I could have a moment with her, but they'd need to be there and she'd have to be in the bag.

TIME STOOD STILL

A few minutes later, I watched them carry the body of the woman I loved down the hall in a heavy duty black bag. I was sitting on the bottom stairs as they softly set her body at my feet and slowly backed away. Respectfully, they remained silent across the room as I gently placed my hand on the middle of the bag.

"I forgive you. I love you. Thank you for being such a good mom. Thank you for being such a good helpmate. Thank you for being such a great example. Thank you Jesus for this woman............. I'm not mad at you. I forgive you. I forgive whatever this was. This will not be used against us."

After standing and wiping the tears from my face,
I looked at them and said;

"This may sound weird, but I'd like to help carry her out."

They let me know it would be OK and it was not a strange request. They said for some people it's part of the healing process. I felt a need to help carry her. I would've carried her by myself if they'd have let me. The three of us carried her body out, set her on a gurney and rolled it into the examiner's truck. Both of them politely said their goodbyes, got in their vehicles and drove away. I turned and slowly walked back into the house.

Standing at the living room window, I watched the examiner's truck drive by again, knowing who was in the back. It's a moment that can not be fully expressed in words. An indescribable and horrific morning, followed by standing alone in the living room of a silent house. The house we'd made a home.

It was a sunny December morning. Most days I'd be saying goodbye to my family and making the drive to work, but today was so incredibly different. I stood poised in the middle of a silent room, and...at the top of my lungs I exclaimed;

"Thank you Heavenly Father! Thank you for this woman! I don't understand this! I don't understand, but I trust you! I trust you! I love her, I forgive her! She is forgiven! I trust you! I trust you! I don't understand this! The devil will not use this against us, we will not give him a foothold! I trust you!"

At the examiner's suggestion, the first call I made was to a company that handles cleanup of scenes like that. So, one of the first to know of my wife's death were the people coming to clean it up. Then, I nervously sat down in my office and began calling family. "Joy went to be with Jesus today." It was the most basic statement I could make. How could I possibly describe that morning? "It wasn't the Joy we know, but something inside her took her life."

Sometime during the barrage of phone calls, a man from the cleanup company showed up and got to work. It was extremely important from the beginning to protect our kids from knowing too much before the right time. I needed to keep them out of their play room until it looked normal again, which was easier said than done.

That evening, I drove the 45 minutes to our friend's house to pick them up. I had a wide range of emotions, from incredibly sad to dumbfounded of what happened that day. *Did that really happen? ...What am I going to tell the kids?'*

Arriving at the house, I put on a good face for all the kids I was about to see, especially mine. Our friends have four young kids who were all eager for Christmas. They started showing me all their presents they would soon be opening. I was very grateful my kids were able to spend all day having fun with them. Their parent's faces were the first ones I'd see in a long line of *'I'm so sorry'* faces. That's the face friends and family make when they don't know what to say, but obviously care.

Not knowing what else to do after picking them up, the three of us stopped at a Dairy Queen on the way home. It was one of the most memorable meals of my life. I was so torn up inside, yet needed to keep it together for the kids. I got them whatever they wanted and even some ice cream.

It's a strange feeling. Being in public and interacting with people as normal as possible, after seeing and experiencing the profound loss I did earlier that day. Knowing this is the silence before the storm, and *everything* changes now. The kids were just about to learn they'll never again see the person they were closest to in this world. The woman that loved them so much and spent every single day with them.

We came home to a dark, quiet and empty house. I had them get ready for bed like any other night. After they were ready, it would usually be both Joy and I reading a book and tucking them in. *The question was coming*...the one I'd been dreading all day. I got down and sat crossed legged on the floor. I set my daughter on my left leg and my son on my right. That's when that little guy looked up at me and said it...the hardest question I've ever been asked;

"Where's Mommy?"...

"Mommy went to be with Jesus today buddy..."

"...That's good. It's good to be with Jesus." He replied.

Obviously at four years old, he didn't fully understand, but he understood enough. His response was so innocent and faithful. He'd been wanting to listen to CDs about Jesus for a month leading up to that moment. We talked a little more and then they went to bed.

As I laid down in my room, I was completely engulfed with the horrors of that morning. I couldn't get the macabre sight of Joy from behind my eyelids. Every time I closed my eyes, it was there, and I could still hear the sounds of death...how could I ever sleep again? I was haunted by the worst sight and experience of my life. In tears I prayed;

"Lord, please take this sight away from me, please make it go away! How can I close my eyes again? Please take this from me!"

Needless to say, I didn't sleep much that night. The next day I did my best to have a good attitude and make things as normal as possible for the kids. At one point I happened to look out the window to see someone walking up the driveway. I didn't recognize who it was at first. To my surprise, it was one of my brothers. He didn't say he was coming. It turns out, he dropped what he was doing after I called him the day before. He caught a couple flights, rented a car and showed up at my door. It was a relief to see him.

A few days later, my mom showed up (she wanted to come sooner, but I asked her to wait). Shortly after that, the five of us drove back to Montana for Joy's service.

Two Important Tips:

I will share more helpful lessons as we go through this book. But at this point I want to share *two very important things:*

1.

For you survivors reading this; any thoughts that start with *"If only I had..."* are very normal, but also *very dangerous!!!* A major effect suicide has on the survivors is they're left feeling like they could've somehow prevented their death. The person who committed suicide dumps their issues onto the very people that love them most.

In a nutshell, one person's problems often become many people's problems, with an added layer of shame and guilt.

'If only I had called...'

'If only I had stopped by...'

'If only I had said...'

When people feel they somehow could have prevented their loved one's death, they put themselves in an emotionally devastating lose-lose scenario. Filling themselves with shame and guilt they should not have. I did everything I could have for Joy with what I understood at the time. Obviously in hindsight, I would have done some things differently, but I didn't know what I didn't know. Since losing her, I refuse to take the fork in the road marked, '*If only I...*' Nothing good comes from walking down that road. Being your own punching bag solves nothing, *it's not your fault!* Say it with me;

> "It's not my fault. They made their own decision. Their problems are not my problems. Their death is not my fault! Their struggle with suicide was theirs, not mine!"

If you're considering suicide, just know that in your delusional state, you'd only be hurting those that love you the most. You would seal your fate and find yourself face to face with Jesus, having to explain yourself. Your problems would then be your loved one's problems, and they would likely feel deep guilt thinking they should've done something to stop you. Is that how you want to treat those that love you most?

2.

One takeaway from my testimony is to keep guns away from anyone that may be suicidal. If you or a loved one is suicidal, whether male or female, I strongly suggest the minimum of making guns and other obvious methods inaccessible.

This is not to bring shame or guilt on anyone who has experienced something like I did. This is coming from a place of wanting to do all we can for our loved ones. If I could go back, I certainly would have made guns inaccessible to Joy. However, that does not mean it would've changed the outcome, possibly just the method.

Strong temptation
+ impulsive moment
+ quick tool
= *death*

In this equation, if you eliminate the quick tool, *it buys time.* In my situation, if I ensured she couldn't access any guns, it could have bought time. Time for me to find her alive had she used another method, or time for her to come to her right mind.

As the statistics show, the majority of people that attempt suicide don't actually want to die. At least remove a quick and permanent tool from the equation. The "Jumpers" article quote earlier in the book makes much more sense when we think about it this way. If someone does not have a quick tool, they may look for another method, but while contemplating it, their impulsive moment may fade away, they come to their right mind and survive the strong temptation.

Chapter 3: Kids

Watching my kids come into this world was the most amazing experience. After months of anticipation, seeing them for the first time was indescribable. The hope and expectation of watching our children grow is the foundational element that (almost) all parents share. For those of you that don't have kids, the love a parent has for their child can't be fully comprehended. You have to experience it for yourself to understand.

To me, the thought of kids killing themselves is as horrifying of an image as I can imagine. The natural order of life is for the younger generation to bury the older, not the other way around, and certainly not a child dying by choice.

As I type this, there was yet another suicide of a local high school student over the weekend. There's been a suicide trend at both the local high schools. The news is calling it a "suicide cluster."[15] I only remember ONE fellow high school student committing suicide in the late 90's, *I will discuss that particular friend of mine later.*

Chapter 3: Kids

These two quotes are from local articles about what is currently happening here at the time of writing this;

"Flathead County is facing a crisis among youth. Seven local teens ages 15 to 19 have died by suicide since May 2020, tragedies that mirror a major public health issue nationwide."[16]

"According to the 2019 Flathead County Youth Risk Behavior Survey, during the 12 months before the survey, **12.2%** of Flathead County students from ninth to 12th grade made one or more suicide attempts. That number was **11.7%** for seventh and eighth grade students."[14]

In this chapter, let's dig into the main reasons I believe we're seeing an increase in kids committing suicide across the Country, and what we can do to help them before they get to that point.

Acceptance

I've heard it said that the order of importance to sustain human life goes; air, water, acceptance, food. We crave and desire acceptance, at all ages. A newborn baby relies on the acceptance and embrace of a loving mother. The old man on his death bed craves the acceptance of loved ones around him, while teenagers hope for acceptance at school. Throughout our entire lives, we all desire to feel accepted. Our need for acceptance is always there, it's just more obvious when we're young. For instance, kids worry about things like;

> What clothes to wear ....so they *feel* accepted.
> What hair style to have ....so they *feel* accepted.
> What friends to have ....so they *feel* accepted.
> Who to interact with ....so they *feel* accepted.
> What image to portray
> on social media ....so they *feel* accepted.

59

TIME STOOD STILL

What sports to play .... so they *feel* accepted.
How to talk .... so they *feel* accepted.
How to act .... so they *feel* accepted.
What car to drive .... so they *feel* accepted.
What phone to have .... so they *feel* accepted.
How to stand out .... so they *feel* accepted.
How to not stand out .... so they *feel* accepted.
How to do well .... so they *feel* accepted.
How to not do well .... so they *feel* accepted.

After a certain age, kids go from being their own person to seemingly being controlled by one question;

"What will they think of me?"

This simple question seems to sit at the forefront of nearly everyone's mind during the transition into adulthood. In my opinion, this question is the #1 cause of most people's inner turmoil and uncertainty in life. How many people would follow their dreams if they didn't let the opinions of others stop them? But it goes a step further than that. Not even the actions of others, just the *idea* that someone may think negatively about them halts most people in their tracks. This ties right back to the need to *feel* accepted.

"You wouldn't worry so much about what others think of you if you realized how seldom they do."

-Eleanor Roosevelt
Longest serving First Lady of the United States

I've seen countless people ruled and dominated by this simple and paralyzing question. Endless amounts of people avoid wonderful opportunities because; *'What will they think of me?'* This is also why I believe Jesus speaks of child-like faith. Younger children believe what their parents tell them without question. They're often very blunt and say whatever comes to mind. *'What will they think of me?'* doesn't yet filter their communication. They simply believe and are not afraid to say what they mean. (We could all learn this lesson from children by the way).

Instead of doing what's right or wrong, easy or hard, many people base their actions on how they *think* they will be perceived by others. Their default process is to filter and censor their life through gaining or losing acceptance. The funny thing is, they may not even like the people they're wanting to gain acceptance from. Most people simply want to avoid additional shame put on them because they're already full...of shame (a deep, subconscious sense of wrongness).

Imagine an ever balancing scale, representing our lives. On one side sits rejection, while on the other side, acceptance. Most people have a hard time feeling rejected. Rejection can weigh us down and make us feel wrong. Keep in mind though, sometimes rejection is proof we're actually on the right track. Jesus was rejected by the religious people who thought they were perfect. However, He was accepted by the lowly people who knew they were not. If we strive for acceptance from everyone, we're doing something wrong. (Galations 1:10)

This reminds me of another great Roosevelt quote;

"It is not the critic who counts; not the man who points out how the strong man stumbles, or where the doer of deeds could have done them better. The credit belongs to the man who is actually in the arena, whose face is marred by dust and sweat and blood; who strives valiantly; who errs, who comes short again and again, because there is no effort without error and shortcoming; but who does actually strive to do the deeds; who knows great enthusiasms, the great devotions; who spends himself in a worthy cause; who at the best knows in the end the triumph of high achievement, and who at the worst, if he fails, at least fails while daring greatly, so that his place shall never be with those cold and timid souls who neither know victory nor defeat."

- Theodore Roosevelt
26th President of the United States

In my opinion, most people have only experienced varying degrees of rejection, never feeling truly accepted by anyone. When people don't feel genuine acceptance, they'll continue to seek it out. Sometimes this leads someone to being accepted by people they shouldn't. For instance, there are many vulnerable women in the world, craving acceptance. The trouble is, there's also horrible men that tease them with acceptance in order to take advantage and abuse them.

There are other examples, but an obvious one is kids and adults in gangs. Things could be terrible at home, but their fellow gang members welcome them with open arms. We crave to fit in...somewhere, anywhere. Let's play a game, how many different words can you place on this line?

People _____ to feel accepted.

It can be very damaging for children to be shown conditional love at home, where acceptance comes and goes depending on how they perform. When they don't feel accepted, kids often act out to get attention. They may not be able to vocalize it, but to them, negative attention is better than no attention at all.

Like God's view of us, there's nothing my kids can possibly do to diminish my love for them. I love them no matter what choices they make. If my children misbehave, it does not effect my love for them, but it can effect our relationship. This is how our relationship with God is. He loves us no matter what, but our actions will determine the relationship (or lack thereof) we have with Him.

The world often blends relationship and unconditional love, when they're actually two separate things. For instance, I've met many people that feel guilty for staying away from an abusive parent, like they're being unloving and dishonoring them. What the world doesn't understand is that we can unconditionally love them, while having little to no relationship with them. In this example, it is completely possible to honor and respect a parent (or anyone else for that matter), while maintaining strict boundaries out of necessity. *This ties right into the forgiveness section later in the book.*

Children that have grown up in an unloving and unaccepting environment tend to attract unloving people into their lives as they grow, because that's all they've known. They often continue being subject to playing the game of performing for acceptance. The familiar rut of abuse is often less scary than unfamiliar love from an outsider.

There's a great book called *The 5 Love Languages of Children* by Gary Chapman and Ross Campbell. Gary and Ross discuss more about showing conditional love vs. unconditional love to children. If you have kids, I encourage you to read it. The bottom line is this; kids need to be genuinely accepted and loved. The most important people they need to be accepted and loved by are their parents. If you're not giving your kids love and acceptance, they will likely look for it elsewhere.

Another aspect of acceptance to mention here is about romantic relationships. From experience, the first break up between boyfriend and girlfriend can feel devastating. Break ups can cause people to do foolish things, especially when we're young and inexperienced in relationships. We lack perspective on the big picture and are often engulfed with emotions. Break ups can hurt so much because it's a form of rejection, after being previously accepted.

For those of you that are having a hard time after a break up, know that it gets much better. Eventually you won't even think about the person. I had a very hard time after a break up with my first serious girlfriend. We were together for almost three years. It took a while, but over time I realized we were not right for each other. I was trying to force a long term relationship with the wrong person. In hindsight, it was a very good thing, though at the time it hurt so bad. Remember, this too shall pass.

The Fad

How is a lack of acceptance
playing a roll in kids committing suicide?

Some kids today are getting a twisted form of acceptance by talking about killing themselves. It's not good, but even feeling accepted by a group called *the depressed and suicidal* can scratch a certain itch. Here's a quote from Brooke, a 14 year old relative of mine;

> "Collectively this generation has made it a trend to be sad.
> They brag about mental illness and the meds they're taking."

There's a terrible trend happening today; kids feeling acceptance by talking about being depressed and killing themselves. It's also being used as a sick way of gathering a following on social media.

> This reminds me of a line from the
> villain in the kids movie *The Incredibles;*
>
> "And with everyone super...*no one will be.*"

If you think of this terrible trend in business terms, the market's being flooded and eventually...no one cares. Are we glorifying mental, physical and spiritual issues into a sadistic fad? Are we letting the world teach our kids about right and wrong? What's normal and abnormal? Keep in mind how the Bible describes the wisdom of this world. (1 Cor. 3:19)

Some of these kids even kill themselves live on social media for anyone watching to see. Their final act being a horrific form of acceptance by their 'followers.' In my opinion, children used to be more compassionate and generally wanted to help a fellow kid in need. Now it seems there's more prodding and pressuring, hoping someone follows through with it to give themselves something to talk about.

Think of it like a drug. Many kids have been desensitized by watching countless sensational videos over the years. It takes more and more to get the same 'rush.' Are we that cold? Do we turn a blind eye to what our kids are exposed to? Are we that passive to the horrors of children's suffering? Do we not see their desire for acceptance? There's even a social media game for kids I heard about that's particularly disturbing. Apparently, it starts by having kids do seemingly innocent tasks. However, as the game progresses, the tasks get increasingly more dangerous. The final task; it has the kids kill themselves!

What kind of wicked person thinks up something like that? There are sick, evil people in this world that only want to steal, kill and destroy, (like their father the devil). We must guard our kids and be ever vigilant as to what and who they're exposed to. The main tools I believe being used in this suicide fad are social media and kid's *devices*.

Brooke went on to say this;

"Many kids today can't see past their issues and are just absorbed in the moment. The problems they think are so big now, they probably won't even remember in the future."

I remember being a teenager and I agree with this statement. It certainly is hard to see past the immediate issues of a day in middle and high school. Looking out of place and not fitting in may cause an older child to feel like their world is crashing in. The reality is, even if you did something really embarrassing, it will go away. Things come and go and eventually people won't remember whatever it was. The funny thing is, *neither will you*. What seemed like such a monumental issue will one day fade from memory, but its lesson will last a lifetime.

Things seldom go the way we think they will. We often have a pessimistic view of the world we live in. Usually we expect the worst and rarely hope for the best. When I was young I let many things bother me that I shouldn't have. I put stock in opinions of people I didn't even want to be like. Why'd I do that? People can only teach what they know, so why was I taking them credible?

If you're young and reading this, whatever feels like an insurmountable obstacle today, will get easier...and easier. Eventually you probably won't even remember how you're feeling now. But through it all, you'll grow stronger and be more prepared for the next of life's obstacles.

Devices

There's a great documentary that came out in 2018 called *Connect*. At the time of writing this, it's available at connectmovie.com and Amazon. It's the best video I've seen explaining the dangers of kids using devices.

Chapter 3: Kids

One of the people in the documentary is Doctor Kathy Koch. She's the author of the book *Screens and Teens* and the President of Celebrate Kids, Inc. In the documentary she said there's five lies children are believing because of social media and technology.

They are;
1. I am the center of my own universe.[39]
2. I deserve to be happy all the time.[39]
3. I must have choice. Choices are expected.[39]
4. I am my own authority.[39]
5. Information is all that matters, so I don't need teachers.[39]

Obviously, these five lies can be very damaging for those who believe them, young or old. Kathy encourages everyone to get off their devices as much as possible, and be fully present with each other. If we want our kids to do that, we must set the example first.

A friend of mine had random guys showing up at his house late at night, then driving off. It took him a while, but guess what he eventually found out...his 13 year old daughter had an app on her phone that was allowing pedophiles to track her.

Did you know that 42% of US children ages 0 to 8 have their own mobile device [20] and 90% of tweens (9-12 years old) use social media or gaming apps?[18] The idea of giving a child a device that can access nearly anything about anything, and trusting them to make good decisions with it, is absolutely foolish. With a few presses of their thumbs, kids can access videos, photos and information from almost anywhere in the world. This could range from cat videos to murder. What percentage of what they access is actually good for them? 50%, 10%,...less than 1%?

No generation in the history of the world has had this ability, until recently. An 8 year old on a smart phone has more information available to them than the most powerful kings in the history of

67

the world, (pre internet). In my opinion, all of this 'connectedness' is mostly producing *disconnected* and fearful children. This often leaves them feeling isolated from the real world, because they are. Connection is actually producing disconnection. There are countless things children should not be aware of until they're older, if at all. They're exposed to far too much at too young of an age.

'But I need to be able to get ahold of my child...'

Of course you do. But what's wrong with a flip phone? You know, the affordable ones that won't become a terrible addiction for them. The kind that doesn't expose them to porn, pedophiles and propaganda. Those call and text just fine. But why wouldn't we do that? That's right, we don't want to hear them say; "But what will my friends think of me and my dumb phone?" And there lies the truth! Most of us parents don't want our kids feeling unaccepted by their peers. If we're completely honest, we'd say the biggest reason is we don't want to hear them complain.

As time goes on, I see more kids parenting their parents. Progressively, households revolve around the emotions of children rather than parental decisions. Most parents today cave to the tantrums of children. Who's actually in charge? The Bible says God disciplines those He loves and that if we don't discipline our children, we actually hate them. The problem is, are most parents even disciplined? We can't give what we don't have. Chaotic parents expecting orderly children are hypocrites. We must first get in order, before we teach our children about order. (Matthew 7:3-5)

In my opinion, most kids today are raised to be soft and opinionated, yet very dependent (although most would argue that). They've been coddled too much, disciplined too little and are completely unprepared for the real world.

Regarding devices, many parents purchase their child a very expensive pocket computer (they likely don't want them to have in the first place), knowing they're not ready for it. Children don't appreciate what it's capable of and they certainly can't comprehend the expense. When you were 12, did you have an $800+ walkman (that cost $60+ per month to use) in your pocket? Of course not. It's not a big deal though, right? It's just a low, monthly, interest free payment for the foreseeable future from mom and dad. All of that expense, to provide a fear inducing, bondage device to a (most likely) unappreciative child. A child who is incapable of navigating its dangerous waters and the deceptive snare it is.

The next time you go out, look around and see how many kids are glued to a device. At restaurants, in shopping carts, in cars, standing in lines, it's almost everywhere. Kids, addicted to a screen from a young age and *it's not even their fault*. Let's stop letting devices raise our children, that's the parents responsibility. It's OK not to go along with what everyone else is doing. Not giving into our kid's every desire, just because other parents are, is OK. That's actually a sign of a good parent. Personally, I will not be purchasing a device for my kids to pacify them or as a way for them to fit in.

In my opinion, if a child insists on having a smart phone, why not do what our parents would have done? I suggest you tell them they can have one, as long as they pay for it, its insurance and its service plan. Why not teach them accountability and hard work with this lesson? You'll find out just how serious they are about wanting one.

When I was 17, I really wanted a particular car. It was a two door 1965 Ford Falcon. It was $2500. I worked two jobs, 7 days a week, up to 15 hours a day, all summer break to be able to afford it. If your kid really wants a smart phone, I'm sure they'd find a way to pay for it themselves. They'd also take better care of it, appreciate it more, and develop a better work ethic.

Narcissistic [nahr-suh-sis-tik]:

having an undue fascination with oneself; vain. [135]

Many kids and adults are becoming increasingly more narcissistic, especially online. Again, devices and social media are fueling this problem. People acting phony, making fools of themselves for an audience of strangers that'd turn on them in a heartbeat. It's the classic story of trying to fit a square peg in the round hole of their heart.

It's a vicious cycle that millions of people are stuck in. Until they drop the facade and seek out what they're truly lacking, the void in their heart remains. It reminds me of the term; *the spotlight effect.* It's where people believe they're being noticed more than they actually are, like they're in the spotlight.[26] Millions of people behaving like they're in the spotlight is causing many issues.

First of all, people with a poor self esteem are feeling even worse about themselves. They think nearly everyone around them is judging them, when in reality they're not even being thought about.

Secondly, many narcissists are acting like they have an audience and influence wherever they go. The terms 'Karen' and 'woke' come to mind here. Two categories of people looking for things to be offended by. They often act like babies who don't get their way, undisciplined children in the bodies of adults.

At the expense of sounding like an old man, I'm grateful to have grown up in a time that didn't have cell phones. A simpler time where people lived much more in the moment. Children played and interacted with each other with much less distraction and worry. I hope those times are cultivated again.

In my opinion, people used to be smarter. We had to read through books in a library or seek experienced people to teach us. We put in the work and in turn, retain information. Nowadays, we're lazily spoon fed whatever we want from a device in our pocket. Most young people today probably couldn't tell you which way is north without looking at their phone.

Can you imagine the anarchy that'd happen if everyone had to go a month without the use of their addiction device? People are far too dependent on technology. Thinking ourselves wise, we become fools. Majoring in the minor things of life and minoring in the major things. Most young adults are excellent at navigating their phone, but have no idea how to change a tire, start a business or even stand up straight and look someone in the eyes. They are so used to living through their phone, they don't understand the real world.

With all of this said about devices and social media, I'm not implying you should walk into your teenager's room and take their phone away. That would almost certainly cause more harm than good. I am suggesting however that you pay attention, ask questions, be diligent and open to listening to them and their issues. In my opinion, they should allow you access to their device, (the one you're likely paying for anyway). If they don't, they're probably up to something they shouldn't be. It could be minor, or it could be major. You'll never know if you simply turn a blind eye to your suspicions.

There are also parental controls that limit what sites your kids can visit as well as be able to see what they're up to. I believe if you supply your child with a device, it's your responsibility to make sure they're doing what they should be. Inspect what's expected. Would you throw them the keys to your car and not later ask them where they went and what they were up to? Operated dangerously, cars can kill quickly, I've seen it in person. Operated dangerously, devices can kill....a....little....at....a....time.

Keeping two way communication with your child is very important. If you do things to damage that communication, it will likely lead to them hiding things from you. If you have younger kids, you may want to re-think getting them a device in the first place.

Why am I talking about kids having cell phones in a book about suicide? In my opinion, the suicide rates would be lower for kids if they weren't on social media and didn't have smart phones. Kids are not meant to handle the type of negativity that social media produces. They're also not meant to put on a fake persona just to feel accepted online. If you look at graphs of suicide rates over the last twenty years and compare them to graphs of smart phone ownership during the same time period, they both go the same direction, *up*. I find that interesting, and not in a good way.

Bullying

Hurt people, hurt people.

Did you know that *BOTH* bullies and their victims have an increase in suicidal behaviors?[19] This world is full of hurt people and some of them 'deal' with their hurt by hurting others. For kids, this is called *bullying*. There are many reasons why a child may feel justified in bullying another, but in reality it's never justifiable. Creating victims as a way to cope with internal issues is never right.

Sometimes a child has one or two terrible parents that abuse them, so they take it out on other kids. Other times, a kid is bullied and to deal with it, turns around and bullies others. Whatever the reason, just because a child has endured terrible things, does not give them any sort of right to take it out on someone else. Victimizing kids that have nothing to do with what's causing their pain is wrong, plain and simple.

If you were a builder and wanted the tallest building in town, how would you do it? Well, you could work hard and build yours taller than everyone else's. Or you could do what some people do and tear everyone else's down and yours would wind up being the tallest. I've learned over the years that when people lash out at others, it is often out of jealousy. They want the tallest building, by tearing everyone's down.

Here are some statistics about kids and bullying;

- One out of every five students report being bullied.[18]

- "41% of students who reported being bullied at school believed the bullying would happen again."[18]

- Girls are subject to dealing with rumors from bullies twice as often as boys.[18]

- 46% of bullied students report notifying an adult at school about the incident.[18]

- 49.8% of tweens (9 to 12 years old) said they experienced bullying at school and 14.5% of tweens were bullied online.[18]

- "Students who experience bullying are at increased risk for depression, anxiety, sleep difficulties, lower academic achievement, and dropping out of school."[18]

- "Youth who self-blame and conclude they deserved to be bullied are more likely to face negative outcomes, such as depression, prolonged victimization, and maladjustment."[18]

- "Reports of cyberbullying are highest among middle school students, followed by high school students, and then primary school students."[18]

- "The percentages of individuals who have experienced cyberbullying at some point in their lifetimes have more than doubled (18% to 37%) from 2007-2019."[18]

- "Tweens reported using a variety of strategies to stop the bullying including blocking the person bullying them (60.2%), telling a parent (50.8%), ignoring the person (42.8%), reporting it to the website or app (29.8%), and taking a break from the device (29.6%)."[18]

- "Students who are both bullied AND engage in bullying behavior are the highest risk group for adverse outcomes."[18]

- "The false notion that suicide is a natural response to being bullied has the dangerous potential to normalize the response and thus create copycat behavior among youth."[18]

- "Almost all of the studies (in this particular Yale study) found connections between being bullied and suicidal thoughts among children. Five reported that bullying victims were *two to nine times more likely* to report suicidal thoughts than other children were." [19]

- Bullies have an increased risk for suicidal behaviors[19]

If you're the victim of a bully, it's not your fault. It's also not your responsibility to try to fix the person bullying you. The bully is likely miserable inside and dealing with it by making you miserable too. It's like a drowning scenario. A drowning person will often drown other people in a panicked effort to stay afloat.

If you're being bullied, I suggest you write down in detail what's going on. Who is the bully? What did they say or do? Who was around to see it? Where was it? What time was it? Anything else you can think of, write it down. Then, talk about it. It's very important to talk to the right people about this. This was my mistake when I was bullied as a teenager, I didn't talk about it. I kept it bottled up and it eventually built up too much pressure.

You can get through being bullied. It's very important to know and believe that you will get through it. Being bullied can even make you stronger, it did for me. Bullying is one subject that I really take issue with. I will discuss it later, but after being bullied when I was younger, I believe I have become 'un-bullyable.' I refuse to be bullied.

Secure people have no desire to bully other people. Only insecure and hurt people bully. Insecure people that want to bully others look for reasons and openings to attack them and dump their insecurities onto that person. An example could be an insecure hurt boy wanting to talk to a particular girl. He sees someone with the courage to talk to her, instead of building his own courage, he picks on the kid that actually had courage (he tears down, to be the tallest).

Bullies overcompensate because they're jealous and/or they know they're lacking something. They choose cowardice over courage. Instead of being honest with themselves and dealing with their personal problems, they resort to tearing others down.

A friend of mine shared a story with me about a boy named Drayke Hardman. His sister found him hanging from his favorite sweatshirt in his bedroom...*he was 12 years old!* His dad immediately started CPR and he passed away the next day. There were pictures of Drayke and his family in the hospital. One of them showed his dad crying while embracing his dead son. Another showed his son's hand resting on the hands of two family members. After I read the article and saw the pictures, I began sobbing. As I type this I'm still crying.

I love my kids so much, they're so incredibly precious to me. I know this boy Drayke is just as precious to his parents as well. My heart goes out to him and his family. I immediately started praying for comfort for him and his family, and that what happened be used for good.

I don't want to imagine the emotions Drayke went through, or the helpless panic his sister and dad experienced. How can this be? Why would such a young boy full of life resort to suicide? It turns out, Drayke was being bullied at school. I picture a caring child just wanting peace, yet was confronted with bitterness and was unable to process it.

With permission, I mention Drayke and his family by name because his parents, Andy and Samie Hardman, have started a campaign called #doitfordrayke to help bring more awareness to bullying. They're using the tragic loss of their son to bring light to the subject of bullying and how serious it can get. They want to prevent other children from enduring what Drayke did and other parents from experiencing what they have.

You can learn more at doitfordrayke.com

In the aftermath of unimaginable loss, finger pointing and placing blame is only natural. *"What could we have done,"* or *"If only I would've..."* or *"How could you do this?"* The world can be very cruel and dangerous. As a parent, it's a very interesting thing. We want to prepare our kids for the world, so when they're old enough to be on their own, they're ready. If we isolate our kids too much, they may never be ready, but if we do nothing, the world may beat them down before they've reached adulthood.

When a child simply wants to be kind and get along with others but has to deal with someone that wants the opposite, it's like two worlds colliding. It reminds me of someone who wants to give, interacting with someone who wants to take. The giver's usually taken advantage of, yet continues to give because it's in their nature.

How do we teach our kids the right way to resist a bully? How do we give them the ability to hold their head high and make a bully leave them alone? I believe bringing things out of the dark and into the light is the first step. (Luke 12:3)

One tactic bullies use is staying under the radar. They want to hurt others, quietly. If they make a show of things, it brings attention to themselves and exposes how hurtful and insecure they actually are. This doesn't mean they may not try to retaliate if they're exposed, it just means *they don't want to be exposed*. We need to be bold and speak the truth. A bully is a bully and should be called out as such. This part can look different to various people.

There were two main hurdles for me
when it came to dealing with bullies;

1. Most of the time, I didn't have the confidence to say what I needed to say at the time, and...

2. I didn't have the confidence to follow up with anything physical if I needed to.

Chapter 3: Kids

I'll discuss this in more detail later, but I must mention part of it here; shortly after graduating high school, I started learning Brazilian Jiu-Jitsu and Muay Thai (Similar to kickboxing). There was great physical health benefits, but the biggest benefit to me was that over time, I grew more confident. I began to hold my head higher. Not that I was some kind of tough guy, it just felt good to get over one of the hurdles I mentioned above.

As the years went on, knowing I had the ability to get physical with someone if necessary, helped free up my tongue. In a confrontation, I was finally able say what needed said. I knew that if things were to get physical, I could handle it. Getting over hurdle #2, helped me get over hurdle #1. The physical preceded the verbal.

<blockquote>
In Dr. Jordan Peterson's bestselling book *12 Rules for Life*, he had this to say;
</blockquote>

"If you can bite, you generally don't have to. When skillfully integrated, the ability to respond with aggression and violence decreases rather than increases the probability that actual aggression will become necessary. If you say no, early in the cycle of oppression, and you mean what you say (which means you state your refusal in no uncertain terms and stand behind it), then the scope for oppression on the part of the oppressor will remain properly bounded and limited."

-Dr Jordan Peterson
12 Rules for Life, P. 23-24

If this sounds appealing to any of you parents for your child, I strongly suggest going to YouTube and looking up "Gracie Bullyproof." (The Gracie family is credited for making Brazilian Jiu-Jitsu what it is today). In the "Bullyproof" videos, you'll watch kid's confidence grow as they learn how to handle bullies if they get physical. Just like my experience, this allows kids the freedom to use words to hopefully stop a bully before things get physical.

In the event the bully gets physical, kids have the tools to help protect themselves. One great thing about Brazilian Jiu-Jitsu (BJJ) is with the right training, size makes much less of a difference. A smaller person can hold a much larger person in a position to talk to them without having to hurt them. There's also a nice comradery with most BJJ schools and it's a great place for kids (and adults) to develop friendships. It doesn't have to be a Gracie school, but in my opinion a good BJJ school with a kid's class is excellent for kids, especially for kids being bullied.

Another option for dealing with bullies is to actually compliment the bully, what some would call 'flattery.' Complimenting a bully is a great tool for disarming them and de-escalating the situation. This may sound strange, but think of it this way...everyone loves a compliment, and it's hard to give someone a hard time that's being nice to you.

This method starts by first swallowing your pride. Even though you don't deserve to be treated the way they're treating you, look for opportunities to give them genuine compliments. Bullies look for confrontation. They look for openings with vulnerable people to let out their unstable emotions. However (like Jiu-Jitsu), you can take their verbal momentum and use it against them...here's a simple example:

Bully (looking for an altercation): "What are you staring at? ...you got a problem?!"

Response (calm and unthreatening): "No, no problem. I was looking at your hat, it looks really cool. I wish I had one like that."

It's important to keep compliments simple and don't overdue it, or it could come across fake. Another example of this is a kid being bullied at school walking by their bully (when their bully is alone), and give them a *brief* genuine compliment. A few *calculated* times of this could lesson the bully's desire to pick on them and instead move on to someone else.

Sometimes it can be very difficult, but it's possible to swallow our pride and take the high road. What's better...to win an altercation or avoid an altercation? I'll spare you a cheesy *Karate Kid* quote :)

Instead, I'll share this;

Blessed are the peacemakers,
for they will be called children of God.

-Matthew 5:9 (NIV)

Or how about this;

If your enemies are hungry, give them food to eat. If they are thirsty, give them water to drink. You will heap burning coals of shame on their heads, and the Lord will reward you.

-Proverbs 25:21-22 (NLT)

Lastly, but certainly not least, pray for the bully (Matthew 5:44). This is not native to us and can often be hard to do. It takes purpose and having empathy for the person. About 2/3 of the New Testament of the Bible was written by a former bully. He was a terrible man named Saul. Extremely religious, he hated Jesus and his followers. He hunted them down and persecuted them (Acts 8:3). After a face to face experience with Jesus in his pursuit to capture His followers, he was completely changed. Saul was struck blind and it took a follower of Jesus to pray for him to regain his sight (Acts 9). What if the man refused to pray for him? He knew who Saul was and what he'd been doing. What would the world look like today if no one prayed for him to regain his sight?

Sure, the bully 'deserves' this or that, but love and mercy can be infinitely more valuable than what we'd like to do to them. God sees the Paul inside of a horrible Saul. He also sees the scared little child inside of a bully and it's that child that we're ultimately praying for.

Cyber Bullying

Let's talk about another aspect of bullying, *cyber bullying*. Most kids in history never had to experience this type of bullying. I certainly didn't. Nowadays, bullies have the ability to be even more cowardly than they already were. They can emotionally hurt their victims anonymously and worse, coerce others to join in.

One tactic cyber bullies do is create fake accounts and target their victim on social media. They have the ability to publicly say terrible things to their young victim, while remaining anonymous. They can make up stories or accuse them of anything for any potential viewer to see. Seemingly without recourse.

There are many other examples of cyber bullying, but parents, try to wrap your minds around this; imagine a kid making a short video about something they're interested in. In their excitement, they're vulnerable on camera and show their heart to the world. The huge downside is they completely open themselves up to ridicule...*by anyone, anywhere.* There are wicked people itching to stomp all over someone, just because they can.

In this hypothetical scenario, a cyber bully feels the need to make a video poking fun of the original kid's video. If the bully's video gets traction, the original kid may get bombarded with horrible comments from potentially thousands of bullies, not just the original bully. Dealing with one bully is bad enough, but what about receiving countless degrading messages from people across the world on top of it?

In essence, a kid had the courage to open himself up to the world, and a jealous coward (who wishes he could be that vulnerable), takes the opportunity to hurt the courageous kid as much as possible, and brings others to join in. (Matthew 7:6 comes to mind here).

I do not believe kids are made to handle this type of ridicule and rejection. Personally, I don't like the idea of kids posting photos or videos of themselves online at all. I can think of hundreds of downsides and very few, if any, upsides.

Like we talked about earlier, just because other kids are doing it, doesn't mean that your kid should. Parents need to understand the technology and issues children are growing up with didn't exist when we were kids. We can't just tell them to 'suck it up and deal with it' when we have zero experience in the matter. We did not go through the kinds of things our children are going through today.

How do we combat cyber bullying?

As you may have concluded by now, I believe kids are much better off staying away from social media altogether. For the most part, social media is the bathroom stall of society. How many people go into a bathroom stall and take a stranger's advice via scribbles on the wall?

My job as a parent is to provide for and protect my kids. My job is to prepare them for adulthood and the rest of their life. Letting them interact with the bathrooms stalls of society doesn't achieve those goals. While our kids may have a better understanding of what's happening on social media, as parents, we have a much better overall perspective of life than our children possibly can.

If you're experiencing cyber bullying, what's keeping you from deleting the app off your device? You are. In my opinion, the sooner you get over the addiction and snare of social media, the sooner you mature and grow into the person God wants you to be.

The Younger Me

From Suicide to Freedom

From the time I was young, I've always had a strong passion for both listening to, and making music. I was nine years old when Metallica's *Black Album* came out. One of my favorite memories growing up was having that cassette playing through my walkman as I did my paper route. Along with the newspaper bag, I'd also attached a pair of speakers to the handlebars of my bicycle.

My young ears gripped the auditory bliss of electric guitars and thundering drums that emanated from my bike. Rubber band clad newspapers flew through the air as I imagined myself playing guitar on a stage somewhere. Oh, if only I could go back to that memorable time, but would I want to? To this day, when I hear *Wherever I May Roam* from that album (probably my favorite song ever), I am brought back to riding my bike through rows of single-wide trailers on a sunny Montana day.

Chapter 3: Kids

I got my first guitar when I was around ten years old. I was taking piano lessons at the time. My piano teacher was a very nice lady who helped me appreciate classical music. Her and her husband owned a small music store in town. Somehow I coerced my mom to take me there one weekend. After we walked in, I was instantly enamored by all the instruments, especially the electric guitars.

I remember the moment I saw what I'd later learn was a Gibson Flying V hanging on the wall. I could tell it was a special guitar and I really enjoyed looking at it. It was different and cool at the same time. Its white paint reminded me of porcelain and I'd never seen a guitar shaped like that before. I was instantly interested in getting an electric guitar, especially *that one,* (I'd still love to get one). But for a ten year old in 1992, the price tag may as well been a million dollars. But then I noticed it...it was another odd shaped electric guitar sitting on the floor. It was covered in a black and white checkerboard pattern. It even had a long fin and a point on it. *"Fifty dollars!"* I thought it was the bargain of a lifetime. To my young eyes, it looked equal to the Gibson and for 1/20th the price, who could pass up that opportunity! I knew nothing about guitars at the time, but I knew one thing. *I wanted it.*

I'm sure I pulled out all the stops when I asked my mom if I could get it. She was a bank teller and my dad was a garbage man, so $50 was a big deal. I don't remember if I promised to pay her back with my paper route money, but whatever I said worked! A few minutes later, we set my very first guitar in the back of our wood paneled station wagon. It ended up spending the next few years sitting in my bedroom closet. Occasionally I'd pull it out and play rock star in the mirror. Little did I know it then, that cheap electric guitar would be a very important outlet for me.

The tougher and more confusing life was, the more important music became. One day I pulled that piece of wood and strings out of the closet and set out to learn how to play it. With the encouragement of my older brother, I'd sit for hours and slowly figure out how to play my favorite songs.

TIME STOOD STILL

I didn't know what notes I was playing. After a difficult time learning piano theory, I enjoyed the simplicity of learning the guitar by ear. After learning about a half dozen of my favorite songs, I ended up with a big problem; I was getting bored and felt like quitting. I'd found out the guitar parts on my favorite songs were mostly just a few chords that repeat, over and over. I know it sounds silly now, but at the time I thought that was the extent of guitar playing. Then, something amazing happened!

There used to be an ad in various magazines where you could purchase a bunch of CDs for next to nothing. So I cut out the ad, checked off the CDs I wanted, added a few bucks and sent it off. About a months later, I received a package in the mail. I quickly opened the box to find a dozen brand new CDs for a cheap price. At 14, I felt like I'd beaten the system.

I was familiar with all of the artists I had requested, except one. I'd checked off a particular album because I'd heard the name before, but didn't know who he was. It was track 2 of *that* CD that exploded the possibilities of the guitar for me. Who knows if I'd still be playing guitar and making music today had I not received that disc all those years ago.

His name was *Jimi Hendrix,* and the song was *Machine Gun* from the album *Band of Gypsys*. It was recorded live on new years eve, 1970 in New York City. To me, it's an absolute masterpiece. The emotion that came through the speakers when I first heard it was indescribable. My desire to play guitar went through the roof.

After that I started getting more of his music and began the task of learning my favorite songs. This time, every one I learned was more challenging, but much more fulfilling. I absolutely loved the challenge of learning and playing those songs.

> A side note; having Billy Cox (the bassist on the Band of Gypsys album) play on one of my songs is on my bucket list if anyone happens to know him ;-)

Chapter 3: Kids

Let me tell you about the two worst years of my life. They were filled with tension, uneasiness, depression and suicidal thoughts. The best way I can describe it is like a long silent scream. No one around knew what I was going through, not even those closest to me. In hindsight, those difficult years were very good for me. Though at the time, enduring them seemed almost unbearable. Through it all, God got me through and I'm stronger now because of it. Let me explain...

I was in high school. It was 10th and 11th grade, (16-17 years old). This particular school was the biggest in the area. I didn't feel like I fit in. At the same time, I told myself I really didn't want to fit in. I was into skateboarding, snowboarding and music. Outside of those things, I just wanted to be left alone.

I was usually pretty quiet and generally preferred keeping to myself. Those years were filled with so many new experiences and new challenges. No matter how much I would've denied it at the time, the combination of feeling rejected and 'What will they think?' was ever present.

One very strong need I felt was the need for a girlfriend. I know in hindsight it's silly, but at the time I wanted one so bad. To this day I don't know why not having one effected me so much. Maybe it was teenage hormones, or thinking a girlfriend to confide in could help with how I was feeling. I'm not sure exactly. What I know for sure is not having one was a depressing issue for me back then.

About that time I started to listen to different kinds of music too. I don't recall how it happened, but I started listening to a lot of heavy metal. I went from playing Jimi Hendrix tunes to learning how to speed pick so I could play fast. Something about the combination of double bass drums, powerful guitars and aggressive vocals really fit the turmoil I was feeling inside. Many people may not understand it, but listening to aggressive music would actually calm me down. It was a way to let out the aggression, sadness and uncertainty I felt inside.

During those two years, things continued to get worse for me. The straw that almost broke the proverbial camel's back was a bully at work. After school I was working at a place rebuilding water filters. I was already in a low and vulnerable place, but there was a guy at work pushing me over the edge. The worst it ever got was when I was 17. He was about ten years older than me. Can you imagine a 27 year old man picking on a 17 year old kid? How could a supposedly grown man think that's OK?

Being so quiet, I think he saw me as an easy target... *and I was.* At the time, he was very intimidating to me. He'd verbally push me around and make me feel small, weak and inferior. Occasionally I'd try to stand up to him, but he'd get in my face and I'd cower. It was so degrading. My life was becoming almost unbearable. As a quiet 17 year old, I'd never been in that position before. I had no perspective or understanding of what to do.

I started sneaking beer into my bedroom. Without anyone knowing, I began drinking myself to sleep with room temperature beers I'd swiped from my dad. It quickly progressed from beer to straight rum and whiskey at night. To this day I don't remember how I was able to get hard alcohol, my folks didn't drink it.

Things went from bad to worse when I started drinking before school. After I parked my Jeep, I'd pull out a flask and drink through a straw so people walking by wouldn't notice. Then, come lunch time, I'd do it again. One time during lunch break a few friends caught me. They chuckled and thought it was funny. But it wasn't funny, I was hurting inside and I didn't know how to handle it. I wasn't concerned teachers would notice. Maybe deep down I was hoping I'd get caught so the hurt I was hiding could be exposed. But no teachers did. Then, in my dark bedroom at night, I'd drink even more. The next step in my downward progression became even more dire.

There became nights where the lonely void and hurt in my heart felt like too much to bear. The chasm of despair and loneliness I felt was beyond words. I would hold a long sharp knife to my wrist and forearm. I would start to cut, but then I'd stop. I imagined what my parents would walk in and see the next morning, it was like a wall for me. Covered in tears, I'd desperately cry out to God for help. I begged and pleaded with Him to fill the void I felt inside.

I never actually wanted to die. I just didn't want to live feeling the way I did. The cycle kept repeating; lonely during the day, bullied at work, then depressed at night...over and over. I was still playing music through it all, but it was not relieving the pressure at the rate I needed. The pressure had finally built to a dangerous level. At the age of 17, I hit the lowest of lows...It was at rock bottom when I had my awakening. Unfortunately, it took a friend dying to receive it.

Do you want to know what God used to pull me out of the horrible place I was in? It was an experience that changed my life forever. Out of nowhere, a 16 year old friend of mine from church shot himself. It was a big shock to the community. He was the only kid I remember growing up who committed suicide. I walked into his memorial service, still at my lowest point. Inside, I began seeing many of my other friends. This is when I had my epiphany....

- *I saw;* How absolutely devastated all of my friends were. That could've been me making them so heartbroken.
- *I saw;* His little brother in confused anguish. I have a little brother about the same age. That could've been him, filled with an unexplainable loss, after I purposely left him.
- *I saw;* His mom and dad, completely distraught. That could've been my parents, mourning the sudden loss of their son at such a young age, after I did that to them.
- *I saw;* The absolutely horrific aftermath of what my friend killing himself did to all those that loved him the most.
- *I saw;* The confused torment his irrational action brought on so many unsuspecting people.

TIME STOOD STILL

I was forever changed that day. I was suddenly snatched out of the dense fog I was in and brought into the light. I had a newfound perspective and began to see clearly. The air smelled fresher, the sun was brighter and I began to notice beauty in the world again. I knew I still had my teenage problems, but I also knew that depression and suicide was not the solution. My life began to drastically change for the better that day. I appreciated people and opportunities more, and I started to view myself in a more positive light. I chose to change after witnessing what I did. I am so grateful God gave me a second chance when I was at my lowest.

If I could go back and talk to my younger self, I'd say this;

"What you're feeling and going through is normal. At this age, you're going to have new emotions and experience many new things. Over time you'll get more perspective and understanding. What seems so difficult now, you'll look back on and be grateful for. It will make you stronger and help shape and form you into the person God wants you to be. Sometimes life isn't easy or fair, but the journey is worth it.

It's OK to let the right people know how you're feeling and ask for help. Find the people that love you, the ones you trust. Even if it's only one person...share what you've been hiding. Every time you tell your story it's like a weight being lifted off. You're no longer carrying the entire load. You have nothing to be ashamed of."

The biggest change I would've made would be talking to the right people about what I was going through, instead of suffering in silence. In doing so, it would have relieved pressure before getting to such dangerous levels. Even though it would've been difficult, talking to my parents and close friends would have helped immensely. I would've also dealt with the bully very differently and been much more firm with him.

If you're in a similar position, do not talk to just anybody about this, especially on social media. You're looking to open your heart to someone trustworthy. You can not blindly trust everyone with your heart. Your current struggle is not everyone's business and some may use the opportunity to hurt you worse. Find the right person/people to talk to, ideally in person.

Even if you've never prayed before, I suggest you find a quiet moment and humbly say something like this; "Jesus, please help me, please bring me the right person to talk to about my struggles with suicide."

Used for Good

A major choice I made years ago was to use suicide for good. Instead of wallowing in shame and guilt for having those previous temptations, I used them to help push me. When I hit a fork in the road where I'd normally cower and want to take the easy way, I would say something like this to myself...

- "What if you would've gone through with it, what kind of life would you be missing out on? Let's find out!"

- "Sure, this may be difficult or embarrassing, but if you had killed yourself, you wouldn't have this opportunity at all! Just do it the best you can, it'll all work out."

- "What can this person possibly do to you that you weren't willing to do to yourself? You have nothing to be afraid of."

- "What can this experience do to you that you weren't willing to do to yourself? You're going to get through it just fine."

With God's help, over the years I've used my experience of depression and suicide to overcome fear. Why would I be afraid of someone's words, when a voluntary knife at my wrist is infinitely more dangerous.

Through repetition and practice, the hard roads got progressively easier. I have since learned that our comfort zone is our failure zone. Sometimes, it takes the hard roads to chip away at the weak parts of us. I've been in so many uncomfortable situations over the years that today, being uncomfortable, feels comfortable. In taking that road over and over, I feel I've experienced more in 40 years than I would've in 200 the other way. I've stood on mountain tops and spoken in front of thousands, followed the dream of music and started businesses, gotten married and had children, and the list goes on. I say all this as an example, it's not about me. It's about you; *you can choose to use suicide for good too!*

Whether you've lost a loved one to suicide or you are struggling with suicide yourself, you can use it for good...and I truly hope you do. You and those you love are worth it. I've certainly made mistakes along the way, but I refuse to let them slow me down like I used to. In those moments I ask myself; 'What did I learn?' I've found that without our mistakes, God would have nothing to work with.

Lazy people use the word 'lucky' as a cop-out for their unwillingness to do the hard things. Calling someone lucky is rude and ignorant. I'm not lucky. I'm very blessed and I work very hard...even when things get tough. I have a God who loves me and has always been there for me. If you choose to accept the challenge of using suicide for good, the wonderful fruit that comes from it will not be out of luck. It will be because you believed the best and hoped the best. You focused on where you wanted to go, not the bad places you've been. What the enemy means for evil, God wants to use for good... will we let Him? Asking myself those *'what if'* questions caused me to push through the paper thin walls of fear and into freedom. If you're reading this and have suicidal thoughts...

> "What if you were to go through with it, what kind of life would you be missing out on? What could you achieve if you used your struggles to help you, rather than destroy you? Let's find out!"

The Outlet

Outlet [out-let, -lit]: *a place or opening through which something is let out: exit, vent* [133/134]

I encourage everyone to find a productive outlet. It's something that helps let out pressure so it doesn't reach dangerous levels. The main outlet God has blessed me with since I was young has been music. Other outlets over the years have been photography, working on cars, woodworking and martial arts.

Your outlet(s) certainly don't have to be any of these, but I know there are at least one or two outlets God has put in you. Picture them like relief valves He placed in you for relieving life's pressures. They should feel natural and calming. You may want to feel guilty for taking the time to do them, but don't. It's very important to have some peaceful 'you' time.

Chapter 4: Life Happens

The Blue Bird

Let's do an experiment; don't think about a blue bird, don't think about a blue bird...whatever you do...

Don't...think...about...a...blue...bird!!!

What are you thinking about?

A blue bird.

It's not enough to 'stop thinking about A', stop doing A, or ignore A. We must stop A, but we must also focus on B. Think about B. Put our energy into B. *We must replace A with B.* Stop 'watering' A and 'water' B. Stop giving attention to A and give it to B. Stop complaining about A and say good things about B.

Chapter 4: Life Happens

If we leave our house vacant, what would eventually happen? Whether we like it or not, something or someone would fill it. It could be rodents, bugs, raccoons, squatters, who knows. This principle also applies to time. If we don't plan what we're doing with our time, things we don't plan, will fill it. The bottom line is this; if we leave a void, it'll be filled. Voids do not stay voids for long. For instance, if someone wants to quit a bad habit, they need to replace the bad habit with something they want. This could look like going for a walk instead of smoking. Reading a book instead of being on social media. Saying good things about people instead of bad things.

How does this principle relate to suicide? Whether you're struggling with suicide or have lost a loved one to suicide, being stuck in the cycle of suicidal thought is common. Suicide can be a sticky subject that keeps us in a place we really don't want to be. It's not enough to simply say 'don't think about suicide.' What does 'not' thinking about suicide leave us with? Like the blue bird example, it leaves us thinking about suicide.

Instead, we must replace those thoughts with something we *do* want. Like I brought up last chapter, what's your outlet? What's something good you can focus on? Instead of watering the weed seed of suicide, how about watering actual seeds in a small garden? Don't have a garden, why not start one? Gardening is a great outlet. I love the process of watching life grow before your eyes after putting in the work. What about volunteering, learning an instrument you've always wanted to, writing, going to the gym, starting a business, learning a martial art, getting a job in a better field, moving to a place you've always wanted to, (or at least taking a trip there). What about opening a dusty Bible and getting to know the Jesus you'll one day meet.

The possibilities are endless, the bottom line is this; *we get what we focus on.* So let's focus on good things we actually want in our lives. This is why they teach white-water-rafters to focus on where they want to go on the river, not the huge boulders in the way. If they focused on 'not hitting the boulders,' they would inevitably...

...hit the boulders. Did you know that in the Bible, Jesus was not the only person to walk on water? A man named Peter was also able to walk on water. As long as Peter looked at Jesus and believed he could walk on water, *he did.* Do you know what happened? Peter got distracted and changed his focus to the wind and the waves...*and sank.* He got what he focused on.

People are rut builders. If we do the same thing day after day, eventually we can't see out of the rut we've dug ourselves into. Getting out of our daily ruts and getting a new perspective on life is extremely important from time to time. It's common to construct a negative view of ourselves, and wind up surrounding ourselves with those that reinforce this pessimistic view. It could easily be family and close friends. In such a case, getting out of the rut could be moving out of it, to a new place, around new people. Or at least taking a vacation and getting out of the rut for a time.

There's an old saying about a crab pot. The analogy goes like this; if you put a single crab in a pot, it'll slowly crawl out. However, if you put multiple crabs in a pot, you don't even have to put a lid on it. As soon as one crab starts to crawl out, the other crabs pull them back in. Life's often like a crab pot. The people closest to us are often the ones that pull us back down when we try to get out. One certainty I've found in life is that people don't like being exposed. If you work hard to get out of your situation, you can bet some people close to you will do their best *to keep you where you are.* They do this because they don't want to be exposed. If you were to actually get free, it would prove they could've done the same thing. The best thing we can do for the people we love is to be an example to follow.

Climbing out of the crab pot will show them they can do the same thing, should they choose to. Some will, some won't. But that's not your choice to make. You made the choice to climb out and they have their own choice to make. God does not make junk. You do not need to accept misery. You do not need to accept depression and the temptations of suicide. You are worth so much more than that. Listen to these words from Jesus:

"Look at the birds. They don't plant or harvest or store food in barns, for your heavenly Father feeds them. And aren't you far more valuable to him than they are?"

-Matthew 6:26 (NLT)

Depression

From my experience, most people connect suicide to depression. A common statement people say when hearing about a suicide is "I didn't even know they were depressed."

According to the NIH; "Major depression is one of the most common mental disorders in the United States. For some individuals, major depression can result in severe impairments that interfere with or limit one's ability to carry out major life activities" (NIH).[25]

While depression may be a factor at times with someone attempting suicide, I don't believe depression is the only factor. An example could be if someone's depressed, then has challenging events heaped on top of it. Another factor could be a spiritual attack while they're already in a low and depressed state. The enemy loves that tactic. *More about this later.*

I've certainly had low points in life, but there's one thing that's always gotten me through. It's one of the most vital things any of us can acquire. *Hope.* Hope is what kept the father watching every day for his prodigal son to return. Hope is what kept Abraham believing he would be a father to many, even though he was an old man without children. Hope is what the bleeding woman had when she touched the hem of Jesus' garment...and was healed.

Hope is essential. Hope is foundational. Hope gives context when we're down or depressed. Hope shines light into our darkest moments. Hope is the lifeline we desperately need when we're barely clinging to life. Hope causes thoughts of improving and a better life.

Hope preserves. Hope restores. If you're in a low and depressed state, hope. Hope confirms we do not have to accept being stuck where we're at. Hope is the vision that draws us forward. It keeps us going. With hope, we know that sooner or later, this too shall pass.

There's an old saying that goes like this; *'When in hell, don't get a motel.'* If you're in a terrible spot, don't just stay there. Believe the best and *hope* the best. Hope causes words...words cause action. Action starts getting us out of our lowly state. Recognizing we're getting out of that state gives us more hope, and the fruitful cycle continues...

Do you see what happened? Instead of a downward cycle of despair, sprinkling the ingredient of hope into our lives starts a movement in the right direction. This turns into a cycle in the right direction. We can't steer a parked car, we need to act. Hope is the nudge that gets the car moving. Hope and keep on hoping. *I'll discuss more about hope later in the book.*

Depression Statistics:

- Depression affects 20-25% of Americans ages 18+ in a given year. (Save)[24]

- Females experience depression at roughly two times the rate of men. (Save)[24]

- Only half of all Americans experiencing an episode of major depression receive treatment. (Save)[24]

- 80%-90% of people that seek treatment for depression are treated successfully using therapy and/or medication. (Save)[24] *(We'll talk about prescription drugs later).*

I believe there's a distinction between potentially dangerous depression vs. a person's selfish fantasies about suicide. Let me explain. Some people have a narcissistic imagery, imagining distraught friends and loved ones mourning over them in some twisted selfish way. I believe this is transitional immaturity. In my opinion, this usually occurs during the change that happens from thinking like a child to thinking like an adult. (Which for some takes much longer than others, *if ever*). An example would be during someone's first time experiencing big obstacles, especially in a body full of increasing hormones. The selfish feelings of suicide differ from that of the dangerously depressed. The very depressed person doesn't think about suicide the same way. They don't get a thrill from imagining loved ones mourning for them.

For the severely depressed, it's like being in a dark hole. An abysmal void where internal screams are absorbed by textured darkness. The cold black is a barrier between them and the obscured light. They can see the light, but barely. People don't understand where they are and getting out seems nearly impossible.

"They'd be better off without me..."

The common words spoken of a suicidal and depressed person. But that's not true! It's a lie...don't buy the lie. Suicide is never the answer. It's absolutely possible to get out of this state. I've done it and if you're in this state, you can do it too!   Do you want out? Do you really want out? Great! *Keep reading.*

Finances:

Financial difficulties can have an impact on suicide rates, particularly in men. First of all, two traits most men have ingrained in them are to provide and to protect. Having major financial problems hinders both. For single men, providing and protecting is much simpler. If they make bad financial decisions, consequences can be tough, but they only impact themselves. However, for men with families, the stakes are significantly higher. A man with a family depending on him has an important weight on his shoulders. The weight is even heavier if he's doing so within his own strength and understandings. (Proverbs 3:5-8) Should a family man find himself unable to *provide*, the household may have to move to a more affordable and generally less-safe area. In doing so, this may also impact his ability to *protect*.

Regardless if the man caused the financial problems or not, this type of event can be one of the most demoralizing things a man can experience. Providing and protecting are huge traits of what it means to be a man. Failing in these areas can easily leave a man feeling worthless and incapable of truly being a man. But that's not all, this type of event can also bring shame, guilt and embarrassment.

'What will my wife and kids say?'

'How will this change the way they view me?'

'What about my friends and extended family?'

This is a brief summary of a study done after the 2008 crises regarding suicide rates during that turbulent time;

"After the 2008 economic crisis, rates of suicide increased in the European and American countries studied, particularly in men and in countries with higher levels of job loss." (Chang)[40]

For husbands and dads out there, your wife and kids need you. They need you infinitely more than they need money. Money can be lost and made again. *You can not be.* You are not replaceable, money is. For you single guys in a tough financial spot, welcome. This is where you mature and grow. Yes, it's tough. But I know you will learn a lot and it'll make you stronger in the long run. For instance, a brother of mine lost everything in 2009, but guess what he did. He took everything he learned...what to do and what not do...and kept going.

Chapter 4: Life Happens

Through the wisdom he gained during those tough times and hard work, he's built one of the most successful businesses around in his industry. Today, he and his family live on hundreds of acres, something he's always wanted to do. He never would have accomplished his successes without enduring hardship.

Years ago, one of the most impactful businessmen I've ever known encouraged me to watch the movie *Cinderella Man,* starring Russell Crowe.

"Most people think it's impossible for them to wind up in a similar position. Somehow, they feel like they're the exception...they're not."

In general, most of us have been spoiled by varying degrees our entire lives. The average person in the U.S. lives better than kings of the past. Don't believe me? King Solomon is known for being the wisest person to ever live, (after Jesus of course). But, did you know he's also the wealthiest person to ever live? (2 chronicles 1:12)

In all of his immense power, wisdom and splendor, did he have a refrigerator that kept his food and drinks cold? Did he have a forced air heated and cooled house? What about something as simple as electricity and the ability to have endless light at the flick of a switch? Could he jump in an air conditioned mobile vehicle and drive down paved streets, all while talking to a friend thousands of miles away at the push of a button? Did he have a hot water heater providing 100 degree plumbed water for a cozy shower?

Could King Solomon listen to any type of music he wanted, just by having a little box play it? Or did he have access to endless information from all over the earth at the click of a mouse? A homeless man with a library card has that. What about traveling clear across a continent in a matter of hours? College kids on spring break can do that.

We don't understand just how good we have it. Did you know if you make $32,000 or more in a year, you're in the top 1% income bracket in the entire world? Did you know that 1/4 of the people in the world don't even have access to safe drinking water?[79] I laugh at the hypocrites who throw the word 'privilege' around these days, they're the very ones who're privileged.

We complain that our iPhone is getting old or we have to wait in line for more than five minutes to get coffee. We have it so easy that many have resorted to a sad game of 'who can be the most offended,' where the person who whines the most, thinks they win. But that isn't how the real world works, unfortunately some have to learn this the hard way. Think of the horrific and challenging things our ancestors had to overcome for us (in general) to be so complacent and apathetic.

Most of the world looks at the U.S. as fat and lazy. One of my concerns is *WHEN* tough times come, how will millions of spoiled and entitled Americans react? My grandparents lived through the great depression. Back then, many people knew how to farm, hunt, barter, make and fix things, and it was still very difficult for them. Movies depicting times past make me feel like such a weakling. *Braveheart?* Check. *Cinderella Man?* Yep. *The Patriot?* Yessir.

Financial difficulties are one of the hardest things to go through. Whether up or down, in good times or bad, it's incredibly important to remain grateful. Focusing on what we have; family, a spouse, kids, life, health, friends, shelter, food, air, water, etc.

No matter what may come in life, all of us have things to be grateful for in any given moment. Finding joy in every moment, whether good or bad, is a worth-while pursuit. Pride is a killer and a thief. Financial difficulties are a great way of humbling us and helping us mature. Count it all joy, this too shall pass.

Chapter 4: Life Happens

Isolation:

Like you, I have my opinions and beliefs about what has transpired in the last few years regarding a health scare, and the actions taken. Instead of getting into opinions, let's discuss obvious facts and their potential implications on suicide rates;

1. Millions of people were in fear of catching a disease they thought could kill them.

2. Millions of people were forced or strongly encouraged to stay at home and isolate from others.

3. Millions of people were forced or strongly encouraged to cover their face when around others.

4. Millions of people were unable to work because their business was labeled non-essential.

5. Millions of people avoided their own friends and loved ones.

6. Millions of people distanced themselves from others and avoided physical contact.

7. Millions of people were divided with each other about what was happening and the large scale methods taken.

8. Millions of people were given government assistance.

9. Millions of people were forced or pressured to take a fast-tracked vaccine to keep their job or to go about life in a somewhat normal fashion.

10. Millions of people believe the vaccine is safe and effective while millions of others believe the vaccine is not safe or effective.

There are many other examples, but let's stop there.

The last handful of years have been more divisive than I ever thought possible. I saw families voluntarily avoiding close loved ones. Even within families, many members were angry with each other over their choice to wear a mask or not, take *'the jab'* or not, social distance or not, go about life normally or not, avoid physical touch or not, etc. I never imagined I'd see my fellow Americans acting the way many of them have. Instead of pointing fingers at each other, let's look at the big picture and think about the potential ramifications regarding suicide.

Check this out from *Psychology Today*;

"We are now seeing some serious consequences of these responses to the pandemic. Mental health difficulties such as anxiety and depression, as well as substance abuse have all increased during the pandemic (Agha, 2021). **Enforced isolation** appears to be a particularly potent trigger for these increases. Reduced contact with friends and smaller households are correlated with increased difficulties (Bland et al., 2021). Those who already struggle with mental health difficulties or substance abuse are likely to experience deterioration during this time.

While these effects on adults are sufficiently concerning, the impact on children may be devastating. In particular, children kept out of school are showing deterioration in their mental health, **with increases in depression and suicide attempts.** The impact of [C-19] on families through loss of employment, financial insecurity, loss of child care services, and available social support for families has resulted in increases in child abuse (Cho, Smith, Cory, & Smith, 2021). Intimate partner violence has also increased during the pandemic (Viero, Barbara, Montisci, Kustermann, & Cattaneo,

2021). Thus, unintended but predictable consequences from the pandemic and the consequent "lockdowns" with the associated social isolation are obvious.

The response to [C-19] and the effort to control the pandemic by isolating individuals and families is exposing millions of children to Adverse Childhood Experiences (ACEs) which we know to be predictive of future difficulties, ranging from increased likelihood of smoking to **suicide and increased morbidity and mortality** in general (Boccia, 2017). The relationship between ACEs and these negative outcomes is quite direct: the more ACEs an individual experiences in childhood, the greater the likelihood that they will experience negative outcomes in adulthood. Maltreatment, substance abuse, and parental mental illness are all ACEs that are increasing through the social isolation imposed on families to deal with the pandemic." [29]

Do you see anywhere in this portion of the article about the effects of being sick? No. It's the effects of people's voluntary or involuntary isolation to the *fear of being sick* that's caused so many issues. We're currently finding out the major negative impacts that can follow such isolation. At the time of writing this, a lengthy paper by the IEA just came out entitled; *Did lockdowns work? The verdict on Covid restrictions.*[68] The paper discusses how ineffective "lockdowns" actually were. But how effective were they at mentally hurting people?

Below are two quotes from the 2023 IEA Paper:

"In addition to their immediate economic impact, lockdowns have reduced the time spent by children in school, decreasing the extent of education, and therefore reduced investment in human capital, increased mental disorders and domestic violence, and caused significant quality-of-life losses. Lockdowns have also reduced personal freedom, caused political unrest, strengthened authoritarian tendencies, increased government corruption, and undermined liberal democracy." (IEA 2023) [68]

"A standard comparison of the costs and benefits of lockdowns leads to a strong conclusion: until future research based on credible empirical evidence proves that lockdowns have large and significant reductions in mortality, lockdowns should be rejected out of hand as a pandemic policy instrument." (IEA 2023) [68]

In prison, isolation is a form of punishment. They also call this type of punishment, *lockdown*. How many times have we heard that word used to describe keeping people stuck in their own homes? Words have meanings. Do you ever wonder why the same word used in prison is also used for the general public? The following was taken from a *Medical News Today*[30] article about potential mental health impacts from solitary confinement:

"Humans require social contact. Over time, the stress of being isolated can cause a range of mental health problems. According to Dr. Sharon Shalev, who authored A Sourcebook on Solitary Confinement in 2008, these problems may include: [30]

- anxiety and stress
- depression and hopelessness
- anger, irritability, and hostility
- panic attacks
- worsened preexisting mental health issues
- hypersensitivity to sounds and smells
- problems with attention, concentration, and memory
- hallucinations that affect all of the senses
- paranoia
- poor impulse control
- social withdrawal
- outbursts of violence
- psychosis
- fear of death
- **self-harm or suicide**

Research indicates that both living alone and feelings of loneliness are **strongly associated with suicide attempts and suicidal ideation.** Additionally, many individuals who experience confinement become incapable of living around other people." (MNT)[30]

Throughout losing Joy and the months that followed of 'lockdowns,' masks, stay-at-home 'orders,' and 'social distancing,' my goal was always to have my children experience a normal childhood. I believe we won't know the full impact the last few years have had on millions of people, especially children, for many years to come. In my opinion, almost all adults in this world carry baggage with them that stem from negative childhood experiences. As the man at the gate of my household, my job is to watch for potential danger from the world that can impact my family in a negative way.

Everything starts in the home. A healthy society starts in the home. A healthy nation starts in the home. A healthy family starts in the home. Healthy relationships start in the home. A healthy culture starts in the home. Healthy marriages start in the home. Happy kids start in the home. We *must* take responsibility for ourselves and our children and not pawn that responsibility off to others, technology, or especially the State. I witnessed countless fellow Americans blindly give their decision making over to the State. Many people's God-given minds are swayed by whatever's popular, usually driven by fear and greed.

I encourage you to pay attention to what is allowed into your household. What mindsets, seeds, ideologies, and fears are allowed to come in and take shape in your household, especially if you have kids. To summarize, isolation is not a good thing. Sure, there are times to be by yourself to relax or collect your thoughts. But no one should be an island, you miss out on the best parts of life.

Veterans:

In my opinion, the way most veterans are treated in this country is an absolute travesty. Most of them went into the military at a young age with a sense of patriotism and a longing to serve their country. They were trained how to fight and how to kill. They were trained how to perform important duties, so their fellow servicemen could achieve victory and hopefully survive their mission. From what I've seen, most veterans seem to be left to fend for themselves after their service is over.

It took about two years for a single day to go by where I didn't envision the terrifying sight of my wife on the floor. Can you imagine the sights and sounds many of our veterans have experienced? Can you imagine the trauma and torment many of them live with everyday?

Whether people agree or disagree with the conflicts the United States is fighting, it should not effect the way we treat our military servicemen and women. They're told where to go and do not have a say in the matter. We should always support the men and women that serve this Country. We must remember that without a military, the United States would quickly cease to be a Country.

Mark Twain said; "Patriotism is supporting your country all the time, and your government when it deserves it." It's important to distinguish the difference between the people that say where to go, and the brave men and women that actually have to go.

I've heard countless testimonies of veterans needing medical care. The amount of hoops they have to jump through to receive proper care sounds horrible. In my opinion, I don't think it's a stretch to say many illegal immigrants in this Country get better health care than many of our own veterans do.

They were once treated noble, valuable and honorable, until they were no longer needed. They often seem to be disregarded and treated as disposable. It's like their government got what they wanted out of them and kicked them to the curb once they didn't need them any more. It's no wonder the suicide rate for Veterans is so incredibly high. To give everything to your country and once you did, be treated so poorly in return. It's wrong, plain and simple.

> Here are some statistics about the
> suicide rate for veterans in the United States:

Chapter 4: Life Happens

- About 17 Veterans commit suicide every day (VA)[27]

- "From 2001 to 2020, the unadjusted suicide rate among Veterans between the ages of 18 and 34 **increased** by 95.3%

    For those age 35-54, the rate **increased** by 12.9%;

    for those age 55-74, the rate **increased** by 58.2%;

    and for those age 75 and older, the rate **increased** by 21.2%" (VA)[27]

- "In the two decades between 2001 and 2020, the prevalence of mental health or substance use disorder (SUD) among participants using the Veterans Health Administration (VHA) rose from 27.9% to 41.9%." (VA)[27]

- "Veterans who misuse drugs or alcohol are more than twice as likely to die by suicide than other Veterans."(AAC)[28]

- "The suicide rate for Veterans is 1.5 times higher than that of the general population."(AAC)[28]

- "More than 1 in 10 Veterans are diagnosed with a substance use disorder. Veterans are more likely to use alcohol; many also have a greater risk of opioid overdose."(AAC)[28]

- "Other common factors leading to increased suicide risk in Veterans as well as other groups;

    1. Anger, rage, mood swings, and episodes of anxiety and agitation.

    2. Expressing feelings of having no reason to live.

    3. Increased alcohol and/or substance misuse.

    4. Self-destructive and risky behaviors like driving while impaired."(AAC)[28]

Here's an eye-opening graph comparing veterans suicides to non-veteran suicides. It shows the methods used and the % change from 2001 to 2020. Remember, these are actual people that have become part of a very sad and misunderstood statistic. These are Husbands, Wives, Fathers, Mothers, Sons and Daughters....

Lethal means used in suicide deaths in 2020 and difference from 2001:

	SUICIDE DECEDENTS, METHODS INVOLVED										
	Non-Veteran U.S. Adults		Veterans		Non-Veteran Men		Veteran Men		Non-Veteran Women		Veteran Women	
	2020	Change*	2020	Change*	2020	Change*	2020	Change*	2020	Change*	2020	Change*
Firearms	50.3%	-2.3%	71.0%	+4.5%	55.3%	-2.7%	72.1%	+4.8%	33.3%	-2.1%	48.2%	+11.2%
Poisoning	12.8%	-5.6%	8.4%	-4.8%	8.0%	-4.3%	7.5%	-4.9%	29.3%	-8.7%	26.8%	-16.0%
Suffocation	28.4%	+7.6%	14.9%	+0.9%	28.6%	+6.2%	14.7%	+0.6%	27.7%	+12.0%	19.2%	+8.8%
Other	8.4%	+0.3%	5.8%	-0.6%	8.1%	+0.8%	5.8%	-0.5%	9.6%	-1.1%	5.8%	-3.9%

*Difference compared to suicide deaths in 2001

Graph and statistics courtesy of U.S. Department of Veterans Affairs, Office of Mental Health and Suicide Prevention. 2022 National Veteran Suicide Prevention Annual Report. 2022. Retrieved 4/12/23 from https://www.mentalhealth.va.gov/suicide_prevention/data.asp.

One big takeaway from this graph is that *firearms are the #1 method used in suicide deaths in 2020 for both men AND women*. However, firearms are used even more often in suicides by Veterans. I must reiterate what I mentioned earlier in the book. Please remove any quick tools (guns, etc.), from the equation if you or a loved one is having suicidal thoughts.

If you're a Veteran, please know that I see you and many other people see you as well. We thank you for your service, courage and sacrifice. You should've been treated better for your service to this Country. Even if you're at the lowest point of your life and feel like you don't have a purpose, you certainly do. Suicide is not the answer. Suicide is never the answer. There are people that need you and need to hear your testimony. Our testimony is likely the most powerful thing we can offer anyone. The younger generation needs to hear and learn from the older. You have purpose. You have meaning. God has a plan for you and it does not involve suicide. His plan is to work in you and through you for good. Will you let Him? I hope you do.

To the non-Veterans out there; if you're out, and run into a Veteran, please take a moment to extend your hand and thank them for their service. I try to do this every chance I can. You never know how much it might mean to some of them. At the very least, they've earned our appreciation and acceptance.

To Hurt and Manipulate

Earlier in the book I shared a story about Sarah and her daughter. That was an example of a teenager using the threat of suicide as a way to hurt her mother. I've heard examples of both children and adults using the threat of suicide as a way of hurting and manipulating others. How many troubled teens threaten their parents with suicide if they don't get certain things they want? How many narcissistic and controlling people tell their 'partner' something like; 'If you leave me, I'll kill myself.'

Sometimes these people may be serious with their threats, but in my opinion, they're often not. They're likely grasping at straws and manipulating the other person's heartstrings to get their way. These threats should not be taken lightly though. Either; a.) they're serious and need help, or b.) they're manipulating someone in a very sick way, and need help.

Whichever it is, it's not acceptable behavior. Whatever is the root cause of the threat needs addressed. Where are roots? Are they sitting up on the surface, easily noticed? No. Roots require some digging to find. These threats are not the roots, there is a cause for the threats. What's deep down in the person's heart, making them believe it's OK to say these things, that's the root. You can not simply go after the words, you must deal with the root of the words. The cause of the emotions manifesting as threats of suicide. Keep reading, as the book goes on, we'll get more into dealing with roots.

For a child, we must obviously help. With that said, let's say a manipulative partner uses the threat of suicide as a tool for controlling someone. That person may not be a 'partner' at all, they may be a captor, and found the tool to keep someone bound. Sticking around trying to 'fix' them may be exactly what they want their subject to do.

The Whistleblower

I'd be remiss if I didn't at least mention the 'whistleblower suicide' or what's commonly known as being *suicided*. This is when someone is murdered in a way that makes their death look like a suicide. The most common premise is that someone has damaging information on someone else, then suddenly the person with the information 'commits suicide' out of nowhere. Obviously this is the kind of thing that'd be very rare, but to say it could never happen is ludicrous.

It's a fictional movie, but in *Shooter*, starring Mark Wahlberg (2007), there's a powerful scene where someone tries exactly this on a character. The man knew too much and was a liability for people that had a lot to lose. It's hard not to, but whenever I hear of a high profile person committing suicide, my first thought is usually...*I wonder what they knew.* Personally, a certain island comes to mind.

Imagine someone having power and/or millions or billions of dollars to lose if certain information were to get out. What could they be capable of? How many movies show someone being killed before they're about to testify against someone in court? Why couldn't something like this happen in real life? Is it because it's not shown on the 6:00 news? In my opinion there are people that believe they lost a loved one to suicide, when in reality that person was trying to expose something, and was murdered for it. Or the family knows they were murdered and no one believes them. It's for these people that I mention this subject here. God knows the truth and in the end, true justice will be served. A justice that is more just and fitting than anything man can possibly do.

Chapter 4: Life Happens

The time is coming when everything that is covered up will be revealed, and all that is secret will be made known to all. Whatever you have said in the dark will be heard in the light, and what you have whispered behind closed doors will be shouted from the housetops for all to hear! Dear friends, don't be afraid of those who want to kill your body; they cannot do any more to you after that.

- Luke 12:2-4 (NLT)

For the record, I'm not suicidal and I don't have dirt or inside information on anyone :)

Chapter 5: Drugs, Alcohol and Mental Illness

> Now, let's talk about these three subjects that I've been all too familiar with in my life, especially during my young adult years. This chapter is not to put shame or guilt on anyone, quite the opposite in fact. I'm speaking from a place of healing, not judgment. I understand the struggles and I want you to experience freedom and restoration, guilt free. With that said...

The connection between drugs, alcohol and suicide may be obvious at times, but other times, not so much. For instance, what's the difference between someone that can have a good time with friends over drinks, and someone that habitually goes down a very dark road to a bad place?

Why do some people seem drawn to drugs and alcohol like moths to flame? Are they destined to walk a miserable road to their own destruction? Is it the fault of the drugs? Is it the alcohol? Or is it something more?

illicit [ih-lis-it]:

not permitted, unlawful [136/137]

> Below are the latest statistics (at the time of writing this) from the U.S. 2021 National Survey on Drug Use and Health;

- "Among people aged 12 or older in 2021, 61.2 million people (or 21.9 percent of the population) used illicit drugs in the past year." (HHS)[43]

- "The most commonly used illicit drug was marijuana, which 52.5 million people used." (HHS)[43]

- 1 in 3 young adults (18 to 25) used marijuana in the last year. (HHS)[43]

- "9.2 million people 12 and older misused opioids in the past year." (HHS)[43]

- "46.3 million people aged 12 or older (or 16.5% of the population) met the applicable DSM-5 criteria for having a substance use disorder in the past year" (HHS)[43]

- "In 2021, 94% of people aged 12 or older with a substance use disorder did not receive any treatment." (HHS)[43]

Keep in mind what was happening in 2021. Fear, uncertainty, anger. After their experiences, how are these millions of people doing today? How will they and their households behave tomorrow? How many people have joined these statistics since 2021? Only time will tell.

There's no shortage of videos online
demonstrating the next subject...

Mental Illness in The United States;

- "Nearly **1 in 4** adults 18 and older, and **1 in 3** among adults aged 18 to 25, had a mental illness in the past year." (HHS)[43]

- "Despite having the highest rate of serious mental illness, people aged 18 to 25 had the lowest rate of treatment in comparison to adults in other age groups." (HHS)[43]

- "13.5 percent of young adults aged 18 to 25 had both a substance use disorder *and* any mental illness in the past year." (HHS)[43]

- "Nearly 1 in 3 adults had either a substance use disorder or any mental illness in the past year." (HHS)[43]

- "46% of young adults 18-25 had either a substance use disorder or any mental illness." (HHS)[43]

- "In 2021, 1 in 5 adolescents had a major depressive episode in the past year. Of these, nearly 75 percent had symptoms consistent with severe impairment" (HHS)[43]

I mourn for the people and the future of this great Country. Think about it, 1/3 of adults between 18-25 had a mental illness in the last year and nearly 1/4 of all adults? Almost HALF of young adults have a substance use disorder OR mental illness? In my opinion, it's very easy to see evidence of these terrible statistics. There are thousands of videos online showing how unhinged and disconnected many people are becoming. Millions of people living in a false reality, yet unlike the years past, this trend seems to be becoming normalized... trendy even.

What do you suppose will happen to the suicide rate after huge amounts of children and young adults with mental illness have destroyed their own minds and bodies? *More on this later.*

Chapter 5: Drugs, Alcohol and Mental Illness

Additionally, I see the exponential rise of artificial intelligence (AI), only making mental illness worse. It's just the tip of the iceberg, but right now it's possible to have manufactured photo, audio and video of anyone you want, doing just about anything (and that's just what the general public has access to). With the rise of AI, I also anticipate an equally exponential rise in the amount of people becoming more disconnected from reality. Sadly, I believe many of them will welcome it. *We'll talk more about the mind in a later chapter.*

> Now, let's look at some statistics regarding drugs, alcohol...and suicide:

- Over 50% of all suicides are associated with alcohol and drug dependence. (Miller)[41]

- At least 25% of alcoholics and drug addicts commit suicide. (Miller)[41]

- Over 70% of adolescent suicides may be complicated by drug and alcohol use and dependence. (Miller)[41]

- 22% of deaths by suicide in the U.S. involve alcohol intoxication. (Samhsa)[42]

- Opiates, including heroin and prescription painkillers, are present in 20% of suicide deaths in the U.S. (Samhsa)[42]

- In general, people misusing drugs and alcohol are more likely:

    To be depressed. (AAC)[28]
    To have social and financial problems. (AAC)[28]
    To engage in impulsive and high-risk behaviors. (AAC)[28]

During my research, many of these statistics surprised me. They're even higher than I predicted they would be. Due to how diverse the subject of suicide is, in my opinion, the roll that drugs and alcohol play must vary from person to person. For some people, drugs or alcohol would have to be a massive factor and for others, a much smaller role...but still a factor. If that factor were eliminated would they have still committed suicide? This is one of those areas where "professionals" would conclude this or that. Most people in white lab coats won't admit to not having all the answers. Obviously God knows, but the person that understood what was happening the best, died. In the upcoming chapters I'm going to bring some things to light that can not be tested in a lab or shared from a psychologist. In fact, most Doctors have no clue these huge factors of suicide even exist.

To those struggling with drugs and alcohol;

"Because alcoholism and drug addiction are leading risk factors for suicidal behavior and suicide, any alcoholic or drug addict should be assessed for suicide, especially if actively using alcohol or drugs." (Miller) [41]

Now we know it's very common for drugs and alcohol to be a factor in someone's suicide. If you or a loved one is feeling suicidal, even in the slightest, please stay away from drugs and alcohol. Please let go of any shame or guilt also. Do not be your own punching bag. You're worth so much and you can persevere through any drug or alcohol troubles if you want to bad enough. You can live a happy life, free from those addictions. It may not be easy, but it's worth it and you can do it. Do you believe it's possible? *Because I do.*

amplify [am-pluh-fahy]:

to make larger, greater, or stronger [138]

Drugs and alcohol often AMPLIFY what's inside a person. The issues of the heart tend to come out when people do drugs or consume alcohol. You can often see what's inside of someone in these moments. If a person's angry, they can become angrier. If a person's sad, they can become even sadder. If a person's suicidal, they can become more suicidal. There's an old saying; "A drunk man's words are a sober man's thoughts."

You're at your strongest before your first drug or drink. Every one after that becomes progressively harder to say no to.

When that strong temptation comes, say *"No!"*

Say it out loud with me.....*"No, I will not!"*

Boldly and vocally standing firm is very powerful. Then, like we've discussed before, replace it with productive thoughts and productive actions. Believe the best and hope the best. It's also extremely helpful to talk to a trustworthy person about drug or alcohol problems. Find someone or a small group of people you can confide in that are qualified to help. Very often, we need others to help remove the load we've put on ourselves. These can be people who've been through similar hardships and can help navigate the waters. Or maybe all it would take is sharing your struggles with a close loved one.

Remember, *you're worth it!* You are worth the struggle. You are worth the fight. You are worth the battle. You do not need to hide in shame. Bring your struggles to the light and let the right people help you.

Say it with me..."*I'm worth it.*"

Ok, now, like you mean it...*"I'M WORTH IT!!!"*

That's right, you are. The enemy wants to keep you in bondage and shame. But, The Ancient Of Days wants you free! *Freedom.* That's the word. Believe and hope for freedom. Freedom from bondage, because that's exactly what addictions and destructive bad habits are, bondage.

> I need to preface the next section by acknowledging something. I understand that many of you are currently, or have taken prescription medications. Although I haven't in years, I too have taken prescription medications in the past. I'm not going to be a hypocrite and imply that no one should ever take them. In certain circumstances, some of them can be very helpful and in some circumstances, they can be very harmful.
>
> This entire section is not to put shame or guilt on anyone. This is a safe place and let's look together into an important subject, free of wrongness. Remember, I'm not a doctor and this is not medical advice. With that said, let's talk about...

Pharmakeia

What about drugs that are not considered illicit? What about pharmakeia? Are you familiar with that word? Perhaps it reminds of you another word...

>   **pharmacy** [fahr-muh-see]:
>
>   *1. Also called pharmaceutics. the art and science of preparing and dispensing drugs and medicines.* [46]
>
>   *2. a drugstore.* [46]
>
>   The origin of the word... "Pharmacy" (two examples):

"late Middle English (denoting the administration of drugs): from Old French farmacie, via medieval Latin from Greek **pharmakeia** 'practice of the druggist', based on pharmakon 'drug'." (Oxford Learner's Dictionaries) [44]

"...directly from Medieval Latin pharmacia, from Greek **pharmakeia** "a healing or harmful medicine, a healing or poisonous herb; a drug, poisonous potion; magic (potion), dye, raw material for physical or chemical processing." (Online Etymology Dictionary) [45]

Why am I bringing up the origins of the word pharmacy and how it came from the Greek word pharmakeia? The word *pharmakeia* is used three times in the New Testament of the Bible. You may not be a Bible reader or believer, but you may still find this interesting...Can you set aside whatever stance you have, at least for a moment, and bear with me? Does this sound like it could apply in the not too distant future?

The light of a lamp will never shine in you again. The happy voices of brides and grooms will never be heard in you again. For your merchants were the greatest in the world, and you deceived the nations with your **sorceries.**

- Revelation 18:23 (NLT)

The word translated into *sorceries* is the Greek word...you guessed it, *pharmakeia*. This part of the Bible is prophetic, meaning it tells of the future...our future. It was written about 2000 years ago when Jesus (after he died and came back to life), met with his last surviving disciple, John. All the rest were brutally murdered for telling others about Jesus. John was exiled on the Island of Patmos when this happened...

"When I saw him, I fell at his feet as if I were dead. But he laid his right hand on me and said, "Don't be afraid! I am the First and the Last. I am the living one. I died, but look—I am alive forever and ever! And I hold the keys of death and the grave. "Write down what you have seen—both the things that are now happening and the things that will happen.

-Revelation 1:17-19 (NLT)

TIME STOOD STILL

During all the amazing things John was told and shown, one of the things he was told about was future nations being deceived with *pharmakeiea*. (Rev. 18:23)

"Pharmakeia" definitions (two examples):

1. Strongs Concordance #5331: *the use of medicine, drugs or spells*[48]

Comes from Strongs #5332; medication ("pharmacy"), i.e. (by extension) magic (literally or figuratively):--sorcery, witchcraft.[49]

2. NAS Exhaustive Concordance...

Pharmakeia Definition: *the use of medicine, drugs or spells*[48]

Word Origin: *from pharmakeuó (to administer drugs)*[48]

The word *Pharmakeia* is also used in Galatians 5:20 in a long list of the results of following our fleshly desires. Lastly, it's used in Revelation 9:21 in another list of bad things people refused to stop doing, (even after experiencing terrible consequences).

So, it's safe to say that *pharmakeia* is referring to medicine and drugs, but what about spells? How does that apply today and moving forward. This is not going to be a deep dive as I don't want to lose people here, but within the last few years, I've seen some crazy examples of drugs and spells. I've seen choreographed dancers in syringe costumes on national TV coaxing people into taking 'medicine.'

I've seen what I believe is 'trauma based mind control' (brainwashing, look it up) used on billions of people across the world to willingly or unwillingly push them into 'medicine.' I've seen *fear* used as a spell to cause millions of people to behave completely out of character and reveal what's truly in them. I've seen countless 'celebrities' (paid actors, idols), who, in my opinion were used

Chapter 5: Drugs, Alcohol and Mental Illness

as puppets to change the stance of millions of people to go along with 'medicine.' I've seen countless ads depicting happy people on drugs, many of which state potentially terrible side effects at the end (meaning those terrible side effects actually happened to people). This reminds me of the pictures of models on adult diaper boxes. Somehow, they always manage to look young and happy. In my opinion, those adult diapers aren't the only things full of crap.

I've seen and heard countless stories of loved ones left to die alone in a hospital bed, unable to see their own loved ones. It's like many hospitals became prisons. The last time I saw my own grandmother before she died was standing outside her hospital window with my brothers. In my opinion, this is one of the many crimes against humanity we witnessed in the last few years.

My friend Rob also died during this same 'protocol.' He was an amazing and healthy man, full of life. His wife Sheila wrote the book; *The Protocol That Kills: A TRUE CRIME STORY* after his unexpected and horrific death. It's available on Amazon at the time of writing this. She details the *weeks* of torment they both went through during that time (in the supposed freest Country in the world).

What else would you call hundreds of millions of people blindly following tyrannical measures? Or the countless people going against their own conscience, but them...being in a *spell*? A spell where you cannot question what you're told...A spell where you cannot question the 'science' (which is actually anti-science)...a spell where you cannot question the official story...a spell where you cannot follow the money...a spell where you cannot think for yourself. If you don't see that much of the world has been in a spell, you.... may.....be......in.......a...........

The great part is, we don't have to stay in a spell. We can choose to see clearly. We have to reject lies and accept Truth, replace A with B.

> Below are statistics for The United States regarding prescription drugs (pharmaceuticals);

- "More than 131 million people — 66% of all adults in the United States — use prescription drugs." (HPI)[50]

- 4 out of 5 pharmacy-filled prescriptions are opioids.[52]

- The U.S. consumed about 30% of the world's supply of opioids in 2015. (Politifact, 2017)[51]

- Almost 50,000 people died from opioid overdoses in 2019. (National Institute on Drug Abuse, 2019)[51]

- "The United States is the country with the highest total drug spending and also with the highest per capita pharmaceuticals spending among developed countries."[56]

- 6% of Americans over the age of 12 abuse prescriptions in a year.[52]

- "Prescription drug misuse is highest among young adults aged 18 to 25. (National Institute on Drug Abuse, 2020)[51]

- 1 in 7 teens has taken a prescription drug without a doctor's prescription. (Teens Health, 2018)[51]

- "23% of college students had a lifetime history of prescription drug abuse." (Journal of Substance Abuse Treatment, 2014)[51]

- The United States spent $511 billion on medicines in 2019. (Statista, 2020)[51]

- "Brand-name drugs made up 80% of the money spent on medicine in the U.S. in 2019 (Statista, 2020)[51]

- "Manufacturers of the top six best-selling drugs spent the bulk of their promotional budgets—more than 90%—targeting consumers directly..." (Forbes)[55]

- "The findings could suggest pharma firms are aiming promotional dollars directly towards consumers, rather than clinicians, as part of a *"strategy to drive patient demand for drugs that clinicians would be less likely to prescribe,"* said the study's lead author Michael DiStefano, a researcher at Johns Hopkins." (Forbes)[55]

- "Just two countries in the world allow drug makers to market prescription medications directly to consumers: the U.S. and New Zealand. Most countries ban the practice." (Forbes)[55]

- $6 billion. That's how much researchers estimate pharma spent on direct to consumer ads in 2016. The figure grew significantly from 1996, when consumer ad budgets totaled $1.3 billion. (Forbes)[55]

- "The increasing prevalence of prescription drug abuse in the United States and globally is considered by many experts to be an epidemic. Statistics indicate that prescription drug use is growing, along with prescription drug misuse."[51]

Prescription drug use by age in the USA:

- 18% of children aged 0-11 years old reportedly used prescription drugs in the past 30 days (CDC, 2019)[51]

- 27% of adolescents aged 12-19 years old reportedly used prescription drugs in the past 30 days (CDC, 2019)[51]

- 47% of adults aged 20-59 years old reportedly used prescription drugs in the past 30 days (CDC, 2019)[51]

- 85% of adults aged 60 or older reportedly used prescription drugs in the past 30 days (CDC, 2019)[51]

> "The Centers for Medicare and Medicaid Services reported prescription drug expenditure in the United States came to some 378 billion U.S. dollars in 2021. This amount includes only retail drug spending, excluding nonretail." (Statista)[56]

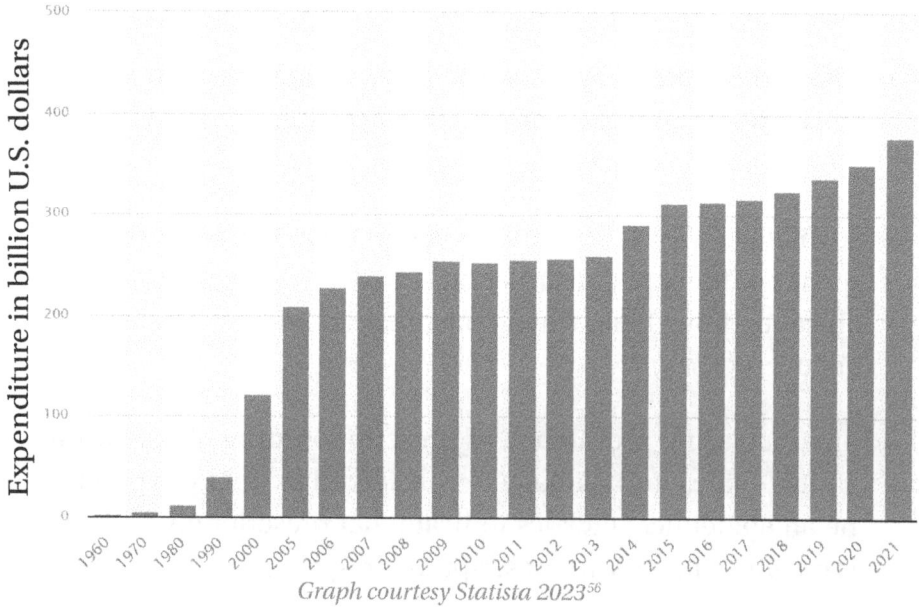

Graph courtesy Statista 2023[56]

Does this graph open your eyes to just how much money we spend in the U.S. on prescription drugs? How many people stop and think, 'What if all these drugs actually cured whatever the underlying issue is?' I've talked to more people than I can remember who've been told by a doctor to take a particular drug...*for the rest of their lives.* Never mind the potentially disastrous consequences of long term drug use I guess (sarcasm).

Having to buy a product *indefinitely* creates exponentially more income than a one-and-done product. If these products actual-

Chapter 5: Drugs, Alcohol and Mental Illness

ly cured the problem for good, people would stop buying it once they're healed...right? In my opinion, this is why I believe there'll never be a 'cure' for cancer. Cancer costs bring in about $200 billion per year in the U.S. alone.[58] It would wipe out trillions of future dollars to people and companies that, in my opinion, wouldn't allow that to happen. In my opinion, discovering *the cure* for cancer could be like discovering how to make a car run on water. They could both likely wind up in someone's mysterious death and the research somehow disappearing.

Many people have the mentality that it's easier to pop a pill than actually deal with a problem. For instance, how many younger people say they're *anxious* and therefore have *anxiety*. There's a pill for that, right? One aspect of being young and immature is wanting to take short cuts. A pill is often an attempt at a short cut. In my opinion though, it can rob you long term, *big time*. Younger folks especially need to realize feeling nervous is normal, especially while maturing. It's because you're experiencing something you haven't before, who wouldn't be nervous?

I remember being nervous on the first day of school, playing an instrument in front of someone, meeting people for the first time, being around large groups of people, or making cold-calls for work. The most nervous I'd get was before and during public speaking. I would get so nervous I'd often be sick. But I found a simple, yet effective solution. I practiced...*a lot.*

No matter how nervous I was about public speaking, my desire to succeed was greater. I've since spoken hundreds of times publicly. The nervousness hasn't gone away completely, but I've learned to be comfortable while feeling uncomfortable. Had I done like a growing number of people today, I would have let 'anxiety' control me. I would have either quit or resorted to taking a crutch (drug). How would either of those benefited me long term?

> "Drug overdoses were the leading cause of injury-related death in the United States in 2019. Over 70% of overdose deaths involved an opioid like prescription opioids, heroin, or synthetic opioids (like fentanyl)." (CDC) [61]

I haven't found a suitable resource that breaks down the ratio of illicit vs. pharmaceutical drug overdoses. However, I have heard and read from various doctors over the years that they believe pharmaceutical drugs are one of the biggest killers of people. Below is a quote from a Danish Doctor named Peter C Gøtzsche from the NIH/Pubmed site. The Title of the article is; "Our prescription drugs kill us in large numbers."

> "Our prescription drugs are the third leading cause of death after heart disease and cancer in the United States and Europe. Around half of those who die have taken their drugs correctly; the other half die because of errors, such as too high a dose or use of a drug despite contraindications." (Gøtzsche, 2014) [59]

> He also had this to say in a 2016 article:

> "There are simple solutions to our deadly drug epidemic. Make fewer diagnoses, prescribe fewer drugs and tell the patients to read the package insert on the internet. Then they might never take the drug. Many years ago I did research on naproxen and when I read the package insert and realized in how many different ways this drug could kill me, I decided never to take an NSAID. A life without drugs is possible for most of us most of the time." (Gøtzsche, 2016) [60]

His last line there, is my stance. Pharmaceutical drugs have a place, but it should be a much smaller place. I'm not saying they're all bad or you shouldn't take them. I am simply saying that in my opinion, drugs should not be a go-to, they should be a last resort.

Chapter 5: Drugs, Alcohol and Mental Illness

The biggest point is; who or what are we putting our trust and faith in? In my opinion, most people place their faith and trust in an industry they should not, and there are some men in white coats playing god. To expound on what Dr. Gøtzsche had to say, most people don't know that Medical errors are one of the leading causes of death in the United States. Here's a recent quote from WebMD in 2023:

"Medical error is the nation's third leading cause of death, behind only cancer and heart disease, according to researchers at Johns Hopkins. They estimate that it causes more than 250,000 deaths each year." (WebMD)[62]

Now, let's compare that quote to this one;

"Medication error is widely accepted as the most common and preventable cause of patient injury. Medication errors include giving the wrong drug or dose, via the wrong route, at an incorrect time, or to the wrong patient." (NIH)[53]

So, it appears that medical errors are the #3 cause of death in the U.S...and medication error is the #1 medical error? If these two quotes are accurate (and they sure appear to be), should we begin to change our view of prescription drugs as a whole? Right now, you may be wondering; 'Why is he putting all this info about prescription drugs in a book about suicide?'

For four reasons;

1. How many people use these drugs to commit suicide?
2. How many of these drugs have an increased risk of suicide as a potential "side effect" and play a roll in people's suicide?
3. How many people resort to suicide after losing someone to these drugs?
4. They can drastically lower our defenses against something we will cover later in the book. Which, in my opinion, can drastically increase someone's risk of suicide.

I want life and that abundantly for myself, my family, you and your family, for this Nation, and people across the earth. In my opinion, taking a bunch of drugs is not how we accomplish that. It may be essential for some people at times, but in my opinion, taking drugs should be rare, not the norm.

I want to make it abundantly clear that I'm not referring to the smaller minority of people with severe mental and physical impairments that require specific medications just to get through the day; ie. nerve damage, severe microcephaly and schizophrenia, cancers, etc. I'm talking about the majority of people who, in my opinion, are unnecessarily medicated or over-medicated for reasons they could most likely deal with in other, more beneficial ways. First and foremost, by seeking God.

Story Time:

I spent a lot of time reading testimonies of people having horrible side effects to their prescriptions. Normal, every day people turning completely out of character. Psychosis, depression, thoughts of murder and suicide, not remembering hours of time, hallucinations.

The question for me is; what do I share with you about all those anecdotal stories? They're everyday folks like you and I. They started taking something that sooner or later caused terrible side effects and they had to live with the results. Some lost marriages, some lost relationships, some lost their jobs, some lost their kids and some lost their lives.

Statistically, some of you are genuinely interested to learn more, while some of you have made up your minds. No matter what, some will say; 'That kind of side effect is rare,' and this whole section will go in one ear and out the other. If you want to know more about this subject, you are going to have to do your own research. There's an endless amount of reputable information online that you won't hear on the 6:00 news.

Here are a few side-effect examples that stand out...

Chapter 5: Drugs, Alcohol and Mental Illness

1.

My friend Ron told me a story about a friend of his. She'd been taking a prescription to help her quit smoking. Want to know what made her stop taking the drug? It caused her to start having strong thoughts about murdering her whole family!

There was one particular drug that used to be very popular. One side effect though was that you could wind up with serious psychiatric problems.[66] It was available to the public starting in 2006[70] and was voluntarily recalled by the manufacturer in 2021 "due to high levels of cancer-causing agents called nitrosamines in the pills."[69] It was widely available to the public, pushed by many doctors and approved by the FDA. Statistically though, a year after people started taking this particular drug to help quit smoking, on average only 10 percent of people were off cigarettes.[67] They took the risk of terrible side effects to have a 10% 'success' rate. Some of the side effects included;

> "...neurological side effects, and serious ones: depression, psychosis, erratic behavior, even "feeling like a zombie." The drug has been linked to more than 500 suicides, 1,800 attempted suicides, and the bizarre death of an American musician." (National Geographic)[70]

That quote was from a 2014 National Geographic article, I wonder what the numbers were by 2021 when the drug was voluntarily pulled off the market. How many normal, loving, caring people went psychotic, committed suicide, hurt someone or hurt themselves after taking this drug? God only knows. Below are first hand quotes from an article written by a NY author. The whole article is worth a read, but here's parts of it:

> "For me, self-destructive fantasies slowly began cropping up as cartoonish flights of fantasy—nagging, almost imperceptible chatter that became a little more concrete and domineering with every passing day." ………

129

"It felt as if the essential barrier between reality and my imagination had eroded." ....

"Maybe I should just go downstairs and leap in front of a tour bus. Or launch my head through the computer screen. All this seemed logical, but also weirdly funny, even at the time: I could see how crazy these impulses were, I could recognize them as suicidal clichés. But I couldn't make them go away." (NY Mag) [66]

In 2009, the FDA decided this drug needed a "black box" warning, (a black box around particular warnings in the paper work). The black box is the FDA's most severe safety warning. (National Geographic) [70]

2.

Check out these warnings associated with another popular drug. This one is supposed to help for sleeping. These were from a Men's Health article;

- FDA Warning: "After taking [Drug name], you may get up out of bed while not being fully awake and do an activity that you do not know you are doing. The next morning, you may not remember that you did anything during the night." (Men's Health) [65]

- "And as for those activities referenced above that you "may not remember"—that list was also printed on [Drug Name]'s Medication Guide: driving a car ("sleep driving"), making and eating food, talking on the phone, having sex, and walking around." (Men's Health) [65]

Can you imagine any possible side effects of someone that took the drug to help quit smoking and this drug to help sleep? Yowzers.

3.

How many drug ads have you seen on TV that say 'talk to your doctor if you have suicidal thoughts or an increase in suicidal thoughts...'? Many of them are supposed to be ANTI-depressants,

Chapter 5: Drugs, Alcohol and Mental Illness

yet a side effect is suicidal thoughts or increased suicidal thoughts? Really? That seems very counter-productive. Relating to anti-depressants for children and adolescents, the FDA had to say in 2018;

> "...FDA has determined that the following points are appropriate for inclusion in the boxed warning;"[71]

- "Antidepressants increase the risk of suicidal thinking and behavior (suicidality) in children and adolescents with MDD and other psychiatric disorders."[71]

- "Anyone considering the use of an antidepressant in a child or adolescent for any clinical use must balance the risk of increased suicidality with the clinical need."[71]

- "Patients who are started on therapy should be observed closely for clinical worsening, suicidality, or unusual changes in behavior."[71]

4.

Recently, (at the time of writing this) there was a horrific story that made national news. It happened in a small town in Massachusetts, you may have heard of it. A father came home from getting dinner for his family to find his Wife lying bloody on the ground. Inside the house, he made the most gruesome discovery. He found his 3 year old son and 5 year old daughter strangled to death. His 7 month old son had also been strangled and died a few days later. His wife survived her cut wounds and the 20 plus foot fall from the top floor.[75]

I can't imagine what this man saw and had to endure. I can't imagine the irreplaceable loss he must feel every day. My heart goes out to him, deeply. How could this have happened? How could a father run an errand and come back to find a horrific nightmare that he can't wake from? Movies can't replicate that kind of horror. The mother was a 32 year old labor and delivery nurse.

She'd reportedly been suffering from post-partum issues.[76] Since that gruesome day, she's had incredible support from friends, family and strangers. Those that know her have written many letters stating she was a wonderful and caring wife and mother. Again, how could she have done such a horrendous thing?

It turns out, she'd been on *12 prescription medications. TWELVE!* I'm not a doctor and I'm not going to start digging into all of the possible side effects from the drugs she was on that they've made public. Shortly before she killed her children and tried to kill herself, her husband went to the doctor for help and told the doctor; "Please, you're turning her into a zombie,"[76]

Does this sound similar to example #1, where one of the side effects for that prescription was people feeling "zombie like," followed with the suicide numbers? The main defense stated by her attorney is that she was over-medicated. In my opinion, how could any doctor expect anyone to function normally with taking that many drugs?

I've heard other reports over the years of loving mothers going off the deep end similar to this after taking many prescription drugs. Personally, I view them as victims. An entire family devastated. For anyone to say she was of sound mind; having post-partum issues and being drugged with a dozen drugs is beyond me. At the time of writing this, the mother is still in the court process. I agree with this statement from a doctor about the case;

> "Every time I think about this case, I sit in amazement, on the brink of tears, considering the magnitude of the tragedy that occurred," Dr. David Benjamin, a clinical pharmacologist and forensic toxicologist, wrote. "Lay people think that if a physician prescribed the medications, that they cannot be hurt by the drugs. Nothing could be further from the truth." (yahoo! news)[77]

> *I'm going to cover another important aspect later in the book of what I believe pushed this mother to do such a terrible thing.*

Chapter 5: Drugs, Alcohol and Mental Illness

I'm not saying to avoid talking to therapists, psychiatrists or doctors. What I'm saying is to be very mindful of who you put your trust in. In my opinion, there are many good, loving doctors and there are also glorified pill pushers in white robes. If doctors had to put patches on their wardrobe to show their 'sponsors' (like a race car driver), I think it'd put things more in perspective. I've heard testimony of good doctors refusing to push certain drugs onto adults and children because they believed they were dangerous. It cost them thousands of dollars in kick backs.

Check out this quote;

"More than 2,500 physicians have received at least half a million dollars apiece from drug makers and medical device companies in the past five years alone, a new ProPublica analysis of payment data shows. And that doesn't include money for research or royalties from inventions. More than 700 of those doctors received at least $1 million." (Propublica) [54]

The Pusher

...You know the dealer, the dealer is a man
With the love grass in his hand
Oh but the pusher is a monster
Good God, he's not a natural man
The dealer for a nickel
Lord, will sell you lots of sweet dreams
Ah, but the pusher ruin your body
Lord, he'll leave your, he'll leave your mind to scream
God damn, The Pusher...

- Partial Lyrics from *"The Pusher"* by Steppenwolf

Chapter 6: Warfare and Temptation

I want to preface this chapter by stating that, more than likely, what you're about to read will be new to you. What's in this chapter is rarely discussed and barely understood. Are you open to learning more, without jumping to conclusions and ridicule? *(Proverbs 18:13)*

I hope you are.

Our natural tendency is to reject anything that goes against what we've already chosen to believe. My challenge to you is this; can you remain neutral and open to the possibility that perhaps, there are important topics that most people are unaware of? Topics that effect everyone.

I believe this is going to be the most insightful chapter of this book. This is a bold statement; it's impossible to understand suicide without having a basic understanding of what's in this chapter. What you're about to read is not understood by doctors or discussed in therapy. It's not preached at church or talked about in college. I am blessed to be able to share all of this with you, but its come at great cost.

Chapter 6: Warfare and Temptation

The difficulty for me is summarizing what could easily be a book, into a single chapter. Unfortunately, this may also be the chapter most people stop reading at. I guess we'll see. With that said, *let's learn more about ourselves...*

The Snow Man

To better understand suicide, we *must* have a better understanding of ourselves. For instance, did you know there are actually three parts of us? They interact with each other and communicate with each other. I refer to these parts as our 'snowman.'

First of all, each of us have a *spirit*. This is commonly referred to as a *heart* in the Bible. A conduit for connecting us to God and to each other. This is where Jesus' spirit resides in the Believer. Most people feel this part spring up as their conscience.

Second, each of us have a mind, will and emotions. In scripture, this part can also be referred to as a soul. (I know it seems the same as spirit, but there's a difference). How often do we feel our 'conscience' (spirit), nudging our minds (soul) to do the right thing? Do we listen?

Third, each of us have a body. This is also called *the flesh* in the Bible.

I'll never claim to be an expert and say that I fully understand all of this and how the three parts interact, because I certainly don't. I do however, know The One who does. I've simply been blessed with a glimpse through a keyhole in a door and I'm describing what I'm able to see on the other side. I don't know if he meant it this way, but a great example of our 'three parts' is described in Zac Brown's song *As She's Walking Away*. There's a particularly accurate phrase that most people probably overlook...

> "When your **heart,** won't tell your **mind**
> To tell your **mouth,** what it should say."

He mentions a heart (spirit), telling a mind (soul), telling a mouth (flesh), what to say. People often wonder how Jesus was able to live over thirty years on this earth without sinning. One big thing to keep in mind; He's the only person to have ever lived that was able to live this way, flawlessly. Listen to His words;

> "I don't speak on my own authority. The Father who sent me has commanded me what to say and how to say it. And I know his commands lead to eternal life; so I say whatever the Father tells me to say."
>
> - John 12:49-50 (NLT)

and...

> So Jesus explained, "I tell you the truth, the Son can do nothing by himself. He does only what he sees the Father doing. Whatever the Father does, the Son also does.
>
> - John 5:19 (NLT)

Just think of it, God created *everything* through Jesus. He made everything perfect...you want to know who messed it up? We did. I've heard countless people over the years say things like; "Why did He make things so messed up?!" He didn't! We were immortal. We walked with God on this earth. There was no death and there was no evil. There was no toiling over hard labor. There weren't even weeds on the earth and childbirth was much less painful.

Mankind messed this world up, yet most people choose to blame God. Even so, *the Creator entered His own creation* to restore what was lost. What did it cost? The wages of sin is death. The Creator had to die to pay the ultimate price...*for His own creation!* We get His rightness and He took our wrongness.

Chapter 6: Warfare and Temptation

You might ask why He'd do something like that. It's actually quite simple, He absolutely loves His people more than we can comprehend. During His time on earth as one of us, Jesus was subject to the same temptations and challenges as us. The Bible says He was tempted in *every way* that we are. He was even tempted with suicide.

I am going to discuss this more later, but if you are full of shame over having thoughts of suicide, you don't need to be. Let it go...*Jesus did after He was tempted.* Are you greater than Him? Remember, temptation is not sin. He is the most un-hypocrite you can imagine. He's not like hypocritical 'religious' people of the world. He lived what He taught, perfectly. In fact, it was the most religious people that murdered Him, *His own people.*

> "Chad, get to the point. Why are you saying all of this in 'the snowman' section?"

Remember how I said Jesus is the exact opposite of a hypocrite...He voluntarily subjected Himself into 'the snowman.' He showed us how it should be operated. Not only did He demonstrate perfectly how to operate 'the snowman,' He also demonstrated perfectly how to treat other people's 'snowmen.'

This is a simple diagram showing how 'the snowman' is supposed to function. God does not usually operate with our understanding (mind). He operates on the frequency of trust and faith. These are matters of the heart, not matters of understanding.

This is exactly why many people don't understand The Bible. They're caught up in their head, while God is speaking to their heart. When the heart and mind line up though, that's when revelation knowledge can flow.

God ↕
Spirit (Heart)
Mind (Soul)
Body (Flesh)

TIME STOOD STILL

Years ago, these sentences changed my life forever;

> Trust in the Lord with all your **heart;** do not depend on your own **understanding.** Seek his will in all you do, and he will show you which path to take. Don't be impressed with **your own wisdom.** Instead, fear the Lord and turn away from evil. Then you will have healing for your **body** and strength for your **bones.**
>
> - Proverbs 3:5-8 (NLT)

Our heart (spirit), is supposed to trust God. We're not supposed to rely on our own understanding (mind, soul). This results in two-way communication between our spirit and His. Then, we're not supposed to be impressed with our own wisdom. This means to be humble and *know that we don't know everything*...but He does. Then, it says to fear The Lord (which means a deep reverence, knowing He is God and we're not), and turn from man's evil ways.

What does this process of having a spirit and mind in correct alignment result in? Among many things, the above example describes health and strength for the body (flesh). This is the process Jesus demonstrated and religious hypocrites killed Him for. It exposed them for their pride and faulty understanding. How are the vast majority of people being led today? If we look around, it's obvious. Most people's version of the above proverb goes something like this;

> 'Trust in man with all of your understanding and lean not to your own heart. Seek whatever makes you feel good in all you do. Ignore your conscience and the God you sense trying to help you. Pride is good and it certainly won't lead to your demise.'

Everyone has a god/God. The only question is; who or what is it? It could be many things, but I believe most people's god is usually themselves (flesh or mind), their spouse, their children, their mother or father, alcohol, drugs, sex, or the State. (The last one has certainly been more obvious to witness lately).

Chapter 6: Warfare and Temptation

> For a time is coming when people will no longer listen to sound and wholesome teaching. They will follow their own desires and will look for teachers who will tell them whatever their itching ears want to hear. They will reject the truth and chase after myths.
>
> -2 Timothy 4:3-4 (NLT)

In my opinion, most people's 'snowman' looks like one of these, completely out of order. It's no wonder the World has been going the way it is. We make terrible gods...history proves it.

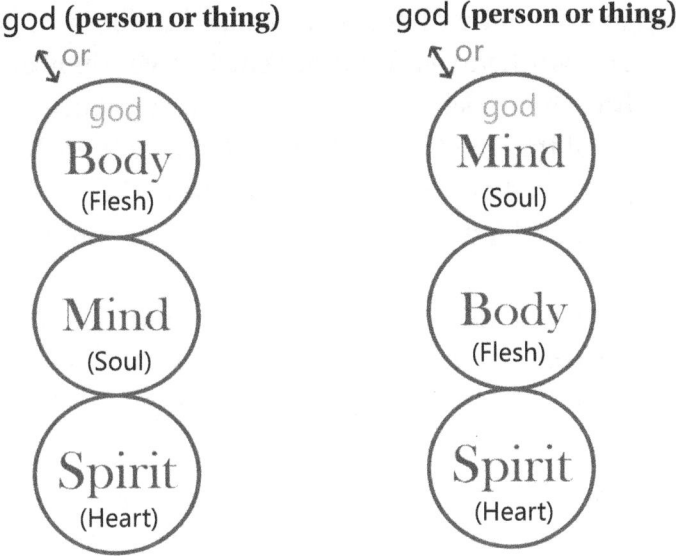

Most people are led by their own body or their own mind. Their body makes a decision, their mind agrees and their spirit is just along for the ride. It was outvoted 2-1. Our bodies only want pleasure and to take it easy. Being led by the flesh usually makes lazy and selfish people.

The other common order is being led by the mind (soul). This time, the mind makes a decision and the body agrees. Again, the spirit is just along for the ride. It was outvoted 2-1. Being led by the mind usually makes people feel like they have to know and control everything.

How often do we do something and *feel* our conscience (spirit) disagreeing,...*yet we do it anyway?* This could be during big or small things. It can be very dangerous to ignore our conscience. It's a glimpse of our spirit inside of us, trying to reason with the two other parts of us that want to do things their way. Jesus said He knocks on the door to our hearts. Not our minds, and certainly not our bodies. Our mind and body need to learn to take a back seat to our spirit, and our spirit needs to speak up. Apathetic acquiescence can be fatal.

The last few years have been extremely revealing. Fear of something happening to their bodies has caused millions of people to go against their own heart and mind. Fear is a very powerful tool. It's like a wildfire. Once it spreads (like it has), it can cause utter devastation. Instead of trusting God and His order, most people traded freedoms for perceived security for their bodies. The result is our children's liberties and futures rapidly eroding before our very eyes.

> "Those who would give up essential liberty to purchase a little temporary safety, deserve neither liberty nor safety."
>
> - Benjamin Franklin

I absolutely hate it when I'm saying goodbye to someone and they tell me to *stay safe*. I know they mean well, but they don't understand what they're actually saying. (Plus, it always reminds me of 1 Thessalonians 5:3). What they're actually trying to tell me is that our bodies are at the top of the 'snowman,' and God is not sovereign. There's only ONE place to have true safety. There are many examples I could use, but here's one;

> This I declare about the Lord: He alone is my refuge, my place of safety; he is my God, and I trust him. For he will rescue you from every trap and protect you from deadly disease.
>
> -Psalm 91:2-3 (NLT)

Chapter 6: Warfare and Temptation

Do I believe that? After everything I've experienced in my life, absolutely! So please, don't tell me to 'stay safe.' And to quote another Founding Father;

"I prefer dangerous freedom over peaceful slavery."

- Thomas Jefferson

Years ago, one Bible story in particular completely changed the way I live. Over time it's helped me gain peace and calm. It did not come easy though. (A struggle in my 'snowman' still springs up from time to time, but progressively it happens less often). It's the story of the fiery furnace. I will summarize this amazing story. You can read about it in Daniel, Chapter Three. The King of Babylon had set up a large statue, and everyone was given a mandate to bow and worship it or be thrown into a fiery furnace.*

*(What would you do in this situation? Really ponder it. I ask, because something very similar to this is going to happen again in the future (Rev 13:15). From what I've seen, most people would stick their heads in a guillotine if it was 'mandated.' Backbones are hard to come by these days).

Anyway, back to the story. Three men refused to bow down and worship the statue. They were brought before the king and said these words...

"...If we are thrown into the blazing furnace, the God whom we serve is able to save us. He will rescue us from your power, Your Majesty. But even if he doesn't, we want to make it clear to you, Your Majesty, that we will never serve your gods or worship the gold statue you have set up."

- Daniel 3:17-18 (NLT)

Guess what happened...*all three were thrown into the furnace...*

but that's not the end of the story. As the King watched, he saw a fourth person appear in the fire. He could also tell they were all unharmed. The King called the men out of the fire. They walked out, completely unharmed. Their bonds were gone, their clothes weren't burnt, and they didn't even smell of smoke. After that, the King made a decree that anyone who spoke evil against the God of those men would be cut to pieces and their house turned into a dunghill (where people brought their poop). The men were then promoted by the Babylonian King.

This story hit me hard in 2015. Before that, in their shoes I would have relied on, and trusted in all the physical things I could do. How I'd fight the guards, get out of town, or as a last resort, make a suit I could wear to possibly survive the flames. I'd have been leaning to my physical strength and understanding. Montana men are survivors. We risk our lives to kill things...and then eat them. We know how to fix things like Macgyver and survive brutal winters. Getting ourselves out of a tough spot is a way of life (this is how I was raised anyway, lol).

> This is what the Lord says: "Cursed are those who put their trust in mere humans, who rely on human strength and turn their hearts away from the Lord.
>
> - Jeremiah 17:5 (NLT)

I did not agree at first (pride does a great job at hiding our shortcomings), but over time, my pastor helped me see I was leaning on my strength and understandings way too much. I'd spent years honing mental and physical skills and realized I had slowly promoted myself as my own god. I was trusting my understandings and abilities. It has not been easy, but my flesh and mind needed to take a back seat and let God in.

I certainly support self defense and having an armed society. We must understand though, all of that comes secondary to True safety. He's God and we're not. True safety only comes from Him. Someone as tough as Rambo can still be wiped out by a 17 year old texting and driving. God can intervene by having the man stop for coffee. Without his even knowing, Rambo the 2nd can be spared an untimely death. But does he listen to his spirit (conscience), and pull over for that coffee?

God certainly can and does use us and our abilities. Who do you think gave us our abilities in the first place? (James 1:17) The daily choice we all make; do we rely on Him or ourselves? Every day we are presented with that same question. We answer it with our actions. He can prevent or thwart what would be impossible in the natural. He can get us through a fiery furnace. He can deliver us through insurmountable odds, completely unscathed. But do we trust and believe Him?

> Though a thousand fall at your side, though ten thousand are dying around you, these evils will not touch you.
>
> - Psalm 91:7 (NLT)

Spirit/Heart

> But there is a spirit within people, the breath of the Almighty within them, that makes them intelligent.
>
> - Job 32:8 (NLT)

We naturally use the words 'spirit' and 'soul' interchangeably. When we do, I believe we're usually referring to the spirit. However, the Bible makes a distinction between the two;

> Now may the God of peace make you holy in every way, and may your whole **spirit** and **soul** and **body** be kept blameless until our Lord Jesus Christ comes again.
>
> - 1 Thessalonians 5:23 (NLT)

and...

> For the word of God is alive and powerful. It is sharper than the sharpest two-edged sword, cutting **between soul** and **spirit**, between joint and marrow. It exposes our innermost thoughts and desires.
>
> - Hebrews 4:12 (NLT)

Our bodies are very lazy and want the easy way out. They want pleasure and rest. We must be in charge of it, not subject to it...

> For the mind that is set on the flesh is hostile to God,
> for it does not submit to God's law; indeed, it cannot.
>
> - Romans 8:7 (ESV)

Our mind, will and emotions (soul) is naturally very selfish. It wants to play god and be right. We must also be in charge of it and refresh it. We need to teach our mind how to think.

> Do not conform to the pattern of this world, but be transformed by **the renewing of your mind.** Then you will be able to test and approve what God's will is—his good, pleasing and perfect will.
>
> - Romans 12:2 (NIV)

Finding our purpose in life is a byproduct of renewing our mind. We're supposed to be in this world, but not *of* this world. We must be careful what we allow into our minds and our children's minds. They're like sponges and can soak up all kinds of things, good or bad.

Now, getting to the heart of the matter, (pun intended). Our spirit is inside of us. It doesn't need sleep like the other parts do (Song of Songs 5:2). We often get another glimpse of our spirit when we're barely awake. That brief moment when our mind and body are out of the way, but still alert enough to understand spiritual things.

Chapter 6: Warfare and Temptation

It doesn't happen often, but I've woken to an effortless stream of understanding that my spirit was getting from God's spirit. In that moment, my mind tries to grab what it can before it's over. It's like standing in front of a flowing stream with a metal pail. In a moment, the stream is gone and whatever the mind grabs in that brief moment, is it. Minds can only comprehend a small amount of spiritual things.

Over time, God's spirit, flowing into my spirit has overflowed into my understandings. For instance, the outline for the song *The Joy of my Life* was given to me while I was in the shower. I jumped out quickly and wrote all the parts to the song down, along with the basic guitar cord sequence. It was effortless and was just...*there*. Two weeks ago I was in the shower (for some reason showers are a common place for this to happen for me), when a song with multiple overlapping classical guitar parts, drums, vocals and bass was suddenly...*there*. I wasn't even thinking about music before that.

Our spirits are so much bigger than our minds, they understand so much. Our minds however are the bottleneck. Minds are like the bossy loud person, sometimes it's hard for the spirit to get a word in. It's not supposed to be a competition between them, they're supposed to be working together. When they work together, they can tell the body what to do, which makes a harmonious 'snowman.'

Our heart is who we really are. It's the spirit inside a flesh body. It's the hand in the glove. Without a hand, the glove dies. Without the glove, the hand lives on. Even though many people try to perfect their body, our body is not who we really are. Man looks at the outward appearance, but God sees our hearts (1 Samuel 16:7). Our mind is also not who we really are, most of us have *stinkin' thinkin,'* even though we're likely not the way we view ourselves.

> Remember him—before the silver cord is severed, and the golden bowl is broken; before the pitcher is shattered at the spring, and the wheel broken at the well, and the dust returns to the ground it came from, and the spirit returns to God who gave it.
>
> - Ecclesiastes 12:6-7 (NIV)

It's not common, but there are people playing with fire in an extremely dangerous way. Let me explain...there's a term called *astral projection*. I mention it here, because to me it can easily be a form of suicide. Some 'new age' people and various religions attempt what is called an out-of-body experience. This is when someone *deliberately* leaves their body. I've also heard testimony of people doing this for nefarious purposes. However, most of the time I believe it's lost and ignorant people dabbling in extremely dangerous territory.

As mentioned in the above example, people have described a silver looking cord that keeps the spirit and body connected (like an umbilical cord), while someone is alive. This is called the 'silver cord.' If this cord is cut while someone's outside their body, the body dies, and the spirit...well...that's a good question.

I heard testimony years ago of a woman who was being tormented at night. Somehow she discerned it was the spirit of a particular person. She prayed against it. Guess what, the next day they found the lifeless body of *that* man.

What happens to a spirit, when it went somewhere it wasn't supposed to go? *Sounds pretty terrifying.* This should be a dire warning for people who think playing with spiritual fire is a good thing. It's similar to playing with a Ouija (weegee) board (which we'll discuss later). Most people don't understand what they're actually doing.

Broken

Spirits can be broken.

Most people have a broken spirit...and don't know it.

I did. I possibly still do.

Most likely, you have a broken spirit.

Chapter 6: Warfare and Temptation

> He heals the brokenhearted and binds up their wounds.
>
> - Psalm 147:3 (NIV)

I'm grateful you've had the courage to keep reading this far. This is where the rubber meets the road in this book. The core of what's completely misunderstood about suicide...is *brokenness*. You'll not hear this at a doctor's visit or in a therapist's office. The majority of pastors don't even know about this; *most people have more than one person(ality) in them.*

> A merry heart maketh a cheerful countenance:
> but by sorrow of the heart the spirit is broken.
>
> - Proverbs 15:13 (KJV)

Physical and emotional trauma is not only hurtful to our body and mind, but it can also cause our spirit to break. This is most likely to happen as a young child. Spirits are more easily broken then. Think of it this way; God created us in such a way that, for our own survival, we can go through a traumatic event and keep living. Part of the spirit breaks off and contains the trauma. When it does this, the broken part also stays at the age and understanding it was when it occurred. As the person grows and matures, this broken part is *always* there. It's another personality, frozen in time. He/she holds the memories and pain of what caused him/her to break off from the main spirit...you.

Occasionally, this broken-off spirit gets stirred up and becomes noticeable *to those paying attention*. Usually they're stirred up by a trigger that reminds them of whatever caused them to break off in the first place. There's also an aspect where the main spirit is protective over the broken spirit, similar to how an older sibling would guard and protect their younger sibling.

There are many ways a spirit can be broken, but some of the most common types of trauma that can cause this are;

- Molestation/rape
- Abandonment/Rejection
- Neglect
- Dominated (never good enough)
- Death of a close loved one
- Divorce

Imagine a person's body as a car. We naturally think there's only one person in the car, the driver. Most people don't realize that often, there's at least one passenger in the car. They may even take the wheel from time to time. Most of the time it's one main driver behind the wheel, but sometimes, even briefly, one of those 'passengers' gets behind the wheel. Sometimes the main spirit knows of the other spirit(s), other times they do not.

We likely didn't know it at the time, but we've all seen this happen. The part that was broken off usually behaves different than the main 'driver,' because it's a different personality. Examples are someone becoming abnormally quiet, loud, angry, sad, hysterical, irrational, bossy, hopeless, etc. The main part to look for is a very obvious and sudden switch after a particular trigger. Some of you may have light bulbs turning on at the moment as you think back on your loved one's actions, or even yourself. "Why do I react this way when...?" We likely don't remember what caused any brokenness, because those broken parts contain the memories and deep hurt. That also goes for our loved ones. Let me give you an example...

Many years ago, my dad had an episode while we were all enjoying a nice time as a family on a pontoon boat. Not long after departing the dock, he became extremely quiet and *very* passive. He just resembled a shy toddler, not dad. We were all very puzzled and concerned as to why he was behaving so out-of-character. The enjoyable

Chapter 6: Warfare and Temptation

boat ride was cut short that day. Things became more concerning in the parking lot as we were leaving, he wasn't himself at all. On the way into town, we decided to swing into the emergency room.

He ended up having an MRI/CT scan (I can't remember which), and looked over from head to toe. *They couldn't find anything wrong with him.* He stayed a couple days in the hospital. Friends and family visited him. I still remember it vividly. He was so quiet and passive, not even questioning why he was there. After a few days, he was back to himself.

This was many years ago. I didn't know then what I know now. I was witnessing something I didn't understand at the time. There was a little broken boy behind the wheel of my dad's body. What caused him to be broken off decades earlier? Why did he show up during a pleasant family boat ride? I'll never know. I wish I knew then what I know now. I know this sounds completely weird, but I would've talked to that little boy. I would have found out his age and talked to him like he was that age...*because he was.* I also would have tried to learn what happened to him to be broken off from my Dad.

Yes, I know most of you think this is nuts or silly but this subject is incredibly real. As I've stated already, you likely have at least one broken part of you too. I believe it's rare for a person to go through life without having a broken spirit. As for me, so far I've had two broken parts come to the surface. They even had names (they often do). Zack and Matt. I don't know how old Zack was, but Matt was five. At the time of writing this I'm 40 years old. That means 35 years ago, something traumatic happened to me to cause him to break off. What was the traumatic event? I really don't know. Someday I might, but maybe not.

You may be wondering how I found out these things about myself (I would be). When I lived in Washington State, there were usually around a dozen of us that would meet every week and have a Bible study. Since having to move back to Montana, I've been calling in to our normal church meetings. (It's not nearly as good as in-person, but still sustaining). Do you ever have those moments where you sense something deep, then receive confirmation that you know in your heart is right? Some time after Joy died, I had a sense of something that was hard to explain. An internal presence so familiar, yet a growing awareness of a coming change.

One evening, during my normal weekly call, *brokenness* became the main focus. My pastor told everyone that he felt there were people in the group that had brokenness and The Lord was telling him it was the right time for some to be made whole. I was certainly familiar with the subject, especially after my experiences with Joy. This time was different though, deep down I had an unexplainable sense and awareness...it was my time.

He asked how many people felt they had brokenness that was ready to be healed. There were around 5 people that raised their hands in the room, but you know what happened...*my hand shot up also*. I was two states away on a conference call and my hand went up, without me consciously doing it. Something or better yet, *someone* inside of me wanted to be healed. Tears started welling up and running down my face. No one knew my hand had gone up, my phone was muted as I quietly listened.

I was laying alone on my bed in the dark. Over the phone I could faintly hear my pastor talking to the broken parts of the others, one at a time. I couldn't hear much, but one was distinct. I heard a four year old girl speaking out of a grown woman. She told the story of how she'd been broken off after being lost in the woods and no one came looking for her. Do you know what her name was? *Forgotten.*

When you're four years old, being lost and no one finding you, that's traumatizing. This was a grown woman with an abandoned four year old personality in her, alongside her main personality. Again, picture a four year old in the passenger seat of a car. The rest of her life had grown around this little girl, but she was always there.

Chapter 6: Warfare and Temptation

Another name for these broken pieces is 'alternate personalities' or 'alters' for short. Like most things, Hollyweird has done a great job of making terribly inaccurate movies that try to depict this. They make it seem strange and rare, but it's not. It's very common.

The next morning, my pastor and I talked on the phone. I described how my hand had shot up and I could feel something inside was ready to be healed. He prayed for a moment and agreed. He asked to speak to the broken piece. *It got really quiet.* It's hard to describe this, but it's like stepping back and relaxing. Imagine a little boy, beaten down, suppressed, and who's spent his life in the dark, unable to speak. I was aware of what was going on, but it was like allowing someone to step in front of me.

My pastor asked a few more questions. The boy could just grunt and make noises to imply yes or no. After a moment, another thing became clear. He had a demon preventing him from speaking. It's like he had someone on his back, almost like a back pack, covering his mouth. We'll talk about demons in a bit, but my pastor kicked him out and then the boy was finally able to speak.

What's your name?

Matt. (Like a young timid child)

How old are you?

Five.

How were you broken off from Chad?

... (pause)...I don't remember...

Do you want to be made whole again with Chad?

Yes.

There's only one way to have a broken part of our spirit healed. A therapist can't do it. A doctor can't do it. In my opinion, either one would likely try to push drugs anyway.

I don't want to imagine where I'd be in life if God had not blessed me with my pastor. He certainly knew I needed someone like him and I'm forever grateful for him. He told Matt this simple military example;

> "You stopped and took a stand to allow your fellow man to get away and live. You did your job amazingly well and Jesus is proud of you. Your mission is complete, it's time for you to rejoin Chad. Do you want that?"

Yes. *(Quickly)*

Speaking to him like a child, my pastor told him about Jesus and that He loved him and was ready to restore him. "He's here for you. Can you see him?" My eyes were closed. This is not an outward sight, this is an inward sight of the spirit. "No." Was Matt's response. "That's OK, keep looking, He's right here for you."

Keep in mind, Matt had spent the last 35 years in the dark, unable to speak. Then, I saw what Matt saw. A faint look of a smiling face in the darkness. "There He is..." More tears poured out. And then, hands. A faint outline of hands reaching for him. "Do you want to be with Jesus and have Him make you one with Chad again?"

"Yes!"

And just like that, it was over. Tears subsided, breathing slowed. I opened my eyes and cleared my throat. I've heard of other people going through something like that, but it was a first for me, 35 years in the making. My pastor and I chatted for a bit after that. He let me know something great. Not only does each broken piece hold the trauma, but they also hold good, God given qualities that rejoin after Jesus heals them. It's like finding lost treasure in a sunken ship.

Over the next couple of weeks I noticed it. I was calmer and more patient with my kids. I would pause and get down to their level and listen to them more. I was more empathetic to them. All because of a little boy about their age.

Chapter 6: Warfare and Temptation

> There's a few things worth noting;

- The restoration is very time sensitive, you cannot force it. It is literally a broken personality that must *want* to be healed.

- Jesus is the only one that can do the healing. Apart from Him, it would only be man's feeble attempts and/or demonic manipulation.

> The Spirit of the Lord is upon me, because he hath anointed me to preach the gospel to the poor; he hath sent me to **heal the brokenhearted,** to preach deliverance to the captives, and recovering of sight to the blind, to set at liberty them that are bruised,
>
> - Luke 4:18 (KJV)

He takes the sorrow from each of the broken pieces of our spirit *that want* it taken. In 1 Corinthians chapter 13, we get a list of things that love is. One of them is; love does not insist on its own way. God is love and He's not going to force his way into healing us. The heart, (our spirit) is where Jesus dwells. That's why the Bible says our body is His temple.

> Then Christ will make his home in your hearts as you trust in him. Your roots will grow down into God's love and keep you strong.
>
> - Ephesians 3:17 (NLT)

- Not every healing is the same process. For instance, the other broken part of me that surfaced was different. His name was Zack, I don't know how old he was. I had a sense he was broken off from something that occurred in the basement of our Sunday school building when I was a kid. He surfaced over a couple of weeks and gave himself to Jesus without letting me know. Like I just gave the introduction and He did the rest.

- We must be vulnerable and open with the right people. Years ago I prayed earnestly for someone like my pastor that understood heavy things like spiritual warfare. He's someone I trust with my life and I can be vulnerable with. When you feel in your spirit you're ready to be healed, it's vital to be open, but *only* with the right people.

As I mentioned earlier, most people don't understand this subject, but some do. Jesus is the first to talk to, He knows exactly what's going on. Ask Him what you need, and what to do. If you don't know Jesus, this is the perfect time. Then, your broken pieces would be next up for meeting Him. Ask Him to lead you to someone that can help. His followers do not operate in isolation.

> Then Jesus said, "Come to me, all of you who are weary and carry heavy burdens, and I will give you rest.
> - Matthew 11:28 (NLT)

"But what about broken pieces that don't want to be healed? Can they even be hostile towards God?"

Yes.

Earlier in the book I mentioned seeing a little girl on Joy's face a handful of times before her death. Obviously this is all in hindsight, but I believe that broken part of her I saw was badly hurt and had very serious issues. I believe she was jealous of Joy and our daughter, and angry at God. She didn't want anything to do with Jesus, and was tricked by the enemy to do what she did (we're getting to that part).

Remember the car with more than one person in it analogy? Well, I believe that broken part of her was able to get behind the wheel that fateful December morning. I believe demons were also manipulating that broken part of her to do what she did. I also believe it was God that prevented the kids and I from dying that day as well. Joy was somewhere in that body, but I wholeheartedly believe she was not behind the wheel. Like sitting in the backseat while a devilish nightmare played out in front of her. She was along for the ride as the driver steered the car off a cliff. (This is just an analogy, I've had people think of this in a literal sense). Can I be mad at my wife for being a passenger in a car, driven by someone else who deliberately ran it off a cliff? Can I have anything but compassion and empathy for the women I so deeply love and shared my life with?

The woman I love would never voluntarily separate herself from her children. She'd never hurt myself or the kids. But that broken piece that I saw...would. It's horrific, but God intervened. It would have been so much worse. This book would never exist if God had not stepped in. You don't think so? Do you remember how I was told by my pastor to focus on her and the kids for 30 days, and all the great times we had? *It was early morning on day 31 that she died.*

By His love and grace, God intervened. He blessed us with amazing family time and because of Him...let me say that again, BECAUSE OF HIM, I have no regrets. In my own strength and understanding the kids and I would be lost. But He knows the end from the beginning.

Most suicide survivors haven't considered that perhaps their loved one was not actually in the driver's seat when they committed suicide. From my experience, it's not like the other personalities were able to take over and be fully in control of my body. It was like allowing a much smaller person to step in front of you at a concert so they can see better. 'If you get out of line, *I can and will step back in front of you.*'

However, I also believe some broken pieces can be a more dominating and larger part of a person's spirit (the term 'bipolar' comes to mind). As mentioned before, Joy had many issues going on, not just a broken spirit. However, I believe the broken spirit played a large roll in what happened to her.

It's possible for a person's spirit to be broken hundreds of times, like it's been shattered. This can happen to children who've been heavily abused and also to mentally handicapped people. I know a severely handicapped man my age that has the mind of a three year old. He has various personalities come up, sometimes they even fight and yell at each other. You'd think you're hearing two different people, but it's coming out of the same body. The medical world would call this schizophrenia. Spiritual brokenness usually follows mental impairment, which can further complicate the behavior of the person.

The Boxer

Imagine stepping into a boxing ring with someone half your size. That should be an easy fight, right? *But what if that person was also invisible?* Even though your opponent is half your size, do you stand a chance? Nope. If you're unaware of what they're up to, you'll get beaten down every time. However, if they were suddenly visible... game over.

> Put on all of God's armor so that you will be able to stand firm against all strategies of the devil. For we are not fighting against flesh-and-blood enemies, but against evil rulers and authorities of the unseen world, against mighty powers in this dark world, and against evil spirits in the heavenly places.
>
> - Ephesians 6:11-12 (NLT)

I'm a Veteran of a different kind of war, spiritual war. I've been through many battles and I will continue to do so whenever necessary. I have experienced both struggle and victory. I'm a man ready to die...and not just die, but to die for Him doing whatever He wants me to do. Jesus calls us to take up our cross and follow Him. To liter-

Chapter 6: Warfare and Temptation

ally accept death, by figuratively carrying what is going to kill you. I make mistakes and fall short every single day, but every day I choose to keep turning to Him. He already won and I choose to be on the winning side.

I want to see my kids grow, so I hope it's not for a long time, but when it is my time, I've already accepted it. I have faced death and therefore do not fear it. It can no longer control me. In my opinion, we can not truly live if we're afraid of death. (This does not mean we do stupid things and put ourselves in harm's way). Remember, this life is temporary and we know what happens after all of this...it's glorious beyond measure. Meditate on these words from Jesus;

> If you cling to your life, you will lose it;
> but if you give up your life for me, you will find it.
> - Matthew 10:39 (NLT)

Whether we like it or not, we're born into a war. The major problem is most people, even those that know of the war, park their butts on the sideline. Can you imagine troops sitting around having a barbecue while war is going on around them? One thing about troops is that they're not cowards. Even with bullets flying past them, they still push forward. They're not fearless, they just don't let fear control them. They've also accepted death. This allows them to move freely, *into danger.*

This is how I see the American Church today...

Asleep

      Distracted

           Lazy

                Apathetic

                      Complacent

complacency [kuhm-pley-suhn-see]:

self-satisfaction especially when accompanied by unawareness of actual dangers or deficiencies [139/140]

The good news is, the tide's changing. The Church is waking up. Bad times have a way of jarring people out of a passive comfort zone. Trivial things like sporting events lose their flavor when evil begins running rampant...*which it obviously is.* The last few years should've been very eye opening, especially to those paying attention.

In churches along railways, Christians in Nazi Germany sang loud to drown out screams of doomed souls in passing train cars on their way to death camps. It's not the same category, but I witnessed the majority of churches in this supposedly free Country cower to fear and tyranny in the last few years. A few resisted, but most; *Stopped assembly. Distanced. Jabbed. Feared. Didn't touch. Masked. Stayed home. Towed the line.*

> And let us not neglect our meeting together, as some people do, but encourage one another, especially now that the day of his return is drawing near.
>
> - Hebrews 10:25 (NLT)

I believe millions of people are being stirred up and beginning to see the growing lawlessness. I also believe millions of people will learn and understand spiritual warfare. People will get off the sidelines of life when they really understand what's at stake. Do people really think the growing evil is natural? It's not, it's supernatural. Therefore, we must understand the supernatural...boldly and without fear. It is not scary. Ignorance is scary...*and deadly* (Hosea 4:6).

I want to start this section off by saying that we're not to fear what I'm about to talk about. It's not necessary. Fear is a very useful tool used against us. Contrary to what it shows in the movies, the Devil doesn't show up in red with a pitchfork and horns. The Bible actually says he was created beautiful, and can disguise himself as an angel of light. He is much sneakier than to show up looking scary, people would run right to Jesus. One of his biggest tools he uses is subtlety, often making people believe he doesn't even exist.

Satan's not omnipresent like God is. This means he can only be in one place at a time. He's a type of angel called a cherub. He caused 1/3 of the other angels to follow him in a rebellion against God. These other angels are referred to as *fallen angels* (bad guys). Lastly, there are demons. I mentioned them earlier in the book. Some people believe the term is used interchangeably with fallen angels. Another belief is that they come from the disembodied spirits of the Giants (Genesis 6), like Goliath.

I know this was a brief summary, but I want to keep this simple. Think of it like a military. Satan is the General of his army. Then you have his fellow fallen angels that are next in charge. You can read about them having power over certain areas on earth. Demons are the main foot soldiers. Even with demons there's a hierarchy. Some of them are stronger than others. Some will stand and resist longer, while others are gone at the first sign of resistance. Demons can operate in, on, or around people.

The Bible also says that Satan entered Judas, like demons can. So angelic beings are physical, but also a spirit that can go into someone. Keep in mind, there are multiple types of angels. Remember, Satan and his minions can *and do* trick people into believing they're the good guys. It's actually very common. They've been around for thousands of years and are very good at deceiving people. They do it every day. Jesus said Satan is the father of lies. We're supposed to test the spirits to see if they're from the Lord (1 John 4).

Even mainstream uses the word demon. Usually something like, 'He had his inner demons...' Most of the time, people use the word more like having bad habits or bad traits. But demons are literal evil spiritual beings that want to steal, kill and destroy. Just like their master. I remember being introduced to the subject of demons. I must've been in grade school, it was in a movie. It was a reenactment of a scene from the Bible, depicting someone being severely demonized. *It scared me.* I didn't know what to think of it. How can you fight something you can't see? Let alone something *inside* of someone...

Over the years, almost like clockwork, there seems to be a new movie showing demonized people. Usually, a religious man in a long robe shows up, attempts some kind of ritual, but inevitably fails. The demon then laughs at the man who brutally dies or runs away. Can I tell you something? That's not how it works. That is fiction. Hellywood also gives people the perception that demons are all powerful and scary things to be feared. But they're not to be feared. They get their power from our submission, fear and especially our ignorance. For example, those of you that suffer from sleep paralysis; those are demons using your fear against you. Boldly tell them to go away in Jesus' name and never return.

Like whispers over our shoulder in the dark, the enemy plots and plans. The enemy comes to steal, kill and destroy. Suicide is the very definition of that. It steals someone's earthly life, kills their body and destroys their chances of living more days. Not to mention the collateral destruction suicide causes to loved ones. Demons want us isolated. If discovered, they want us to think they're scary and all powerful. They'll threaten us to keep us away from those that can actually help.

Different demons have different functions. Some specialize in things like sexual deviance, lying, suicide, depression, anger, and murder. The most common way of getting a demon is giving them a foothold. This is not rare, I believe it happens to almost everyone at times. Picture ravens sitting on a fence, watching. They wait for their opportunity. Imagine someone who's generally an angry person. In the moments of angry outburst, they can make their move. They claw on board and amplify what was a level 6, to a 9 or 10. The level they are allowed to influence a person varies.

I've heard fellow believers say that a follower of Jesus can't be demonized. To that I say, *show me a verse.* Show me in scripture where it says that.....I'll wait. I can tell you for certain, believers *can* be demonized. Usually in the form of attack or oppression. However, I do not believe they can be fully demon possessed like is possible with an unbeliever. It's like to the degree of light is in a person, equals the degree they can not mess with you.

If you're being spiritually attacked, but you believe you cannot be, are you actually giving the enemy free reign to attack you? Will you not even take the first step of casting them away? At least question if that's what is happening. It's nothing to be ashamed of. I have been spiritually attacked by demons many times. Most of the time it's subtle. Like, *"Why am I feeling this way?"* Then I have a sense that it's a looming oppression. I have learned to not sit on it in procrastination. I go to work praying boldly out loud, commanding it in Jesus' name to go away and not return.

> "When the seventy-two disciples returned, they joyfully reported to him, "Lord, even the demons obey us when we use your name!"
>
> "Yes," he told them, "I saw Satan fall from heaven like lightning! Look, I have given you authority over all the power of the enemy, and you can walk among snakes and scorpions and crush them. Nothing will injure you.
>
> But don't rejoice because evil spirits obey you; rejoice because your names are registered in heaven."
>
> - Luke 10:17-20 (NLT)

It isn't the demon we know about that's dangerous, it's the one we don't know about. The one that sneaks through the hedge and plants weed seeds in an otherwise weedless garden of heart and mind. The sneaky devil that's OK with not taking credit, as long as it helps lead to our demise. The one that influences subtly (usually). The one that tries to slowly coax us to the edge. The one that longs to steal, kill and destroy us and all we hold dear.

A person may have started the ball rolling, but the enemy is trying to push it faster across to their end goal, destruction. It's a matter of when we realize we've given him a foothold, to kick his foot off and not allow him back. Some of us have become so comfortable with his foot on us, we're afraid to kick it off. It sounds crazy, but it's true. The Israelites became so comfortable as slaves to Egyptians they actually wanted to go back. Do you think we're much different?

From my experience, I also believe it's possible for the main part of someone's spirit to be free of demons, but for a broken part to be demonized. Meaning that (if or when) that broken part is 'behind the wheel,' it's also being influenced to some degree by a demon.

Always remember this when dealing with the enemy; Jesus has the ultimate authority. As an ambassador of His, when you say "In Jesus' name____," it means "By the authority and sovereignty of Jesus, who has dominion and power over everything, you are commanded to _____."

"In Jesus' name" is a legal term, a power of attorney if you will. It means BY HIS AUTHORITY I say _____. The demons, fallen angels and the devil himself are not subject to you or me, BUT they're absolutely subject to Jesus, He is the highest authority. An important thing to remember is when demons leave a person, if that person doesn't fill that void with Jesus, the original demon returns with more demons, then the person is worse off than before (Matthew 12:43-45).

The Visitation

It was Monday, May 24th, 2021 at roughly 4:30am. I woke to the most intense fight of my life. Someone was trying as hard as they could to kill me. My kids slept cozy in their beds down the hall as I was suddenly plunged into a life or death struggle.

What you're about to read is insight only the dead know. I've never heard testimony of what I experienced. By God's grace these words are here. I believe this is going to be incredible insight into suicide that's never been told, until now.

Chapter 6: Warfare and Temptation

I'll share more about it later, but the year and a half leading up to this fateful night could be summarized in two words; *grief* and *restoration*. Considering our lives had been turned completely upside down 17 months earlier, the kids and I were doing really well. We were living back in Montana near family. It was tough being a single dad, but I was doing the best I could.

We were living in a two bedroom apartment over a shop. I was homeschooling the kids while trying to work from home as much as I possibly could. One great thing is my bedroom was big enough to fit all my studio gear. (I basically had a small recording studio with a bed in it). Most days I was able to spend at least a few hours working on this book as well as future music. I mention all of this before telling this story, because we were in a great place. I was not depressed, sad, angry or any other negative emotion. Things were not easy, but I was happy and grateful to spend all day with my precious kids and work from home. I had also been looking at houses to buy in the area and making a 5 year plan of action. Our small family was in the restoration phase and things were absolutely going in the right direction. It was so great compared to the devastation we'd gone through.

I'd heard from various people that CBD can help people be more calm and think clearer. It's an oil that comes from the cannabis plant. It's not intoxicating or psychoactive and perfectly legal to buy, at least here in the U.S. I pictured it being like certain teas that can help with relaxation. CBD is readily available and is sold just about everywhere nowadays. It's in all kinds of things.

I like to support local businesses any chance I can. I did some looking and found a local business that made and sold CBD oils. I called and was able to talk to the owner. He was very friendly and took the time to answer all my questions. In a nutshell, he said CBD helps people think a little clearer and relax more. He also said I could basically take as much as I wanted without any risk of overdosing. The possible benefits sounded good, so I ordered some to give it a try.

TIME STOOD STILL

They showed up a few days later. To me, it wasn't some drastic difference. Maybe I felt a tiny bit more relaxed, but not really enough to justify buying it again. *Maybe more would work better,* so I tried taking more than I had been. After all, he said I couldn't overdose and could take as much as I wanted. I went about my normal evening routine and went to bed.

Ughh...I suddenly woke in a strange slow motion daze. The room was dark, but if I could see I knew it'd only be a blur. I quickly sat up, trying to get my bearings. What's this? *What...is this presence?* I had an awareness, my spirit knew death and danger was at hand. I laid back down. I could feel it, hovering a few inches over my body. It was like a heavy, oppressive, textured fog. Imagine chopping up a dark gray wool blanket into little strands, and mixing it into a thick blanket of fog.

It was on top of me. Its oppression and intensity was like nothing I've ever experienced. I could feel the evil and intention of death. It was not just over my body, it was literally reaching into my mind and manipulating my thoughts. In my delerious and weakened state, it began tugging at the chains that were somehow embedded into my psyche. What gave him the right to do this? How did he have the ability to attack one of Jesus' own in this way? It had hooks in my brain and was pulling as hard as it could.

It was a demon...and he was there to kill me. He was pulling with everything he had. I do not understand it, but he was able to forcefully and violently place the scenario of me going to the closet and killing myself into the forefront of my thoughts. It was something urgent he wanted me to do immediately, but it was completely illogical and I knew it. In reality, I had absolutely zero thoughts or desire to kill myself, *what is this?!?!*

Chapter 6: Warfare and Temptation

"This is insane!" I thought. But it was not, it was warfare. I resisted with every fiber of my being. I was laying face down, pinning my own hands beneath me in a strange type of hug. I didn't want to budge. I feared that if I moved, it would begin an unstoppable motion towards my inevitable murder, which would not look like a murder.

In the darkened haze, I started praying out loud against the demon that was attacking me. Normally I would've done this sooner, but I can't fully describe the state I was in. Like a slow motion foggy dream. But I was starting to gain more clarity. As I prayed, it lifted slightly, but was still there, struggling with me.

> "Am I going to have to call my brother
> to come here and physically restrain me?!"

After a while, I was able to grab my phone and text my pastor. I let him know I was under spiritual attack and in urgent need of prayer. If I didn't hear back from him quickly I was going to call him. He texted back right away that he received the message and was also praying against my attacker.

I don't know how long all of this went for, it could've been an hour or two. I kept praying against it and was feeling like I could start moving around without being pulled. The demon's presence had gone. What remained was the intense mental hooks and haze.

I quickly went to the shower, put the water on cold and jumped in...it helped. *What did I just experience?* As I type this, these words are not adequate. I can't fully describe the intensity of him forcing an irrational thought into my mind, then trying to make me carry it out.

I mentioned earlier in the book about someone being *suicided*. Where they're murdered in a way that makes them appear to have killed themselves. This was exactly what the enemy tried to do to me. There was no part of me that wanted to kill myself. As I already stated, I was not depressed. The kids and I were healing and going in the right direction. Not to mention the fact that I'd never do that to them. What I experienced was a murderous onslaught.

Had that demon succeeded, people would have said things like...

"He must have missed Joy so much he couldn't live without her."

"I didn't know he was depressed!"

"If only I had...!"

But the reality would have been that I was actually murdered, by a demon. One that somehow was able to have strong momentary access. And the worst part; *no one would've known it.* My kids and family would have thought I deserted them, when that would be completely untrue.

I don't believe many people experience what I did and live to tell about it. The ones who do survive may be very reluctant to speak or even think about their experience. They likely don't understand what happened, think they're crazy, or are embarrassed about it. If you lost someone to suicide abruptly and without reason or suspicion, perhaps your loved experienced something similar to what I did.

Later that day I chatted with my pastor over the phone and filled him in with the details. We both came to similar conclusions, but he had a few more specifics. We both knew one thing. I hope you're ready, because this is big; God had *allowed* me to experience what Joy did. *He wanted* me to experience first hand a taste of what she went through, for two reasons;

- So I could have a much better understanding of what Joy experienced.

- That I would share this understanding with others.

I understood the *why*, but what I didn't understand at that moment was the *how*. *How* was he able to attack me so viciously like that. As I've stated already, demons are usually much more sneaky and subtle. This was a spiritual blitzkrieg. *How* was he able to get that close?

The answers came within a handful of days. It was two-fold;

- The CBD had lowered my natural defenses.

- There was a breach in my hedge of protection.

My pastor also believes it was the same demon that attacked Joy on day 31. It certainly could've been, and that would make perfect sense, but I didn't receive insight into that. At the very least he had the same role or function.

One thing worth mentioning; for a couple weeks after surviving the attack, I felt absolutely amazing. It felt like God was showering me with grace and love. Everything felt easy and flowed. I hoped it would never end because it was so incredibly peaceful. But after a while, it slowly tapered off and I was back to normal.

Lowered Defenses

In boxing and kick-boxing, you're trained to keep your hands up to protect your head. The jaw is especially important to protect. When struck, the impact transfers into the ear area via the jaw bone and can easily cause a person to lose their equilibrium and be knocked unconscious. Someone may be the toughest person in the world, but if they lower their defenses, a small person with experience can still knock them out, or worse.

Drugs lower our defenses against demons. I've known this for a long time. When I took CBD, I didn't think of it like a drug. I didn't think it could lower those defenses. I was very wrong. The interesting thing is CBD has to be very mild compared to powerful prescription and non-prescription drugs many people take.

Earlier in the book, I shared the story of the mother that was on 12 prescriptions and killed her children, then tried to kill herself. After the police and ambulance showed up that horrific day, she was

Chapter 6: Warfare and Temptation

taken to the hospital for her injuries. Later, while undergoing a mental health evaluation, she used her psychiatrist's phone to call her husband. She told him *a voice compelled her to kill the children and herself.*[78] I believe her. Keep in mind, I took something that you can buy nearly anywhere. There's no federal age restriction on CBD in the U.S. at the time of writing this. It's in creams, lotions, gummies, oils, bath bombs, capsules, and is certainly a fad at the moment. Something that appears to be so innocent was able to lower my defenses and allow a murderous demon to attack me. Can we begin to imagine what 12 prescriptions could do? Especially heavy prescriptions? What defenses could anyone have at that point? I imagine someone in that condition is free reign for the enemy.

As I mentioned, he was able to plant thoughts and pull, but I never heard any words. I've heard testimony from many people who've heard demons speaking directly to them, *voices, telling them to do something.* Just like that mother stated to her husband. Earlier in the book I also mentioned this is exactly what happened to Kevin Hines before he jumped off the Golden Gate Bridge. He heard voices compelling him to go to the bridge and jump. I'm sure many psychiatrists would disagree, but in my opinion, those voices are almost always demons.

As I mentioned earlier in the book, occasionally, a particular drug could be a benefit for certain purposes at certain times. In general though, I encourage people to stay off of drugs, whether from Big Pharma or not. Even seemingly innocent drugs can wind up with large consequences, especially when taken for long periods of time. If you're struggling with drug addiction, you can be free of it, *if you want to bad enough.* Drop the shame and guilt and be vulnerable... ask the right people for help. You can do it. You're worth it!!!

Below is a diagram of a dangerous cycle I see playing out. In Chapter 5, we discussed the alarming amount of people taking drugs, not to mention an equally alarming number of people with mental illness. What happens on a spiritual level when millions of Americans have their defenses lowered, and are attacked in ways they don't understand? What do those attacks cause some people to do (not to mention potential side effects of various drugs). If this trend doesn't change, on a large scale, I believe this is what we're going to see more of, and it's not good;

A Breach in the Hedge

King David was one of the most incredible warriors the world's ever known. But he always gave God the credit. David wrote in Psalm 91 about thousands of people dying around you, but nothing effecting you. It's called *the secret place of the Most High*. It was obvious through my experience there was a breach in the hedge of God's protection around me. But what could it be?

Blackberries are my favorite fruit. They're delicious, especially when you can pick them yourself. But have you ever gotten snagged in a blackberry bush? They make rose bush thorns feel like a gentle hug from a down comforter. I picture God's hedge of protection around us like a column of blackberry bushes surrounding a house. No enemy can make it through that. They would tear themselves apart in their feeble attempt. However, if there's a breach in that

Chapter 6: Warfare and Temptation

hedge, the enemy can make their way in. Sometimes it's a small breach and it takes them a while to notice it. Other times it can be multiple wide breaches and the enemy can stroll in willy-nilly.

I knew I had a breach. Somewhere I was off. I could feel it in my heart, *what is it?* I prayed and pondered, but received no answer. I needed an answer. I had to know what needed changing...and change it. Was I doing something I shouldn't? Was I supposed to be doing something, but wasn't? *Weeks went by.* I felt I needed to get a new perspective. My pastor and I talked about me heading west and visiting for a quick vacation. We both sensed and agreed it would be on this trip I'd receive the answer to the important question I'd been asking.

About a year earlier, he'd mentioned a boardwalk on Puget Sound near Canada called *The Taylor Boardwalk* (a fitting name, I know). When he originally told me about it, I had a sense it was a place I was to visit at some point in the future. A year later I could feel in my heart it was time to go there. I believed ahead of time I'd receive the understanding of what the breach was. It was going to be a great trip. I knew that taking it was an act of obedience, and was needed for me to receive my answer. I also knew the kids would have a great time staying in Montana with family. This was going to be a solo trip.

I really like cars and enjoy driving. The time alone on a long drive is a great time to reflect. I've made the drive between Washington State and Montana more times than I can count. On this drive, I had hopeful expectation. After weeks of wondering, I longed for my answer. It was a 10 hour drive with no issues. I checked in to the hotel and relaxed for a bit. The timing worked out great because that night was our normal weekly meeting. I was blessed to be there in person, like I used to be able to. It was a great time seeing everyone. They're a very diverse group of Jesus followers and some of the best people I've ever known.

As the few days unfolded, I could feel that the boardwalk would be the crescendo of the journey. I knew it was very important that I go there. Following through on this part of the venture would be how I'd receive my answer. I woke, took a shower and got dressed. After a quick continental breakfast, I hit the road. *Boardwalk, here I come!*

At my pastor's suggestion, I took a small highway along the water. It wound its way along a steep hillside and gave great views of the water and islands in the distance. You can look up pictures of this road, it's called *Chuckanut Drive*. After a pleasant drive, I reached the parking lot at the north end of the Boardwalk. I wanted to start at the far end, because there's a coffee shop at the start of the walk. My plan was to get a delicious caffeinated beverage and casually walk down the boardwalk, expecting God to answer my question.

I left the cozy coffee shop behind and stepped onto the boardwalk. With a warm coffee in hand I meandered my way southward. The boardwalk is a long and wide dock, about ten feet over the water, paralleling the beach. I don't know the length of it, but it seemed about half a mile long. As I strolled along, I prayed earnestly. "Lord, please tell me what my breach is." .....Nothing. I passed family after family. Some seemed like tourists, others appeared to be locals. The boardwalk was serene with nice views, but I was there for information. *And it wasn't coming.* Eventually the end of the boardwalk came into view. Up ahead there was a curve to the left as the boardwalk met back up with land. I was about to walk past a little wooden bench. I stopped and told God;

> "I'm going to walk to the end of the boardwalk. When I come back, I'm going to sit down at this bench. Lord when I do, please let me know what my breach is."

I arrived at the end of the boardwalk in time to watch a long train go by (I recorded a video of it to send to my kids). Then, I made my way back to the bench. I sat down on the old wooden slats. Little sailboats carved through the water in front of me while people passed behind. I sat there, continuing to ask Him to give me what I was there for. I had waited weeks and driven about 600 miles to be there in that moment and...*silence.*

Chapter 6: Warfare and Temptation

The minutes ticked by. Was I wrong? After about half an hour I leaned over, wresting my elbows on my knees. I didn't want to give up hope, I knew I was supposed to be there. It was like running a race and the finish line being deserted, with no actual line.

Sitting there hunched over, I noticed it. It was painted using a black rattle can and a stencil. Small and easy to miss, it'd been there a while and looked out of place. *What does it say?* I could still read it...*a name*. I didn't think much of it at first, but within a minute, everything changed.

Understanding began flooding in. It was like finishing a jigsaw puzzle, the pieces became obvious and started falling into place. "I got what I came for!" Laying back against the bench, I breathed easier. It was then that I took the time to enjoy the views. I took in God's amazing handiwork. With sincere gratitude, I thanked Him for blessing me with the understanding I'd been asking Him for. I stood up, took a picture of the bench and made my way back down the boardwalk.

Actual Photo

Over the next few days, everything became crystal clear. I knew what the breach was...and it'd been there a long time. It was there nearly my entire life *and I didn't know it.* The Bible makes it very clear that God knows the proper timing of things. It was clearly time to repair this breach.

Distrust. That was the breach in the hedge around me. The name painted at my feet, on a boardwalk I'd never been to, hundreds of miles away, yet knew I was supposed to visit, was that of a close loved one...that I didn't trust. The distrust I had for this person was from a young age. My life had grown around it. Characteristics of myself were due to the fact my life was floating on a sea of distrust. Over many years, this distrust grew into a desire for self sufficiency and relying on my strength and understandings.

Some of you are asking; 'What's wrong with that?' Are you ready for the main point of the breach; *my distrust of this person had grown into a distrust of God.* Slowly over time I did not trust God. I thought I did, I said I did. But I trusted myself more. The cancer of distrust needed removed from my life.

I brought it before Him. I confessed it. He knew I didn't know. Yet, because He loves me, He provided a multi-faceted process for me to learn all of this. Especially in such an amazing and memorable way. He's so good. I've since forgiven the person that caused my distrust issues. I keep a watchful eye on distrust, daily. A big part has to do with setting up boundaries and not allowing myself to be in a position to be hurt again by this particular person. The other part is checking throughout the day who I'm trusting, myself or God.

If you're trying to get free, or discuss these matters, make sure it's with the right person. Jesus warned us not to cast our pearls before swine, because we'll only get trampled on. Do not be vulnerable with people you shouldn't. They'll likely only hurt you. There are those however you can be vulnerable with that will love and help you.

If you feel like it's impossible for you to have a breach in the hedge of your life, your breach is pride. Pride was the original sin. The devil was filled with pride and he rebelled against God, thinking he was better than him. Let's not do the same.

Chapter 6: Warfare and Temptation

The Foothold

In Ephesians 4, we're told not to give the Devil a foothold. What's that? There are many examples given, but let's keep this simple. Things we do that the Devil can amplify and use against us are footholds. Do you lie? Do you steal? Do you have un-forgiveness? Are you an angry person? The enemy wants to turn a foothold into a stronghold, usually a little at a time.

There's an old analogy called *'boiling a frog.'* It's more true today than ever. It goes like this; if you drop a frog in boiling water, it'll quickly jump out. However, if you set a frog in a pot of comfortable water and SLOWLY turn up the heat, it'll continue to slowly acclimate, until it's eventually cooked. *WE* are just like that frog.

Don't believe me? Just look at what's happening in the world today. If what's happening right now had happened quickly, hundreds of millions of people would have stood up and put a stop to it quickly. Yet, because the enemy and the powers that be have slowly been turning up the heat on us, we've continued to acclimate until the point we….well, we'll see I guess.

Now, how does this simple principal relate to the foothold? This is how the enemy works; we *give* him a foothold and slowly he turns it into a stronghold. We acclimate over time and by the end of it, we don't understand how we wound up in such a bad place.

We're made in the image and likeness of God. If the enemy could, he'd destroy each and every one of us right now, immediately. He doesn't have that ability, so he tries to trick us into a cycle of despair and bad habits. Fear is a big foothold. It's the biggest tool used to trick people into giving up their God given rights. Love and trust God more than you fear the enemy. You can't serve two masters. You can not serve the enemy through fear and be submitted to God. It's the classic, fear or faith dichotomy. I'm not afraid of the enemy, their tactics or their attacks they throw at me. Even if the enemy is somehow able to get to me, I will not fear. I trust God more.

Queen Esther is one of my favorite people in all of history. Her boldness to overcome fear and do the right thing has inspired me for years. She said one of the greatest lines of all time right before risking her life. "If I perish, I perish." She went on to save millions of people in doing so.

Nullify the Wrongs

From my experience, it's possible to be born with a breach in our hedge of protection. Issues from our lineage can become our problems. The Bible calls this generational sins. This is one reason why I believe some people say they're 'born this way.' But remember, Jesus calls us to be born again, no matter how we were born the first time.

Before I ever met my pastor, I watched many videos on YouTube from a man named Derek Prince regarding generational sins. They were very helpful. I felt there were things I was dealing with that I didn't cause, but came through my lineage.

This is another common issue, yet very misunderstood. For instance, witchcraft is a very common one. If you had a parent or grandparent that practiced witchcraft, you were likely born with that breach in your hedge of protection. Do not fear it. It's not your fault, but now that you know about it, it's your responsibility to close the breach.

Other common generational breaches are;

- Secret Societies / The Occult
- Entertaining demons with things like Ouija ('weegee') boards. (Demons posing as humans). Mediumship.
- Sexual deviancy
- Astrology / Divination / Psychics
- New Age practices / Mysticism

It's as simple as bringing these things before God. Confessing that people in your lineage did them, and asking Him to cleanse you of them in Jesus' name. He repairs the breach and to Him, it's like it never happened. Even if you aren't sure of anything your ancestors did, you can tell Him something like; "I don't know if they did anything to cause a generational breach, but please forgive any if there are. And cleanse me and my household of them, in Jesus' name."

Why do you think there are family lines spanning multiple generations that duplicate the same destructive patterns? In my opinion, this topic is the root of the problem.

Planting Seeds

> **inception** [in-sep-shuhn] :
>
> *an act, process, or instance of beginning* [141/142]

There's a movie that came out in 2010 called *Inception*, starring Leonardo DiCaprio. At one point in the movie, the main Character (DiCaprio) says;

> "What is the most resilient parasite?...A bacteria?...A virus? An intestinal worm?........*An idea*. Resilient, highly Contagious. Once an idea has taken hold in the brain, it's almost impossible to eradicate. An idea that is fully formed, fully understood, that sticks. Right in there somewhere."

> Then, later on he says; "The seed that we plant in this man's mind will grow into an idea. This idea will define him. It may come to change...it may come to change everything about him."

It was a popular movie, more than likely you've seen it. But next time you watch it, I encourage you to imagine the team of people trying to plant seeds in other's minds...*are demons*.

I believe months ago God told me to do this very thing. It was interesting watching it again from that perspective. It gives us a better understanding of the sneakiness of demons. Watch how they plot and scheme how to get someone to do something.

As I mentioned earlier, their most common tactic is to sneak in through a breach, plant seeds in our garden (heart and mind), then escape without being seen. Did you know that not all our thoughts we have are ours? Some have been placed there intentionally, hoping they take. Will they?

There's a difference between watching a bird fly by, and allowing it to land and build a nest on our head. This is a message especially for the younger generation that believes every thought and feeling is right...*they're not.* Many thoughts and feelings are very destructive. Entertaining every one is a sure fire way to live a miserable and destructive life.

What's especially interesting in the movie is that DiCaprio's character actually planted a seed into his wife, of *killing herself.* Spoiler alert, after he placed the seed, it was stuck there. It grew in her mind like a cancer and eventually she acted it out. It was a planted thought that grew and became fully formed. She thought it was her thought, a good idea. She didn't know he (a demon in this analogy) planted it there.

Even though seeds are small, if left alone and watered, some can grow into horrific nightmares. This is why it's very important to be careful how we talk to people. We don't want to be a delivery system for the enemy and plant seeds in loved ones that shouldn't be there.

In Joy's final moments, the closest example I can think of is DiCaprio's wife in the movie. Sitting on the ledge thinking she's doing the right thing. She was so twisted up and confused. Add in brokenness, out of whack hormones, lack of sleep and demon manipulation...

Chapter 6: Warfare and Temptation

Do we get weeds to die by watering them? Of course not. We get weeds to die by attacking them, ripping them out, roots and all, and burning them up. Like the movie, a deep rooted thought begins to grow and bear fruit in real life. The question is, what kind of fruit is it? Is it good fruit or bad fruit? Of course, any fruit from the enemy is bad fruit. But can we recognize bad fruit? By what standards can we tell? After all, there are beautiful looking fruits in the world that will kill you if you eat it, and there are ugly looking fruits that are incredibly delicious and good for you.

Jesus said you'll know them by their fruit (Matthew 7). What does good fruit and bad fruit look like? If it's; love, joy, peace, patience, kindness, goodness, faithfulness, gentleness, and self-control (Galations 5:22-23), then it's good fruit. However, if it's; hate, turmoil, fear, wrongness, resentment, disorder, and chaos, it's bad fruit. If we want good fruit in our lives, we must plant good seeds in us, while rejecting bad seeds. We must be aware of what's allowed into our minds and our hearts, and of those in our household.

The Moment of Clarity

From experience, once a demon and their oppression leaves, there's a moment of clarity. It's like having a dark fog lifted. The oppression usually comes on slow and we become normalized to it, (like the boiling frog). But once it's gone, everything instantly becomes clearer and easier.

One sad thing is some people spend their entire lives under demonic oppression. They've never actually experienced their life free of them. I've met people like this. They're so used to demonic influence, they actually think it's themselves. But in reality they've been subject to demons their entire life. Would you be surprised if I told you half the people I've met like this are very religious church goers? The first person I remember experiencing like this was actually a pastor. Jesus said there'd be wolves in sheep's clothing. Did you think He was joking?

I mentioned examples from the Golden Gate Bridge earlier. For some people that have jumped, their only moment of clarity in their entire life happened too late. There's no way to know for sure, but I imagine right after they jump, the demons leave the person. Then they have the entire fall to think clearly about the horrible act they just did.

> This reminds me of two important future examples where people see clearly, without any filters;
>
> - At some point after He returns, ALL of mankind will be able to clearly see and understand who Jesus is. Every knee will bend (including yours) and every tongue will confess (including yours) that Jesus is Lord (Philippians 2:6-11). To me the question is; who will say it with gladness and who will say it in terror, knowing they spent their lives opposing Him?
>
> - Man's condition at the Great White Throne judgment. (Revelation 20:11-15)

The first deliverance I did was on myself. I went into the woods and began praying and casting out demons in Jesus' name. This was after months of becoming familiar with the subject, mostly through Derek Prince videos and reading the Bible. While kneeling on the ground, praying and puking my guts out, I was able to get rid of much of the oppression I'd felt for God knows how long.

Unfortunately most churches and pastors are grossly inexperienced with spiritual warfare. I prayed for at least a couple years to meet a pastor or group that understood spiritual warfare. I knew I needed deliverance but didn't know anyone. As always, God came through and brought me a pastor who understood.

As a general guide, I encourage you to not do deliverance by yourself. There's a reason Jesus sent out His disciples two-by-two, healing the sick and casting out demons. If you feel like you or someone you know is in need of deliverance, I strongly encourage you to pray to be led to someone that understands the subject and has experience. It's important to bring in reinforcements, especially when you're new in the Lord and spiritual warfare.

Chapter 7: Getting Personal

Let's get real about a subject plaguing humanity with the highest suicide rates...*19 times higher than average. But first, let's set the scene...*

The Land of Confusion

When I was young, one of my favorite places to go was the music store in the mall. They sold vinyl records, cassettes and eventually CDs. I vividly remember walking up and down the isles, looking at all the new and unknown music. My favorite part was going there with my dad. It was a fun bonding time for us, and I enjoyed seeing his interest in music. I'm sure that's where I got it from.

On one particular cassette hunting trip, I bought *Invisible Touch* by the band *Genesis*. One of the songs was called, *The land of confusion*. Like the lyrics, the music video also portrays very odd, strange and confusing circumstances. It reminds me of modern history. At this point in time, I believe many adults (including many parents), are subjecting children to massive amounts of confusion, and calling it 'reality.'

> "There's too many men, too many people
> Making too many problems
> And not much love to go 'round
> Can't you see this is a land of confusion?"
>
> - Part of the song, *"The Land of Confusion"* by Genesis

Confusion robs people of peace and hope, vital attributes of a fulfilling life. When people don't have a fulfilling life, they're more prone to suicide. Therefore, if we remove the cancer of confusion, I believe wholeheartedly we can reduce suicide rates. Life and that abundantly...we can't have it while living in confusion. Do you want an abundant life? One filled with peace, joy and fulfillment? Do you want that for your children, and their children? I do too! Let's clear up confusion, so it's possible.

> "For God is not a God of confusion but of peace..."
> -1 Corinthians 14:33 (ESV)

and...

For where envying and strife is, there is confusion and every evil work. But the wisdom that is from above is first pure, then peaceable, gentle, and easy to be intreated, full of mercy and good fruits, without partiality, and without hypocrisy. And the fruit of righteousness is sown in peace of them that make peace.

> - James 3:16-18 (KJV)

Do you see much envying and strife in this world? Um, does a zebra have stripes? Well then, there's *confusion* and *every evil work*. But look at the characteristics of the wisdom from above; pure, peaceable, gentle, full of mercy, without partiality and without hypocrisy. In my opinion, much of the confusion we're seeing in this world is not by chance, nor by accident. Confused and fearful people are easy to control. Look at the worst atrocities in history, the people were confused and fearful. Powers-that-be can get away with genocide if the people are mired in confusion and fear.

History shows that we do not learn from history.

Is this Real Life?

There's an old, popular YouTube video called *David After Dentist*. In the short video, a boy's coming off of anesthesia. His dad recorded him saying silly things, one of which, the boy asked; "Is this real life?" This is a very important question. In my opinion, many people are so confused, they actually live in a 'reality'...that isn't real. The 'reality' they experience between their ears is very different from what's *actually* real. Imagine someone living their life wearing 'virtual reality' (VR) goggles. Just because it's how they perceive things, doesn't mean it's actually so.

This all comes back to living in confusion. When people's lives are not built on a solid foundation, the storms of life have their way with them. In my opinion, most of the storms we're facing are planned and orchestrated, or not even a storm at all.

This is the greatest and freest country to ever exist in the history of the world. Yet millions of Americans are being seduced into hating their own country, hating themselves and their bodies, and dismantling the very things that make us so incredibly free.

On January 27, 1838 Abraham Lincoln gave what many believe was his first great speech.[95] In it, he said these words;

"At what point then is the approach of danger to be expected? I answer, if it ever reach us, it must spring up amongst us. It cannot come from abroad. If destruction be our lot, we must ourselves be its author and finisher. As a nation of freemen, we must live through all time, or die by suicide." [95]

- Abraham Lincoln

For good reason, a paraphrased version of this speech has been very popular the last few years;

"America will never be destroyed from the outside. If we falter and lose our freedoms, it will be because we destroyed ourselves." [95]

- Abraham Lincoln (Attributed)

In my opinion, millions of Americans are so confused they're actually viewing freedom as dangerous, and are calling on their new god, *the State,* to quell the 'danger'...a.k.a. freedom. The funny thing about the State is by its very nature, it's happy to oblige this request. To quote the 19th Century British politician Lord Acton; "Power tends to corrupt, and absolute power corrupts absolutely." The more power the people give the State, the more corrupt it will be. It's politics and human nature 101. In my view, the incredibly sad part is; if maintained, this course only leads to the downfall of a great Nation and countless lives lost.

Unless people wake up, I see this course leading to the younger generations being oppressed and killed by the very establishment they're putting their faith in. The one many of them have placed as their new god. Look at the last word Lincoln used in his quote; *suicide.* He could've used many words, but he chose *that* one. He used the analogy of a nation having two options; continually living free, or purposely killing themselves. As a Country, the act of giving up living free is equal to killing ourselves.

How then must we stay alive? Using Abraham Lincoln's logic, *WE MUST LIVE FREE!* We must choose to live free and follow through with it, *while we still can.* Will we be the generation that lost this amazing Country? What side of history will you and I be on? We all have a part to play. This is an overly used quote, for good reason...

> "I would rather die on my feet than live on my knees."
>
> - Euripides

This is the attitude our ancestors had. If they didn't, we wouldn't be here today. Can we begin to imagine the hardships our relatives lived through for us to be living such spoiled and carefree lives? They couldn't begin to imagine the amount of freedom and luxury we take for granted every single day. Remember what I said earlier; "the average person in the U.S. lives better than kings of the past." Yet we often act and complain like spoiled toddlers.

I can only hope to live a life of purpose that would justify my ancestor's immense struggles to simply survive. They toiled in ways I can't imagine, hoping for prosperity for their descendants...*me.* Your ancestors did the same...what are you doing with what they provided for you? It doesn't have to be something grandiose, but God has a purpose for you. Are you finding out what it is? If not, forget the past and start today! I know you can.

Dying on their feet was also the attitude the founders of this Country had when they stood up to the British. Every person that signed *The Declaration of Independence* was signing a death sentence. They were committing treason against England in their plan to form this Country. Many of them suffered dearly for placing their names on that most important document.

Today, these same founders are increasingly viewed more as racist bigots than courageous visionaries. They helped start the greatest Country the world's ever known, yet a growing number of Americans spit on their memories and legacy. You want to know who I like most out of all the signers? John Hancock.

Chapter 7: Getting Personal

You see, John heard the King of England had poor eyesight, so he signed his name very large. Because of this boldness, hundreds of years later, our signature is still referred to as our 'John Hancock.' He was a man that was willing to die on his feet. This Country was paid for by the blood of courageous Americans, willing to die on their feet. Will we be the cowardly generation that let's it all slip away? Will we let our children and grandchildren pay for our cowardice?

Here's a famous line from William Shakespeare's play, *The Tragedy of Julius Caesar...*

"A coward dies a thousand times before his death, but the valiant taste of death but once. It seems to me most strange that men should fear, seeing that death, a necessary end, will come when it will come."

- William Shakespeare's *Julius Caesar*

Act II, Scene 2

I encourage you to live free, boldly free. The same kind of boldness Queen Esther had when she saved millions of people, *with her words*. The same kind of boldness Peter had when he walked on water. The same kind of boldness history's heroes have mustered up through the ages. *Choose freedom.*

Stand firm against evil. A big reason we're in the mess we're in, is because we've tolerated evil. In tolerating evil, we condone evil. When we stop being selfish, and instead start caring for others, we can have a life of significance and purpose. Lives of significance and purpose have meaning. In my opinion, a growing trend like this would certainly lower the suicide rate, not to mention change the world...for the better.

You can quote me on this;

Nonsense ends, when compliance of nonsense ends.

Duality

Divide [dih-vahyd]: *to separate into parts, groups, sections, etc.*[143]

&

Conquer [kong-ker]: *to be victorious* [144/145]

Divide and Conquer: *a way of keeping yourself in a position of power by causing disagreements among other people so that they are unable to oppose you.*[81]

In my opinion, there are many ways the 'powers-that-be' keep the general public fighting with each other. They want us divided. They want us feeling separate and un-unified as a people. I believe they want the *Un*-United States of America. They want Americans to have an 'Us vs. Them' mentality and view each other as the enemy. The worse things get, guess what people call and vote for? More government. More restrictions. More taxes. Fewer rights. Therefore, in my opinion, it's actually in the interest of the 'powers-that-be' to incite turmoil, violence and discord. It results in them gaining more money and power, at the expense of the people.

> Let's look at an example of what can happen
> when people are 100% on the same page...

"Look!" he said. "The people are united, and they all speak the same language. After this, nothing they set out to do will be impossible for them!"
-Genesis 11:6 (NLT)

Do you know who said that? God said that. It was about the people, speaking the same language, working together for one purpose. Their purpose was to build an extremely tall tower. You may've heard of it, it's known as *The Tower of Babel.* So, according to God Himself, the people were unified to a degree that they could accomplish *anything* they set out to do. Keep in mind, they were also doing a bad thing, but that's a story for a different day. The point is, agreement is a very powerful thing. Here's a couple more examples;

"Five of you will chase a hundred, and a hundred of you will chase ten thousand! All your enemies will fall beneath your sword."

-Leviticus 26:8 (NLT)

5 vs. 100 = one person chasing 20.

But,

100 vs. 10,000 = one person chasing 100.

"How could one person chase a thousand of them, and two people put ten thousand to flight, unless their Rock had sold them, unless the Lord had given them up?"

-Deuteronomy 32:30 (NLT)

1 vs. 1000 = one person chasing 1,000.

But,

2 vs. 10,000 = one person chasing 5,000.

Both of these examples show one simple fact; by adding people in complete agreement, you receive a *multiplication* of the desired outcome. I believe this is a principle that can be used for good, or for evil. How does this apply today? Well, if many people are unified for a good and righteous purpose, there'll be a multiplication of good fruit. However, if many people are unified for an evil purpose, there'll be a multiplication of evil fruit.

By fighting with each other, we are un-unified and therefore unable to produce good fruit on a large scale. As a people, how are we divided? How are we manipulated into arguing, fighting and hating

TIME STOOD STILL

one-another? This reminds me of the classic story of the fighting ants;

> "I can't remember what all Frank had fighting in the jar that day...red ants against black ants. They won't fight unless you keep shaking the jar. And that's what Frank was doing, shaking, shaking the jar."
>
> -From Kurt Vonnegut's 1963 novel *Cat's Cradle*

I've got a big question; who's shaking *our* proverbial jar? Why are they promoting division and making us fight each other? Speaking of bugs, did you know that many 'elites' of the world are pushing for you and I to eat bugs and own nothing? They're calling it 'The Great Reset.'[98] Umm, who's it great for? Certainly not for us 'peasants' who'd be eating bugs while owning nothing. (They're actually adding bugs into modern day 'foods' and labeling it names most people won't recognize. Don't believe me? Look it up).

These 'elites' look like modern day Bond villains. In my opinion, it's only a ploy for you and I to be chained by, and for them to eventually hand the keys to their boss. Remember, life and that abundantly. We won't have it if we're willingly enslaved by evil men deceiving us with what I wholeheartedly believe is *artificial scarcity*...

> **artificial** [ahr-tuh-fish-uhl]: *imitation; simulated; sham*[146]

> **scarcity** [skair-si-tee]: *insufficiency or shortness of supply*[147]

It's OK to say no, I am. I will not eat bugs and I will own things. When you can't own property (meaning physical things), you *are* property. I will not bend the knee to wicked people who want to destroy all that I hold dear. I'll not take the bait that the world is in dire peril and mankind is a plague. I'll drive a V8 vehicle and do burnouts occasionally, I'll barbecue steaks and burgers, I'll enjoy this world God has blessed us with, and I'll teach my children to live free. Life and that abundantly, *it's so nice*. I pray millions of others will remove their 'scarcity glasses,' and start questioning the people at the top. The ones on high horses telling us how we should live, while doing the opposite. This is the very definition of hypocrisy and I believe millions are beginning to see it.

Listed below are other topics that I believe have been used historically to incite division among us;

- Black vs. White
- Men vs. Women
- Rich vs. Poor
- Gay vs. Straight
- Left vs. Right
- Democrat vs. Republican
- Pro-choice vs. Pro-life
- Everyone vs. Cops
- Socialism vs. Capitalism
- Haves vs. Have-Nots
- Mask vs. No Mask
- Jab vs. No Jab
- 99% vs. 1%
- Blue Collar vs. White Collar
- Pro gun rights vs. No gun rights
- 'Green energy' vs. Non 'green energy'

In my opinion, these themes pop up at the most convenient of times. 'They're voting on a bill for...' Voila! Like clockwork, a divisive issue jumps to the top of the news and...*SQUIRREL!*...we take the bait and look the other way. The 'news' may as well say; 'Hey everybody, look over there!' In my opinion, it keeps happening...because it works. I picture them as smokescreens for the magician to hide what he's really up to.

> "It's easier to fool people than to convince
> them that they have been fooled."
>
> - Mark Twain *(Attributed)*

There's a very popular compilation video on YouTube. It shows *dozens* of 'local' news stations...all saying the same thing, word-for-word. A scripted, 'intimate' talk to the viewers at home. How ironic, the topic was *the dangers of false news*. It's both comical and disturbing at the same time. On YouTube; "local news stations say the same thing." I believe there's a reason it's called our 'daily programming' on our 'tell-a-vision.'

propaganda [prop-uh-gan-duh]:

information, ideas, or rumors deliberately spread widely to help or harm a person, group, movement, institution, nation, etc.[148]

Listen to this quote from a live talk, by a
brave author and journalist, Dr. Naomi Wolf;

"As a journalist, to say these words, just..I can't tell you with what a heavy heart I say them, but we've entered an era in which it is not crazy to assess news events to see if they're real or not real. And, in the United States, as well as overseas. And, in fact, it's kind of crazy not to." [83]

- Dr. Naomi Wolf
2014 Free State Project's Liberty Forum

To sum up this section; the world wants us divided, while wearing 'virtual reality' goggles (metaphorically speaking). Will we go along with it? Or will we start to question why certain things are pushed the way they are? I've found one certainty in life, *continually and humbly seeking truth always leads to Jesus*. The World is in complete opposition to Him, therefore, those that stand for Truth are hated by the world. If you see the world going after someone, it may be good to stop and ponder why that may be. Jesus said this;

"If the world hates you, remember that it hated me first. The world would love you as one of its own if you belonged to it, but you are no longer part of the world. I chose you to come out of the world, so it hates you."

- John 15:18-19 (NLT)

Men and Women

Q: What's the main 'issue' dividing people today?

A: Men vs. Women

This time however......plot twist!

(pause for suspense)

A man can now *become* a woman. No, seriously. People would buy that right?.....(Note; please bear with me. We are still talking about suicide as you'll see coming up).

Q: How can a man become a woman?

A: He just has to *believe* he, is a she.

Q: How does that work?

A: Stop being a transphobe! Why do you hate 'trans' people?

How we fall for these traps would be laughable, if it weren't so deceitful and destructive. As I write this, guess who just won the *'Miss Netherlands'* beauty contest? A man. *He* will be going on to compete in the '*Miss Universe*' beauty contest.[85] Hello McFly, am I the only person that sees the glaring problem with this? How can a man win a women's beauty contest, let alone be allowed to enter it? Do you really believe *he* was of greater beauty than *actual* women in the *women's* beauty competition? Or do you suppose there was political influence involved? People, wake up! It's like pizza winning a chili cook off. It doesn't make any logical sense.

> Guess who holds the *women's* power lifting world record...*a man*.[91] Guess who's going into women's bathrooms nowadays... *men*. Great...what could possibly go wrong? Guess who's taking opportunities away from women in sports, business, academics...*men*, and some women are helping them do it. What's the point of women having anything if men can just call themselves a woman and take it from them?

When I was at my strongest in my twenties, the most I could ever bench press was 305 lbs. (I'd probably struggle to bench half that nowadays, lol). That may sound like a lot of weight, but I doubt I would've been in the top 1000 men in the state back then. But guess what, the current Montana state record for women's bench press is 225 lbs. That's right. Had I known it back then, I could've *identified* as a woman and smashed the Montana State record. Who knows, maybe I would've been the strongest woman in the Country. Can you imagine that?

Enter dreamy music here... Just picture it, the star spangled banner playing as they put the gold medal around my neck. Oh, my parents would've been so proud of their 'daughter.' Maybe I would've been invited to meet the president or gotten a Nobel Prize. Perhaps even a guest spot on the tonight show. Oh, what could've been...lol.

Do you think that sounds absurd? Of course it does! That'd be me cheating women out of what is rightfully theirs. I would have gotten laughed at and told to go away for even trying something like that... *and they would have been right.*

Chapter 7: Getting Personal

But sadly, this is a big part of the confusion children are being normalized with today. But it's *not* normal. This will never be normal. This is all happening because a small number of people are pushing this evil idea, and millions of complacent cowards...are letting it happen.

One of my favorite movies growing up was *Kindergarten Cop*, starring Arnold Schwarzenegger (1990). There's an insightful line in the movie, spoken by a little boy. It has the power to clear up all the so-called 'gender confusion' happening in the world today.

"Boys have a penis, girls have a vagina."

Whew, I'm glad that settles it. But you know what, some people may need a little more than that...

Men cannot become women. A man *believing* he is a woman, does not make him a woman. He is a man, with problems.

Women cannot become men. A woman *believing* she is a man, does not make her a man. She is a woman, with problems.

Boys cannot become girls. A boy *believing* he is a girl, does not make him a girl. He is a boy, with problems.

Girls cannot become boys. A girl *believing* she is a boy, does not make her a boy. She is a girl, with problems.

Which leads us to the subject with the highest suicide rates...

Erased

There are many people today calling themselves 'feminists.' The incredible irony is some of these so called 'feminists' are actually destroying women. They're rallying around men pretending to be women, while real women suffer for it. They're supporting the destruction of women's rights, achievements and possibilities.

If you support men stealing from women, I have a question for you; *why?* Why do you believe that's OK? Women's safety and opportunities are becoming secondary to the feelings of a very small minority of men playing dress up. They demand inclusion where they have no business being. It's taking advantage of women by stealing what's rightfully theirs.

Let me give you a simple analogy;

Growing up, there were nearby Indian Reservations that had large amounts of wild game. As an outsider, I could not hunt on their land. That would be illegal. But you know what, to take advantage of what's *theirs*, what if I *identified* as being from *their* tribe. I could walk right onto *their* land and take *their* game. Who cares if I'm on *their* ground taking *their* property, while pretending to be from *their* tribe.

That would be OK, right? After all, if we can willy-nilly choose our gender, why not race? Why not profession? Why not age? Why not lineage? The possibilities are endless....Maybe the next time I fly on an airplane I could *identify* as the pilot and jump in the Captain's seat. Better yet, a fighter pilot. I've always wanted to fly a fighter jet. I'm sure the Air Force would be OK with that, right?

What about a 50 year old man who identifies as a 12 year old? It would be OK for him to date a 12 year old girl right? Of course that's absurd, but it's just as absurd as a man winning a women's beauty contest...it's the same logic, *or lack thereof.* People are perverting reality, and mutilating the impressionable. They're lost sheep in a confused world of gray.

This is about human rights and what rightfully belongs to defined groups of people. If everyone supports the idea that you *are* something because you *feel* something, Pandora's box is opened wide. A box with a never ending supply of stealing, killing and destroying.

Chapter 7: Getting Personal

affirm [uh-furm]:

validate, confirm [150/151]

The fact there's something called 'gender affirming care' demonstrates how nonsensical all of this is. Why would someone need a complete stranger to endorse someone's problematic feelings? Feelings that can lead directly to irreversible bodily damage and astronomically high suicide rates. Is that person God? Can they tell within minutes of meeting a perfect stranger that mutilating their own body is a good thing?

"The therapists now are instantly affirming these genders, these opposite genders. As opposed to exploring what's going on...the trans thing I think is a great excuse to avoid issues that are really painful. And if a therapist is affirming therapy, the one person who's supposed to actually face things that are painful, then that's going to send them more into this *trans path*, because that's what feels good in the short term."[94]

-Pamela Garfield-Jaeger
Therapist, Social worker
From the docudrama, *Gender Transformation*

Imagine 'alcoholic affirming care.' You go to a therapist where they affirm you with a problem. Afterward, they hand you a bottle to support your problem under the guise of 'health care.' A bottle you have to drink every day for the rest of your life. Oh yeah, and they want you to cut your penis or boobs off...so you don't kill yourself. Come on people, wake up!

"I'm 82 years old. I'm still talking about the harm that was done to me 78 years ago. Well it all started when I was a four year old boy and my grandmother started cross dressing me...

Well the truth was, it was never about gender. I learned this after I was 50 years old. After living the life of Laura Gensen, female transgender. It was always about what happened with a purple dress and being sexually abused. And no one was addressing this adverse childhood experience that caused this trauma...

Many young people who've been subjected to sexual abuse, actually want to remove their genitalia, because they never want to be sexually abused again. It's not gender dysphoria, you know it's body dysmorphia, or it's sexual abuse, or it's schizophrenia or it's a bipolar disorder. The fact of the matter is, there's many other people who go to therapy and find out that they can treat these disorders and they don't have to live this way...

We need to understand, this isn't about helping people. This is about making money. There's a surgeon in California that makes around 1.5 million dollars a year doing the surgeries. The presidents of these clinics have come out and said *'we need to do this because it's so profitable.'* They never talk about how much harm that's being caused and that it's causing **19 times** more likely for you to commit suicide." [94]

- Walt Heyer, Detransitioner
Founder of sexchangeregret.com
From the docudrama, *Gender Transformation*

Walt has helped over 1000 people and continues to help people every day.

Chapter 7: Getting Personal

Your Conscience

The world is pressuring people to go against rationale, their conscience and their God-given senses. Below are two images; one car, and one truck. Can you tell which is which?

This is; **a.** A Car
b. A Truck

answer: b. A Truck

This is; **a.** A Car
b. A Truck

answer: a. A Car

Of course that was silly, but so is calling someone who's obviously a man, a woman. It's a blatant lie. The World is trying to get people to go against obvious truth. Just because a truck has been altered to have features of a car, doesn't make it a car. The same is true for a car that's been modified to resemble a truck. Even though it has big tires, it's still a car...with big tires.

This is exactly what's happening today. People are being pressured to go along with obvious lies. It doesn't matter how many modifications a man or woman has, just like these vehicles, they will never be the opposite. Deep down, I believe most people understand this, but lack the fortitude to resist the absurdity. In their cowardice, they pretend to agree with nonsense to avoid potential backlash.

One similarity to vehicles and people regarding heavy modifications is this; they break down more. They have different roles in their design, for important and specific reasons. A truck can haul more than a car, but a car goes faster and handles better than a truck. The more a truck or car is modified, the less reliable and capable they become at what they were originally designed to do. Similarly, men and women who are 'heavily modified' often have severe medical problems and become incapable of performing what they were originally designed to do. For some, the outcome is death.

The T. Segment

Q: "Chad, why are you talking about this subject in a book about suicide?"

A: "In all of my research, THE HIGHEST suicide rates I've found are people in the 'LGBTQ' community, particularly the T ('trans') segment. This is an extremely dangerous trend. In my opinion, and what statistics show, if this trend continues it will likely result in huge suicide numbers."

Chapter 7: Getting Personal

What does 'LGBTQ' stand for?

L: Lesbian - Can change without permanent physical issues

G: Gay - Can change without permanent physical issues

B: Bisexual - Can change without permanent physical issues

T: Trans - CAN RESULT IN LIFE LONG PERMANENT ISSUES

Q: Queer - Can change without permanent physical issues

I've read testimony from many in the 'LGB' segments that do not condone the 'trans' ideology, *especially for children.* The T ('trans') segment is the big push now. In my opinion, the useful pawns who push its ideology have no idea they're pushing for a runaway suicide rate. Countless lost people are being swept into a current that will not carry them to the utopia they envision. By sharing all of this information, I'm hoping to prevent some from jumping into these dangerous waters.

Many of those that take the plunge eventually realize the problems they felt were on the inside (mind and spirit), and didn't go away by modifying the outside. Once they awaken to the fact they made a huge mistake after permanently altering their body, what do you think many of them might do? This is why we must talk about this confusing and destructive subject.

'Trans' is short for *transition*. The biggest mistake and fallacy in all of this is believing it's possible to *transition* from one gender to another. Regardless of how many surgeries someone has, or the amount of hormones they put into their body, it's impossible to switch from one to another.

'Trans' Statistics:

- People who have 'transitioned' are *most* suicidal 7-10 years AFTER 'transitioning.' (PLOS)[102/103]

- The only long term study available at the time of writing this (from 1973-2003), shows that after 'transitioning,' 'trans' people have a **19 times** higher suicide rate than the non 'trans' average. (PLOS) [102/103]

- "41% of trans adults said they had attempted suicide, in one study. The same study found that 61% of trans people who were victims of physical assault had attempted suicide" (National Transgender Discrimination Survey).[24]

- "Each time an LGBTQ person is a victim of physical or verbal harassment or abuse, they become 2.5 times more likely to hurt themselves" (National Transgender Discrimination Survey).[24]

- "Transgender individuals are also at increased susceptibility for various suicide risk-enhancing factors, as a growing body of literature suggests that transgender individuals face a high burden of chronic health conditions, psychiatric illnesses and their comorbidities, substance use, trauma and victimization, and housing and employment discrimination." (NIH)[85]

- "Persons with transsexualism, after sex reassignment, have considerably higher risks for mortality, suicidal behaviour, and psychiatric morbidity than the general population."(NIH)[101]

So, if nearly half of 'trans' people attempt suicide, what does that tell you? They thought 'transitioning' would fill the empty void inside, but what actually happened? Keep in mind, statistically they are the most suicidal 7-10 years *AFTER transitioning*.[102/103] This is not feelings or opinions, it's factual statistics.

I've said this before and I'll say it again. I want life and that abundantly for everyone, including people who call themselves 'trans.'

Jesus commands His followers to love people. If that's true (and it is), how should we look at people in the 'LGBTQ' community? With compassion and love of course. I certainly don't agree with their lifestyle, but I love them enough to speak the truth to them. Of course some will call me names and say I'm being hateful, but that's just not true. I have empathy and compassion for them. I want them to wake up and realize it's not the right path to take.

I expect to be called the typical names; transphobic, homophobic, etc. Most people are incredibly childish though, they don't even understand the definition of phobia...

phobia [foh-bee-uh]:[149]

"A phobia is a persistent, excessive, unrealistic fear of an object, person, animal, activity or situation. It is a type of anxiety disorder. A person with a phobia either tries to avoid the thing that triggers the fear, or endures it with great anxiety and distress." [84]

-Harvard Medical School

By the very definition, it's impossible for me to be 'transphobic,' 'homophobic' or any other type of 'phobic.' These 'phobic' words are overused so much these days that they're actually becoming meaningless...*which is a good thing.* Do I really sound like I'm afraid of anyone in the 'LGBTQ' community? I'm hoping to help the few who will listen and prevent as many children and adults from falling prey to this dangerous seduction that leads to a high suicide rate.

This is not about adding shame to anyone. We've all fallen short and done things that are not right. If you view yourself as part of the 'LGBTQ' community, just know that I don't condemn you for it. I have great compassion for you and I want you to feel *true* acceptance. The allure of the 'LGBTQ community' is primarily acceptance. As we covered earlier in the book, we crave it. We absolutely need to feel and be truly accepted.

Legalized Abuse

One summer when I was young, I vaguely remember my mom going through old boxes she had stored in our basement. I found some of their contents interesting. One of the boxes was full of her old Barbie toys from when she was young.

I don't recall how old I was at the time, but I remember having fun playing with them off and on for a couple days. Do you want to know what my mom did after seeing me playing with them? Nothing. She finished going through her old things, then put the boxes away. Do you want to know what a growing number of horrible parents would do today? They'd begin to mentally and physically abuse me by trying to turn me into a girl...*something I could never be*...and likely destroy my life. Gone are the days of coercing and manipulating kids into being gay. Today the new frontier of corrupting kids has escalated into mentally and physically mutilating them.

It's also about genocide. I believe what's being done to children IN THIS COUNTRY and across the world under the guise of 'healthcare' is some of the most evil and despicable actions in the history of mankind. In my opinion, there's literally a generation being made guinea pigs, many of which will not be able to have children. Will there even be a next generation after them? God knows how many CHILDREN will suffer permanent mental, physical and spiritual damage.

> "We have no research on long term hormone use. We will be seeing the first generation of long term hormone use. And, we already know at least with ten years of hormones, you're giving yourself cancer." [93]
>
> -Sara Stockton MA, LMFT
> Clinical Supervisor
> From the documentary; *What is a Woman?*

Chapter 7: Getting Personal

> Let me tell you a fictional story to help you understand where I believe we are in history...

Bobby is a young boy who likes dinosaurs, especially the T-Rex. He grew up watching TV shows and movies about dinosaurs with his parents, who fully supported his interest. They thought it was cute when he'd walk around the house pretending to be a T-Rex. As time went on, Bobby's bedroom turned into a dinosaur themed play room. Friends and family thought it was strange, but Bobby's parents defended their son's interest and promoted it.

They would take Bobby to dinosaur parades and museums where his mother would make a big deal to everyone about how much her son liked dinosaurs. Young Bobby thought about dinosaurs so much that in his young influential mind, he was becoming convinced there was a mistake, he was meant to be born a dinosaur. He felt he was a T-Rex in the body of a boy. After a discussion with his parents, the three of them found themselves in a therapist's office. The therapist explained to the trio that Bobby had *dino-dysphoria* and if they didn't affirm Bobby's identity as a T-Rex and begin his transition, he would have a high probability of suicide.

The mother was supportive and even persuasive to Bobby's longing to be a T-Rex. Deep down, she liked the idea of the attention she'd get with a son turning into a dinosaur. She also thought it could be a great way to ensure Bobby was always dependent on her. The Dad was the typically passive man, afraid of his wife's emotions and backlash. He kept relatively quiet and didn't really care as long as it didn't disrupt his time watching TV. After all, he figured; 'The therapist must know what he's talking about.' The three of them left the meeting with the proper paperwork to schedule the 'life saving' surgery after the therapist affirmed Bobby as a T-Rex. Then, the surgery date was set.

We all know that the T-Rex has short useless arms, so after strong sedation, they removed Bobby's arms below his elbows. Then they filed his teeth down to sharp points and gave him prescriptions that would permanently effect his throat, so he'd sound raspy and lower pitched...prescriptions he'd have to take the rest of his life. Lastly, after a quick trip to the courthouse, Bobby's name was changed to...Bobasaurus.

Three months later...

Bobasaurus and his parents were mortified when people didn't react the way they anticipated. They thought; "How can people be so *'hateful?'*" They expected everyone would see a beautiful T-Rex, but instead people saw a heavily abused child. The parents went to the school principal and demanded that everyone no longer refer to their son as a boy named Bobby, but instead, as Bobasaurus the dinosaur.

Afraid of politically correct backlash and losing his job, the cowardly principal sent a scathing email to all the parents. It stated that the school would not tolerate 'hate speech.' So, with threats of legal action, expulsion and retaliation, parents and students were coerced to go along with something almost all of them thought was horrific. They had to ignore logic, biology, criminal level child abuse and common sense.

Does this story sound ludicrous? Of course it does. But this is basically what's happening in this country and across the world *today!* Young impressionable kids are being mentally and spiritually twisted into corrupting and mutilating their own bodies. No one, including the children themselves, have the right to do permanent physical damage to a child.

Do you know who the youngest person to jump off the Golden Gate Bridge was? A five year old girl...*FIVE!* Her name was Marilyn DeMont.[31] Why you might ask...why would such a young girl willingly jump to her death? *Her dad convinced her to.* He coached his daughter to jump, so she did. Then, he jumped.[31] Now, if the dad happened to survive the fall, what would he be charged with? Murder, that's what. The girl would be completely innocent, but why? It's because little children are not capable of making permanent, life altering decisions. Kids can be talked into just about anything, they're kids. They're naturally trusting of people, especially their own parents.

But, what happens when teachers and parents twist a child's strong faith into their own destruction? What do you call someone that pushes sexual ideas and topics onto kids? *A predator.* In my opinion, a growing number of parents and teachers across the world are becoming child predators. Testimony after testimony are coming out from young people who were 'transitioned' *as a child.* The biggest tool used to scare them into going through irreversible and permanent surgeries has been...*suicide.*

> "I medically transitioned as a minor, between the ages of 13 and 16....They told my parents..if they didn't affirm my identity that I would be at risk of suicide. They gave them the false premise of, 'would you rather have a dead daughter, or a live son?' But this wasn't true.
>
> Before I transitioned, I never had any suicidal ideation, until I started taking testosterone and that was when I was about two years on it and it got worse the further I progressed into my transition." [94]
>
> -Chloe Cole, Detransitioner
From the docudrama, *Gender Transformation*

Chloe had both of her breasts removed during her 'transition.' She has consistent medical problems and does not know if she'll ever be able to have kids.

> "'Would you rather have a dead daughter, or a live son.' That question is asked over and over again in therapy sessions by therapists. And therapists are trained to say that." [94]
>
> -Pamela Garfield-Jaeger
Therapist, Social worker
From the docudrama, *Gender Transformation*

Suicide is mentioned many times in this docudrama. One of the mothers interviewed lost her 17 year old daughter to suicide *after* she 'transitioned.' There are therapists today that will gladly suggest to parents to start the process of sterilizing their child, 'because if they don't they may kill themself.' Let that sink in for a second. Irreversible body modifications to *thoughts*. Thoughts that if left alone, and not fostered, *would almost certainly go away.*

Dr. Susan Bradley, who helped pioneer 'gender affirming care' in Canada, has spoken out against the popular model of 'gender affirming care.' Where children are placed on puberty blockers.[86] She had this to say;

> "We were wrong. They're not as reversible as we always thought, and they have longer term effects on kids' growth and development, including making them **sterile** and quite a number of things affecting their bone growth...
>
> We thought that it was relatively safe, and endocrinologists said they're reversible, and that we didn't have to worry about it. I had this skepticism in the back of my mind all the time that maybe we were actually colluding and not helping them. And I think that's proven correct in that, once these kids get started at any age on puberty blockers, nearly all of them continue to want to go to cross sex hormones." [86]
>
> - Dr. Susan Bradley

Blind Trust

Some doctors used to;

- Perform lobotomies[155]
- Promote cigarette smoking[156]
- Believe in milk transfusions[157]
- Remove part of someone's tongue to treat stuttering[159]

Chapter 7: Getting Personal

- Prescribe mercury pills and ointment to treat syphilis [158]
- Perform bloodletting [158]

How many doctors look at someone and picture dollar signs vs. doing what's right? In my opinion, it can be like going to a drug dealer and asking if you need drugs. They make no money if they say no. I know there are great doctors who truly help people, I have met some. My pediatrician growing up was a great guy. I also had another wonderful doctor go above and beyond when I needed surgery after a snowboarding accident. This is not a blanket statement against all doctors, because that wouldn't be true. We must not throw the baby out with the bathwater. I'm stating that amongst the good ones, there's also evil greedy monsters hiding behind white suits and walls adorned with degrees.

> I think the biggest influence on why this is being infiltrated into my field and the medical profession, is money. And this is coming from top-down. And then the propaganda and the messaging fools people to believe that what they're doing is kind and nice and helpful." [94]
>
> -Pamela Garfield-Jaeger
> Therapist, Social worker
> From the docudrama, *Gender Transformation*

There's a dangerous slogan being perpetuated that has no reputable long term data to support it; *'Gender affirming care saves lives.'* Please don't buy the repeated lie. Among psychologists this tactic is known as the *'Illusory truth effect.'* It's the tendency to believe false information after repeated exposure. [105]

> "If you repeat a lie often enough, people will believe it, and you will even come to believe it yourself." [154]
>
> - Joseph Goebbels
> Chief propagandist for the Nazi Party

209

> **'LGBTQ' Youth Suicide Statistics:**

- "The CDC says the number of LGBTQ students went from 11% in 2015 to **26%** in 2021."[104] (That's one in four!)

- "Youths with nonheterosexual identity have a significantly higher risk of life-threatening behavior compared with their heterosexual peers." (NIH)[23]

- "Lesbian, gay, and bisexual kids are **three times** more likely than straight kids to attempt suicide at some point in their lives." (di Giacomo et al. 2018)[24]

- "Lesbian, gay, and bisexual young people who come from families that reject or do not accept them are over **eight times** more likely to attempt suicide than those whose families accept them." (Pediatrics (Vol. 123, No. 1))[24]

- "Medically serious attempts at suicide are **four times** more likely among LGBTQ youth than other young people." (CDC)[24]

Schooling

"If anyone causes one of these little ones—those who believe in me—to stumble, it would be better for them to have a large millstone hung around their neck and to be drowned in the depths of the sea."

- Matthew 18:6 (NIV)

Do you want to know what it's like today at the high school I graduated from? When addressing a student, the office staff is expected to go along with whatever 'pronoun' the student wants to be addressed by. *What?* Some parents are even calling the school, demanding their *child* be called by different 'pronouns' than they actually are. Keep in mind, it's a school in small town Montana. A state with one of the lowest populations of 'LGBTQ' people in the entire Country.[99] If it's happening there, where would it NOT be happening? According to a person I know that works there, guess what else happens nearly every day at the school. At least one student walks to the office with blood soaking through their pants because they've been cutting themselves.

If 'gender confusion' and self harm have skyrocketed there, then what does that say about the youth of this Country? 80 years ago, kids their age were boldly fighting for the fate of the entire world. Today, many of them can't even look someone in the eyes, have a normal conversation or even confidently say if they're a boy or a girl. Have we really fallen that far into darkness in such a short span of time? It's no wonder home schooling has been skyrocketing in popularity in recent years. Who'd want to send their kids to an atmosphere like that? If you have kids in school, please be attentive to what they're being taught. I'm sure some schools are better than others, but I've seen many videos of 'teachers' being caught grooming children. They used their position to influence evil ideologies onto unsuspecting and vulnerable kids.

Some of you'd be horrified if you learned the kinds of things promoted and endorsed as 'normal' to children. If you have kids in government schools, you likely get an hour or two to influence them in a day. Teachers (strangers), have most of the day to influence them. Even if they have a great teacher, the curriculum may be corrupted by the modern 'woke' agenda.

Why do you do what you do? Is it because you love your spouse and kids? Then don't be so distracted by daily duties, be aware of the thoughts getting into their minds, which will flow into their hearts. For what comes out of their hearts, determines the life they will have (Proverbs 4:23). Many parents view their child's schooling as tax payer funded daycare. They're just happy to have them out of the house. If this is you, please change. You're the last line of defense between your child and the world.

Would it be a good idea to go into classrooms of little kids and discuss adult themed details about sex? Of course not, but why not? Because that would be sexualizing children. Any form of sexualizing children is wrong, not just the modern 'trans' agenda. There are schools *in this country* and across the world, teaching children sexual topics I don't even want to list here, things only adults should know about.

The Comprehensive Sexual Education curriculum (CSE), should be extremely alarming for parents. This isn't the same 'sex ed' you and I grew up with. It's a 'sex ed' curriculum provided by the United Nations (UN). Some of what the CSE curriculum teaches children is gender fluidity and anal sex.[7] The "It's All One" Curriculum from CSE has its main focus being *abortion,* mentioned 112 times and *sexual pleasure* 62 times... for children! [7] It promotes multiple sex acts and instructs children on how to stimulate themselves and/or their 'partner.'

The Root

In my opinion, what was covered in Chapter 6 with the 'snowman' brings clarity to the root of what's happening. People are so focused on the 1/3 of the snowman that's not the problem (the body), and are failing to address the 2/3 of the snowman that is the problem (mind and spirit). Outward attempts will never solve the underlying issue. It's like pruning a weed. It will not solve the problem. The roots of the weed need to be dealt with, or the issue will simply continue to come back.

Until the actual problems in the mind and spirit are dealt with and healed, in my opinion, no amount of changing someone's appearance will solve anything. They're only temporary band-aids of hope that fade away as the inner turmoil remains. My greatest concern is when people realize the outward changes didn't fix how they felt. The answer is back in Chapter 6.

Lastly, there's the subject of people wanting to be called by different 'pronouns.' This is another absurdity I will never participate in by the way.

Jesus demanded, *"What is your name?"*

"Legion," he replied, for he was filled with many demons. The demons kept begging Jesus not to send them into the bottomless pit.

-Luke 8:30-31 (NLT)

This is what *they/them* looks like. A single person has no need to be called as if many, but the demons inside of them do. When people demand to be called 'they/them,' I believe it's very telling and more accurate than most people realize. This is the type of activity that attracts demons to someone. If they don't have them yet, they will... It's basically begging for them without realizing it.

People can reject the body God gave them, but people cannot get a new body through any human means. I picture someone trying to be 'trans' similar to suicide. They want to escape their current body and are willing to do destructive things to it. Anyone struggling with this issue will be very happy to hear that there is a point in the future where we actually get *new* bodies;

But let me reveal to you a wonderful secret. We will not all die, but we will all be transformed! It will happen in a moment, in the blink of an eye, when the last trumpet is blown. For when the trumpet sounds, those who have died will be raised to live forever. And we who are living will also be transformed. For our dying bodies must be transformed into bodies that will never die; our mortal bodies must be transformed into immortal bodies.

Then, when our dying bodies have been transformed into bodies that will never die, this Scripture will be fulfilled: "Death is swallowed up in victory. O death, where is your victory? O death, where is your sting?"

- 1 Corinthians 15:51-55 (NLT)

If you want a new body, that's the only way to get it.
And it will be a perfect body that will never die...*imagine that.*

Authority and Cowardice

There was a famous experiment conducted at Yale University in the early 1960s. It was headed by an Assistant Professor named Stanley Milgram. Mr. Milgram was a social psychologist and wanted to conduct an experiment to see how far people would give in to authority.

World War Two and the Holocaust had occurred just years before and "He had expected that Americans, known for their individualism, would differ from Germans in their willingness to obey authority when it might lead to harming others."[57] Oh, how wrong he was... today his experiment is known as *The Milgram Experiment*. There's a video online by Derren Brown called 'The Heist' where he replicates the experiment, with similar results.

Mr. Milgram had approximately 780 recruits participate in his study. To summarize, the experiment was to see if a person would eventually administer lethal amounts of electricity to someone, just because an authority figure tells them to. The test subjects (referred to as teachers), thought they were administering electrical shock to the person, but in reality no one was being shocked. Here's the results;

> "Milgram and his students had predicted only 1–3% of participants would administer the maximum shock level. However, in his first official study, 26 of 40 male participants (65%) were convinced to do so and nearly 80% of teachers that continued to administer shocks after 150 volts—the point at which the learner was heard to scream—continued to the maximum of 450 volts." [57]

Chapter 7: Getting Personal

This experiment, Derren Brown's version of it, and the last few years have proven to me that most people will go along with whatever an authority figure tells them to do. If we look at atrocities throughout history, I think it's safe to say that people 'just doing their jobs' are often the tip-of-the-spear for tyrants. People interested in this subject would do well to research the term 'democide.'

> "Chad, what does all of this have to do with suicide?!
> Why don't you stay on topic?"

Let me ask you this, what do you think will happen to the suicide rate if humanity continues down the road it's on? Do you really think we are so advanced that we can't experience the same, or worse horrors our ancestors went through?

It's important to question authority. Just because someone is an authority figure in education, medicine, religion, government, science, or any other field, doesn't mean we blindly submit. That's a recipe for a horror movie. As an example, when an authority figure is telling us to do something that goes against God's will for us, we have an important decision to make. The Bible's full of examples of God's people defying wicked authority, here's one;

> "We gave you strict orders never again to teach in this man's name!" he said. "Instead, you have filled all Jerusalem with your teaching about him, and you want to make us responsible for his death!"
>
> But Peter and the apostles replied, "We must obey God rather than any human authority."
>
> - Acts 5:28-29 (NLT)

We must submit to authority that's under and submitted to God's authority. However, when an authority is contradictory to what God wants (which is always what's best for us), it's our duty to say no, regardless of the earthly cost.

> "Therefore put on the full armor of God, so that when the day of evil comes, you may be able to stand your ground, and after you have done everything, to stand."
>
> -Ephesians 6:13 (NIV)

Christians in Germany learned this lesson the hard way during Hitler's rise to power. Before they resorted to force, the growing Nazi regime cherry picked verses to convince Christians to submit to them. Once they'd compelled enough people and grown strong, the Nazis showed their true colors by resorting to military might on the remaining dissidents.

Look how complying with evil worked out for the people of Germany and most of Europe. I'm glad us Americans would never do anything like that.......*(can you sense the sarcasm?)*

Apart from God, mankind is a beast. In my view, mankind has been rejecting God more every day and we're seeing the rotten fruit of it. On top of that, if documentaries like *Died Suddenly* (2022) have any truth to them, hopefully an increasing number of people wake up and seek God and His healing. He's the Great Physician after all. He knows how many hairs are on our heads (Luke 12:7). He can cure what man cannot. He can cure dead...think about that!

Freedom of Words

Words are vital and extremely important. Words need to be protected. People have been oppressed and killed in horrific ways, because of words. Jesus was killed because of words. Words that powerful hypocrites didn't like.

The first Ten Amendments to the Constitution of the United States are known as the Bill of Rights. There's an important reason the First Amendment is this;

Chapter 7: Getting Personal

"Congress Shall Make No Law Respecting an Establishment of Religion, or Prohibiting the Free Exercise Thereof; or Abridging the Freedom of Speech, or of the Press; or the Right of the People Peaceably to Assemble, and To Petition the Government for a Redress of Grievances."

- The First Amendment

Freedom. The Founders of this Country wanted freedom. Freedom to exercise their religion. Freedom to gather. Freedom of the press to speak the truth (even if it exposed corruption), freedom to petition the government and the freedom of speech. The very thing I'm doing right now.

"Once a government is committed to the principle of silencing the voice of opposition, it has only one way to go, and that is down the path of increasingly repressive measures, until it becomes a source of terror to all its citizens and creates a country where everyone lives in fear."

- Harry Truman [80]
33rd President of the United States

Or, what about...

"If large numbers of people believe in freedom of speech, there will be freedom of speech, even if the law forbids it. But if public opinion is sluggish, inconvenient minorities will be persecuted, even if laws exist to protect them."

- George Orwell, author, c. 1945 [80]

Today, many people don't understand the importance of the Second Amendment to the Constitution (#2 of bill of *Rights*). It's there for when words fail. The second protects the first...and the rest of our rights. It has nothing to do with hunting or sporting, those are just nice benefits of it. It has to do with the security of this free Country.

TIME STOOD STILL

The Founders of this great Country knew history very well and knew most governments eventually oppress their own people. It makes you wonder why there's been such a strong push to diminish or remove this vital right over the years. You'd almost think some in charge are trying to disarm the American people.

> A well regulated Militia, being necessary to the security of a free State, the right of the people to keep and bear Arms, shall not be infringed.
> - The Second Amendment

Do you wonder why Government schools seem to care more about pushing gender identity politics onto our kids than teaching them the history and heritage of this Country? Passive, feminized and ignorant boys turn into passive, feminized and ignorant 'men.' They do what they're told and only complain when their Starbucks order is wrong.

Words are vital, I cannot overstate that. We can't give anyone, including governments, the power to dictate what words can be used and what words cannot be used. It becomes a cancer. Censorship grows and grows until the off limit words are...*whatever they say they are*...which is inevitably anything that threatens their political domination.

I learned this a long time ago about voting. Does whatever it is reduce the rights of others? If so, then the answer's no. It's sowing and reaping. Diminishing the rights of others will eventually diminish our own. In my opinion, the powers that be want the opposing views silenced, because they look like wicked fools with their evil and insane ideologies (because *they are* wicked and evil fools).

Life is but a vapor, we're here and then gone. The worst kind of censorship is self censorship. It's a tamed wild animal that no longer needs a cage. We all have a voice, we need to use it when necessary.

The Wrong Approval

> Obviously, I'm not trying to win the approval of people, but of God. If pleasing people were my goal, I would not be Christ's servant.
>
> - Galatians 1:10 (NLT)

I want to finish this chapter by posing a question; What kind of future do we want to leave for our Children and Grandchildren? Do we want to leave them with more or less opportunities than we had?

I believe we must leave our descendants with an atmosphere they can prosper in, not suffocate in. Personally, I want my Children to be able to take off from my shoulders. I want them to learn from my successes and failures, and leave them with the opportunity to go farther and do more than I possibly could. I want them to work hard, treat people right and represent Jesus (with His help of course). I don't want them to have to clean up my mess or deal with my debts after I'm gone.

There's also traits of what it means to be free that I want them to understand and exercise, because those that fail to exercise freedom, eventually lose freedom. There are foundational principles as to why America has been the freest Country in the history of the world. The American heritage and spirit of freedom *must* live on. Parents passing this freedom to their children and grandchildren is the only way it's possible. Government schools, the internet and movies certainly won't do it.

Leaving the possibility of prosperity for our posterity (I know that's a tongue twister). Those are the three P's I want you and I to leave behind. Listen and ponder this quote. I hope it shakes you, like it did me;

"A democracy is always temporary in nature; it simply cannot exist as a permanent form of government. A democracy will continue to exist up until the time that voters discover that they can vote themselves generous gifts from the public treasury. From that moment on, the majority always votes for the candidates who promise the most benefits from the public treasury, with the result that every democracy will finally collapse due to loose fiscal policy, which is always followed by a dictatorship.

The average age of the world's greatest civilizations from the beginning of history has been about 200 years. During those 200 years, these nations always progressed through the following sequence: From bondage to spiritual faith; From spiritual faith to great courage; From courage to liberty; From liberty to abundance; From abundance to selfishness; From selfishness to complacency; From complacency to apathy; From apathy to dependence; From dependence back into bondage."[100]

- Alexander Fraser Tytler (1747 – 1813)
This cycle is known as *"The Tytler Cycle"*

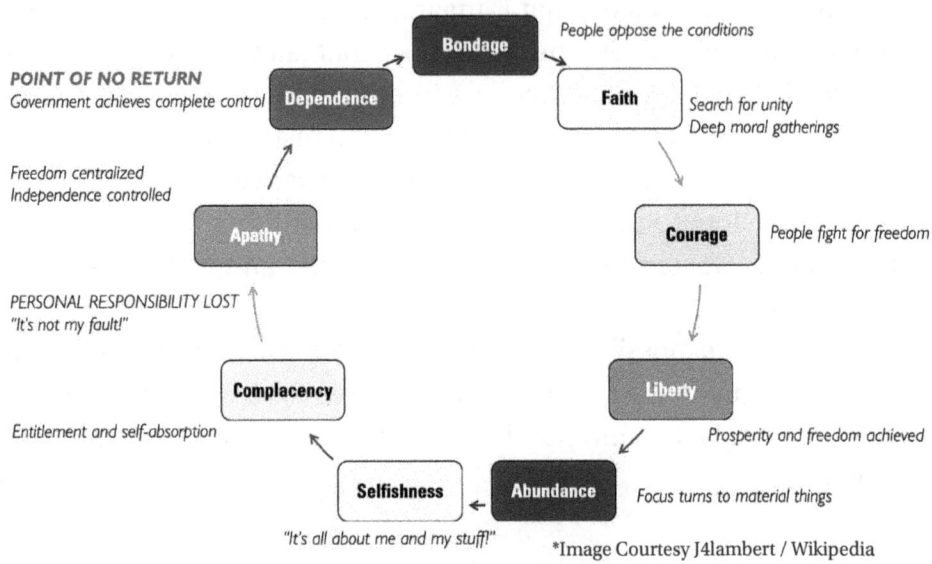

Chapter 7: Getting Personal

I believe innately, part of us knows we need a savior. In substitute for the real Savior, many people look to their government to save them. As I write this, there's a Presidential election coming up. Can I save you some time, regardless who gets in office, they're not going to save you. *YOU* have the most effect on *YOU*. I'm not saying the President isn't important, I'm saying *your* choices and actions have exponentially more effect on you than whoever's in the White House. Even if you're wanting more handouts (gifts from the public treasury) from the government, it'll never be enough.

> Unless you're severely handicapped,
> the rest of this chapter is for you...

Look in the mirror...that's the person responsible for you. I'm very much pro good (smaller) government, but I believe our government only really cares about us at voting time...

> "The most terrifying words in the English language are:
> I'm from the government and I'm here to help."[116]
>
> -Ronald Reagan
> 40th president of the United States

Personal responsibility needs to be brought back into the households of this Country. I mentioned it earlier in the book, but please watch the movie *Cinderella Man*. It's based on a true story. We need that kind of spirit back. The main character was forced to accept assistance, but look what his attitude towards accepting it was. He later even paid it back. Our Grandparents would've been embarrassed to accept handouts and would only have taken them as a last resort.

Nowadays, I see ad after ad on YouTube from people showing how to get 'free' money from the State. Money they supposedly 'deserve.' First of all, you don't deserve anything. You already have everything you need, and there's no such thing as free money. Someone's paying for it, current and future tax payers. I encourage you to be part of the solution, not part of the problem.

You don't feed wild animals, because eventually they become dependent on handouts and are unable to take care of themselves... but for some reason we don't think this principle applies to us. It certainly does. I understand that sometimes we can wind up in a very difficult spot and truly need help. The problem is when we become dependent on that help out of laziness. We'll do anything we can to cling to that 'help.' In that instance, the 'help' is actually a trap, keeping us dependent.

YOU are the only person responsible for you. I firmly believe when we take responsibility for our lives and stop blaming others, we can live lives of purpose and meaning. *This is the type of life that drops the suicide rate.*

Years ago someone told me this; "You're at where you're at, because of you." I was broke and overweight at the time and it felt like a slap in the face. But you know what? *He was right.* I could've been upset with him and pointed the finger of blame here or there, but instead I took responsibility and did something about it. I pray my fellow Americans will regain the gift of responsibility...it's very fruitful.

Chapter 8: What now?

Someday

Many people live in *The Land of Someday*.

Someday things will get better.
Someday I will take a vacation.
Someday I will be happy.
Someday I will call that person.
Someday I will get a better job.
Someday I will win the lottery.
Someday I will open a Bible.
Someday I will spend time with my kids.
Someday I will tell them I love them.
Someday, after I retire, I will...
Someday I will change.
Someday...

I've got news for you, *someday* doesn't exist. The word *someday* keeps people living in a fantasy world. The here-and-now is forfeited for a feel-good daydream called *someday*.

Someday is a thief, it steals *today*. *Someday* lulls people into the idea they'll always have more time. *Someday* robs millions of people...of their life. Now. Right now. All we have is now. All we can change is now. We can't change yesterday and undue past mistakes. We can't change tomorrow, it hasn't happened yet. *We have now.* If we choose to live in the now, the only moment we have any control over, we can change our tomorrows.

If we choose to remain in *The Land of Someday* and let our *nows* slip by, we lose both our tomorrows and our now. Let's be deliberate and purposeful with our Now, it's all we've got. (Philippians 3:13 and Matthew 6:34)

Forgiveness:

Forgiveness is not native to man, it can feel very difficult and unnatural. Sometimes it seems impossible to forgive someone, after all; 'do you know what they did to me?' The reality is, holding unforgiveness is like drinking poison and expecting it to hurt the other person. The person that wronged you usually isn't sitting around feeling bad about how they mistreated you. But from experience, we hold onto that hurt and anger towards that person, expecting something beneficial to come from it, but it doesn't. All it does is sit there festering. How we let it go is by...*forgiveness.*

Forgiveness does not mean putting yourself in the same position to let them hurt you again. Jesus said if someone slaps one cheek to give them the other cheek also. How many cheeks do you have? Did He say to let them hurt you repeatedly? Are you supposed to be a punching bag? I don't think so.

Forgiveness can often look like forgiving someone, and then not putting yourself in a position of being hurt by them again. In

Chapter 8: What Now?

hindsight, these can be great experiences of learning and growing. Through emotional pain, we learn over time not to be vulnerable with people who'll only hurt us (pearls before swine). Really let it go. But who or where do we let it go to? Give it to God. Our hurt and pain. Our vengeful thoughts. Our sadness. Our worries. We give it all to God.

Over the years I've developed a process of forgiveness. When someone comes to mind I realize I've not forgiven, I say something like this;

> "Lord, thank you for bringing this person to my attention. They were _____ to me. I forgive them and I pray that your will be done in their life." (Go ahead, you can try it right now too).

Then, I let it go. At that point, it's between them and God. What He does with them will be infinitely more appropriate and just than I could possibly do. No matter how my mind and flesh may want to do something, the Bible says vengeance is God's. I cannot do the kind of vengeance God can, nor would I want to.

I've had many people in my life that were hard to forgive. As an example, remember the man I told you about that bullied me as a teenager? I used to see him in passing every so often. As I learned and trained MMA after high school, I really wanted to show him how bad I could hurt him...by hurting him. But as the years went on, my anger towards him changed.

There's an old Chuck Norris lore with a great line; "What would it prove?"...That training to do something makes you better than someone who doesn't? Sometime in my mid twenties I realized I needed to let it go. I needed to forgive him and stop letting the anger I felt towards him control me. It wasn't easy, but I turned to God and told Him everything I was thinking and feeling towards that man. I gave it all to Him. Now, it's between him and God. I'm a child of God and I choose to let my Father deal with him. What God does with him is none of my business anymore.

Every couple of years I see him, and the anger's gone. I have no desire to hurt him or even say anything harsh to him. In contrast, I actually have compassion on him. After all, someone that treats people the way he treated myself and others can only be a truly miserable person. I use my experience with him all those years ago as an example in life. This is called wisdom. As we grow, we should increasingly gain more wisdom. Forgive and move on. Life's too precious and important to be unforgiving.

Jesus spoke extensively about forgiveness. Even after being brutally tortured and hung by nails to slowly suffocate to death, He asked The Father to forgive those that committed the brutality. *He had compassion on them.* I can't imagine that kind of love and compassion...*but I want to.*

> "For if you forgive other people when they sin against you, your heavenly Father will also forgive you."
>
> - Matthew 6:14 (NIV)

I've used the word "process" multiple times in this book. Many things in life are a process, *because they have to be.* If we could flick a switch and instantly have an extreme change, I don't believe most of us could handle it. Like countless other topics, forgiveness can also be a process. Let me give you a profound example that happened to me recently, it was decades in the making.

About a month ago (at the time of writing this), I was talking to my friend Dennis, who I wrote about in chapter two. We were discussing the subject of forgiveness and the process God used to help him forgive Caroline. He told me that many years ago, God had instructed him to pray for her and forgive her every time she came to mind. He said it was very difficult, but he did it anyway. Day after day he prayed for her whenever she came to mind, which was frequently. After a few weeks he realized his negative feelings for her were going away. Eventually he was released of the negativity and had even

Chapter 8: What Now?

grown compassion for her. Years later he learned his prayers for her came to fruition, word-for-word.

How does this apply to my story? Earlier in the book I mentioned the distrust I had for a particular person and the large issues it caused for me. I told Dennis that I'd forgiven that person, *many times.* Deep down though, I still had tension and resentment towards (him/her) and it was actually slowly *increasing,* like it was coming to the surface. He suggested that I do what he did with Caroline. I agreed with his advice. So, day after day (about a dozen times a day), when the person came to mind, I'd say something like this;

"Lord, I forgive _____. With every part of me, I forgive (him/her). Would you please cause (him/her) to be a blessing to (himself/herself) and to those around (him/her), especially family. Lord, I bind up any strong men in (his/her) life and trample them under my feet. Please work in (him/her) and bless (him/her) with a spirit of repentance. In Jesus' name."

After about three weeks and countless prayers like this, I was becoming increasingly *more* tense. About a week ago the tension began to exponentially increase. "Why am I feeling so tense?" There was no reason for me to feel that way, everything was going really well.

Then, a few days ago the most amazing thing happened! (This is another shower story, so bear with me, lol). There's a tile bench in our shower. I was kneeling on the floor praying, while resting my elbows and forearms on the bench. Over those weeks I realized I probably had another broken part of me, likely the source of the tension. While asking the The Lord to help with the tension, I was reminded again of the person. Without hesitation I started talking to the broken part inside of me, like I was his big brother;

"It's OK. We can forgive (him/her) now. (He/she) will never hurt us again. We will never put ourselves in that position again. We can let it go, it's over."

Picture two small water puddles in the bottom of a shower. Watch how they slowly slide together and become one. I felt that broken and hurt part within me forgive, and relax into me. Like an exhausted child falling into a parent's arms. My hands that were gripping each opposite elbow instantly relaxed. The strong tension I'd felt for days suddenly vanished. Peace flooded in. I've already stated that repairing brokenness cannot be forced. It's very time sensitive. The broken part in me was holding unforgiveness and had eventually gotten to a point where he wanted to forgive, and let it go. Jesus was right there and effortlessly melded us back together when he did.

Earlier I mentioned the passenger in a car analogy. Is it possible to have a tense and upset passenger effect the mood of a driver? Of course it is. I was feeling *his* tension. I believe the many prayers of forgiveness had caused him to eventually deal with the unforgiveness he was holding onto.

Can I fully explain all of this? Again, no. But what I can tell you is that since that moment I've felt so much better. I haven't felt this calm for as long as I can remember. Each night I have slept better and have actually woken up easier. The lower back discomfort I'd usually wake up with has drastically reduced. It's hard to describe. I feel lighter and more at peace than any time I can remember. *'Is this how good most people feel?'* I can even think clearer than before.

I mentioned this earlier; I don't fully understand how the spirit and body interact. From scripture, experience and testimonies, a healthy spirit seems to radiate outward and often improve the body. The most pertinent thing is that, for the first time in my life I feel like I've actually forgiven the person completely. The negative feelings I've felt deep down towards (him/her) for decades are gone and I feel like a major weight was freed from me.

Now, let's talk about the person that's usually the hardest to forgive…yourself. Even after forgiving those that've done terrible things to us, forgiving ourselves is usually harder. It's said that every cell in our bodies is slowly replaced every seven years, except our brain cells. I've always found that interesting. It would mean that our bod-

Chapter 8: What Now?

ies are moving on, not living in the past, but we are...*in our minds*. Our brains stew on the foolish things we've done. It brings them forward periodically to remind us of the error in our ways.

Please forgive yourself. Life is not a sprint, it's a journey. A very long marathon. As we learn to forgive others, we must also forgive ourselves. Many people try to live a double life of being nice to others, while being unloving and unforgiving to themselves. This is not how we have a fruitful life. You're worth it. Go ahead, forgive yourself. And when you find you're holding things against yourself, let 'em go. Every single person that ever lived (except Jesus), has done bad things. We've ALL done things we shouldn't have, and not done what we should have. Let it go.

I know this is a heavy book and a heavy subject. The fact you're reading this most likely means you've lost a loved one to suicide or you have had suicidal thoughts;

For those that have lost a loved one...

Losing a loved one to suicide is extremely overwhelming, especially early on. Moving forward productively in life can feel like an insurmountable task. Everything feels sucked into the void of the loss, but over time, life must go on. A big part of moving forward is forgiveness. I know it's very hard, but please bear with me. Over time, we *must* forgive our loved one, AND ourselves. Forgiving them doesn't mean you agree with what they did. I'm sure you don't, and neither do I. Suicide is never right.

There's no cookie-cutter template for the aftermath of losing a loved one to suicide. I'm sure you've had a wide range of emotions toward your loved one, but the very fact you love them shows they're worthy of your forgiveness. As I've already mentioned, holding unforgiveness towards them only hurts you.

We can't handle unforgiveness on this large of a subject, whether it be unforgiveness toward our loved one, or unforgiveness toward ourselves. This is not like forgiving someone for damaging a new car. This subject can eat us alive if we cling to it. In forgiving them AND ourselves, AND giving it all to God, we can begin true restoration in our lives. I say begin, because this is all part of the process. There's no magic wand, it takes time.

There's a fork in the road I refused to go down early on, and I suggest you do the same. If you've already started down that road, please make your way back to the fork and take the other road. It's the road that leads to shame, guilt and condemnation. I've already discussed this, but it needs to be mentioned again. I refused to let myself go down the road of "I should have..." I did the best I could, with what I knew at the time. Obviously in hindsight I would've done some things differently, but I've forgiven Joy and I've forgiven myself for not doing more. Remember, all we have is now. We can't change what happened, but we can choose how we allow what happened to effect our now, which will ensure our best possible tomorrow.

As a side note; I've met a handful of people that have a morbid fondness for clinging to shame and guilt as a twisted way to punish themselves. They feel so bad inside already, it gives them an excuse for bathing in misery, like a pig wallowing in mud. Some people crave sympathy in death, and want to remain doused in grief. I pray this isn't you, because that course is a great way to waste what could've been a perfectly good life. Do you want life to improve for yourself and for those around you? Then forgive your loved one AND yourself.

For those with suicidal thoughts...

Forgive yourself for having those thoughts and temptations. I encourage you to do what I did; rebel against suicidal pressure and use your resistance to make you a better person. What kind of life would you be missing out on? Go out and experience just how wonderful this world is. You are very valuable. Your life has meaning and you're worth it. *Keep reading...*

I want to keep this brief, but there's also the subject of headship regarding forgiveness. For instance, a husband has headship over his wife and can nullify and forgive her errors on the day he hears of it, just like a father can for his daughter on the day he hears of it (Numbers 30). For some of you, today is the day you hear of it.

I knew that because I was head over Joy and God's spirit dwells in me, I could not only nullify what she did, but also forgive her. Pastors, as headship over those God has instructed in your care, your forgiveness of that person is also extremely important.

> "If you forgive anyone's sins, they are forgiven.
> If you do not forgive them, they are not forgiven."
>
> - John 20:23 (NLT)

I nullified and forgave Joy before her body was even taken out of the house. This may be the first you've understood or heard this, but it gives a deeper understanding of the importance of forgiveness.

Temptation, Shame and Guilt:

Being tempted to do something is a very normal part of life, even if it's something terrible. For instance, we've all been tempted to steal, but just being tempted does not make us thieves. I remember feeling guilt for many years because I was tempted by suicide. It all went away though, like popping a bubble, when I realized that Jesus himself was tempted by suicide, yet lived a perfect life.

Let me explain. In Matthew 4, the Devil tempted Jesus in various ways to get Him to do the wrong thing. One of them was to commit suicide by jumping off the top of the temple. Even though He was tempted (and would've thought of suicide for it to be a temptation), He never beat Himself up, or felt guilty about having that thought.

> The temptations in your life are no different from what others experience. And God is faithful. He will not allow the temptation to be more than you can stand. When you are tempted, he will show you a way out so that you can endure.
> - 1 Corinthians 10:13 (NLT)

An easy way to know if God is leading us through a tough situation is this; *is there a way out?* God will always show us a way of escape. If there's no way of escape, it's not God...period. The devil loves to beat us up and make us feel shame and guilt for 'even thinking such things.' Jesus isn't in the business of shame and guilt. Jesus is in the business of showing us the way out and setting captives free.

> Therefore, since we have a great high priest who has ascended into heaven, Jesus the Son of God, let us hold firmly to the faith we profess. For we do not have a high priest who is unable to empathize with our weaknesses, but we have one who has been tempted in every way, just as we are—yet he did not sin. Let us then approach God's throne of grace with confidence, so that we may receive mercy and find grace to help us in our time of need.
> - Hebrews 4:14-16 (NIV)

What does the author Paul say then, knowing that Jesus fully understands and empathizes with our weaknesses? To confidently approach God's throne of...*grace.*

Chapter 8: What Now?

grace [greys]:
> *mercy; clemency; pardon*
> *the freely given, unmerited favor and love of God* [152/153]

Grace; knowing we deserve to pay, but the debt's wiped clean. *So good.* The solution for our shame, guilt and condemnation is, you guessed it, forgiveness. Let it go, give all the baggage to God. These issues effect everyone, young, old, man and woman.

For instance, women with lots of shame and guilt can have a strong sense of worthlessness. Women who feel worthless are open season for terrible things like drugs, sex, abuse and suicide. They often put up with being mistreated, because they feel worthless. It's very important to crack the facade of worthlessness and let the light start shining in. God does not make junk, you're worth so much!

Grief

> For godly grief and the pain God is permitted to direct, produce a repentance that leads and contributes to salvation and deliverance from evil, and it never brings regret; but worldly grief (the hopeless sorrow that is characteristic of the pagan world) is deadly [breeding and ending in death].
>
> - 2 Corinthians 7:10 (AMPC)

If you lost someone recently and are in the grieving process, I'd like to suggest something. Find a nearby mirror and take a picture of yourself. The purpose is to document this extremely difficult point of your life. Imagine it like taking a picture of yourself before going on a workout program. Sometimes it's hard to see how far you've come, without seeing where you were. This photo is a gift, for the future you. It's also acknowledging where you are, but knowing it's only a temporary season.

TIME STOOD STILL

I took this picture three days after Joy's memorial service. My brother had invited the kids and I over one evening. At one point I went to use the bathroom. I knew I was at such a tough and low point. I'd spent weeks planning Joy's service and now that it was over, I found myself in a completely unknown chapter of life. It was in this moment that I pulled out my phone and took this impromptu picture of myself.

Chapter 8: What Now?

    This is the face of a man at an extremely low point. This is the face of a man in pain. This is also the face of a man who believes things will get better. Even though it may be unseen, this is the face of a man who still has hope in his heart. I now look at this picture with gratitude. Throughout this entire process of restoration, God has blessed me with the strength to endure. Is your desire to get better? Then get real with yourself and capture where you're at right now. You can look back on it with gratitude as well. From this day on, I believe each day for you will be slightly better than the day before.

The grieving process is extremely important! Some parts of this life can be so incredibly hard...this is one of the hardest. Grief demonstrates how precious of a gift life is, because when someone loses their's, it can be devastating to their loved ones. Grief is a necessary ingredient to our healing. Even though at times it can feel like we're dying, it's necessary to go through it. It's an essential stage for dealing with the strong emotions of losing someone we love.

    Some people try to avoid grief altogether, attempting to bottle up what should be let out. This inevitably results in instability as life goes on. *Please grieve.* As we grieve, remember that in the depths of our sadness, the enemy wants to use it to destroy us. We must be mindful of this. The enemy wants to use these heavy emotions to push us down a self destructive and hopeless path. But, Jesus wants to use it for good.

    From experience, focusing on gratitude was a huge help. I continued to keep the good things in mind, being thankful for the time I had with her and our family. Through the grieving process, I thanked God every day for bringing me Joy and our time together. This positive focus helped immensely. Instead of focusing on what I didn't have, I chose to focus on what I did have. I did the same thing when my dad died unexpectedly. I chose to focus on being grateful for our wonderful time together, and the memories we made. I chose to focus on what a huge blessing he was to me and I wouldn't be who I am without him.

I miss them both very much, but I choose to stay on the road of gratitude and thankfulness. I will not set foot on the road called despair, I know where it goes.

Everyone grieves differently and I encourage you not to compare yourself to anyone else. I had people try to trip me up and get me to repeat parts of grief that I'd already been through. Just because they'd been stuck in a stage of grief for many years didn't mean I had to be. I suggest you be very careful with who you allow to direct your grief. The verse earlier talks about God directing our pain and grief, not our friends and relatives.

God certainly uses our friends and relatives at times, but so does the enemy. All I'm saying is to be cautious. Does the person have good fruit on their tree? Are they qualified to be giving you advice on the subject? Or is it a friend or relative you'd never want to be like, still mourning over someone they lost years ago? Misery loves company. Whether they admit it or not, miserable people love the opportunity to drag someone even deeper into misery.

Cry, yell, break something (inexpensive and replaceable), let it out. Men in particular have a hard time letting out emotions, but do it. The shortest verse in the Bible is this; *"Jesus wept."* You're not better than Jesus. Cry, let it go. Try to stay busy with productive actions at the same time. Go to the gym, clean the house, mow the lawn, all the while making sure you have time to yourself to let it out. Remember that you are in a fragile state. Don't put yourself in potentially bad situations. Acknowledge that you're going through heavy emotions and prepare accordingly.

For instance, while grieving it could be wise to;

- Stay out of bars and be careful how much alcohol you consume, or maybe avoid it altogether. We often do dumb things when we drink, especially when emotional. This could be a great time to switch to tea or sparkling water. This goes likewise for drugs.

Chapter 8: What Now?

- Be more careful and attentive while driving, even if you're a good driver. Limit your driving if you feel it'd be irresponsible during this time. With that said, driving and getting out of the house can be a great way to help with grief. I suggest to be more attentive than normal behind the wheel and know it's ok to admit when you really shouldn't be driving. Also, if you have fast toys like motorcycles and other vehicles that can be dangerous on a good day, I encourage you to park them while going through grief.

- Avoid the gun range. Maybe put your guns away altogether during this time. This goes especially for the easy access ones like near the bedroom or in a vehicle. What's more likely; that someone would have a home invasion in the middle of the night, or do something foolish in a down moment during their grief? I think you know the answer. It's OK and wise to tuck them away in a safe place during this fragile time.

Be polite to people trying to help you. Even though you're going through hard times, don't take it out on those around you. If you have kids, find time to be alone and let it out. If your kids are older, help them with their grief. Bottling up these emotions and not dealing with them builds up way too much pressure. We must relieve this pressure, that's what grieving is.

I found times away from my little kids to grieve. For instance, I'd set them in a playpen while a movie played, then go shut myself in the bedroom closet. There in the dark, I'd lay in the fetal position, yelling, crying and sobbing like a little baby. I remember feeling so much stress and pressure that I genuinely thought it would kill me. I was amazed the body can take that much pressure and stress.

I was very careful to always put on a good face for my little kids. I was attentive to their needs and when they wanted to talk about Joy. At the same time I was careful not to spew my grief onto them and make them go through something they shouldn't.

If you have older kids, it may be very important to have moments where you talk and grieve together. Be careful not to overdo it with them directly, save the big outbursts for when you're by yourself. When you are with them, allow yourself to be vulnerable so they can be vulnerable and let it out with you. It may not be easy for you, but show them that grief is normal and necessary. At the right times, cry in front of your kids. Be the example, show them they can too.

It's worth bringing up the subject discussed earlier about drugs. To me, it's foolish to take drugs to 'deal' with grief. In my opinion, that'd only be a feeble attempt to avoid something important we need to go through. As I already mentioned, these emotions are essential to let out, not try to mask with a band-aid called drugs.

I'm reluctant to discuss time frames of grief, because everyone grieves differently. I mentioned it earlier, but some people have a morbid fondness for death and grief and *want to* live in it. They also like the attention and sympathy they get from people. They'll tell you it lasts years, or forever. Please don't believe them. Remember, misery loves company. I'm not saying you should or shouldn't, but outside of the Bible, I didn't read any books or look up anything about grief. I can't recite any clinical stages as some people have memorized. Saying that everyone will go through a particular order of things just doesn't sit right with me.

I am going to share more details coming up, but from my experience with my Dad, and then with Joy, the initial and strongest sections of grief lasted weeks. At first, it was the shock of the loss. Then it built up to the really heavy parts of grieving. After peaking, it began tapering down. From there, it was a slow progressive drop while life returned to a 'new normal.' Every day was a fraction of a percentage easier than the day before. To summarize; the first six months after losing Joy was survival mode and contained the main grief (sadness and frustration lasted longer). The next six months was trying to develop a routine. The 12 months after that was working out the 'new normal.' As I write this, it's nearly the four year anniversary of losing Joy. Grief, sadness and frustration are gone, *but I still miss my friend.*

Chapter 8: What Now?

The First 1000 Days

> Not only that, but we rejoice in our sufferings, knowing that suffering produces endurance, and endurance produces character, and character produces hope, and hope does not put us to shame, because God's love has been poured into our hearts through the Holy Spirit who has been given to us.
>
> - Romans 5:3-5 (ESV)

I want to share some insights from the early stages after losing Joy. This difficult time felt like dropping into a dark valley with pitfalls all around. A time of immense sadness, uncertainty and inner turmoil. If you've found yourself in this valley, know that the sunshine will return. At the moment it may not feel like it, but I assure you, this too shall pass.

Loose lips sink ships...

There are people I don't trust to watch what they say around my kids. Those I believe could easily hurt them *with words,* if I allowed them access. They've not yet learned to control their tongue and be mindful of repercussions from their loose lips. I believe most of it's out of pure selfishness. They stubbornly spew out words, even though it could be detrimental to little ones within earshot.

It's my job to protect my kids. As they grow, they'll be ready to hear and understand more about Joy. But it'll be at the appropriate pace, not from someone blurting out an ill-timed and unloving statement. Just because someone's an acquaintance, friend or relative, doesn't mean I have to risk them being around my kids. Especially if they've proven in the past to be untrustworthy with their mouth.

If you lost a spouse to suicide and you have children, you have every right in the world to say who does and who doesn't get to impart their words onto them. Some of your friends or relatives may be upset about your spouse, but that doesn't mean they get to say anything negative in front of your children. I made this very clear to everyone early on, and I'm still very mindful of this today.

I didn't allow my kids to be at Joy's memorial service for two reasons; there were people I didn't trust there, and I knew I was going to say things during the service they were not ready for. Of course I got heat for it, but no matter how much grief I received, I was not going to budge. It's my responsibility to ensure people don't vomit their worldly grief and understanding onto them. Even with those I trust around my kids, I was careful to tell them what to say, but more importantly what not to say. I let them know not to bring up Joy, but if the kids brought her up, to only say good things about her and keep it short, within reason.

It's easy to add words, but once words are out, you can't reel them back in. I'm the one around them all the time and with God's help, I know what they're ready for, and when. The friend or family member doesn't. Giving my kids personal information about their mother is not their role. The vast majority of my friends and relatives understood what I meant and were very supportive. It's been so great to watch my kids grow and prayerfully respond to their questions. With God's help, I know they will transition into adulthood with a healthy view of Joy.

Since I started writing this book over three years ago, we've moved 2000 miles from home. It's not the main reason, but one of the reasons we moved was to get away from people with loose lips. Strangers we meet don't know our history. We won't randomly see people we'd have to be on high alert with. We can live normal lives with a fresh start, unhindered by concerns of who will say what in front of the kids. Every scenario is different, but for some people, I believe moving away from the familiar rut and familiar people could be one of the best decisions ever. (Genesis 12:1)

Don't let parenting slide...

Being a single parent in survival mode; I get it...I totally get it. It's hard, very hard. It's easy to let parenting slide when you're just trying to survive. It's easy to give into all your kid's demands when you normally wouldn't. You have so much you're dealing with already, why not? After all, who likes hearing kids whine? Or how about the other side of the spectrum...being extremely hard on them, because you're in a hard place yourself. As parents, no matter what position we find ourselves in, it's very important we never take it out on our kids. They're looking for us to lead them, not break their spirits or give into all their demands.

We find out what's really inside us when we're squeezed. When we lose a spouse to suicide, we're strongly squeezed. When we have kids, what's inside us can easily spew out onto them. As parents, we MUST keep these things in check. Just because we're in turmoil, doesn't mean it's OK to lather our children in turmoil. If anger is being squeezed out of you, don't put that onto your children. Find other avenues...hire a babysitter and go learn how to box or go for a run, seriously. Channel that anger into something productive.

One mistake I made early on was being too loose and not having enough structure with the kids. I remember doing legos with my boy after midnight and letting them both stay up way too late watching kid's movies. I'd tell them to do something and not follow up to make sure they did it. They knew I was distracted by other things, so they didn't really have to listen to me. They were really young and I obviously had a lot I was dealing with. In hindsight though, it would have been much better for all of us had I provided more structure. I'm going to tell you about her in a little bit, but a special lady came into my life and helped me regain structure with my kids.

Our duty is to prepare our children for the world. I know it's difficult, but stay diligent. If you have children and lost your spouse like I did...I know it sucks, I know it's difficult, but your children are worth it. You don't have to be perfect, none of us are, but be present. It's your responsibility, and it's a noble one. *They need you now more than ever.*

A few years of 'survival' can produce bad habits in a child that are hard to break. The first couple years without Joy was a huge and obviously unexpected learning curve for me. I was too soft on the kids, but I was slowly learning. I was trying to home school them while working from home at the same time.

I don't regret it, but it was very difficult, especially emotionally. One parent was not made to do everything. Regardless what the P.C. culture says, kids need both a Mom and a Dad, it's extremely important. I sucked at doing the things Joy made look easy, and still do. I've had to work hard at certain areas, just to barely tread in the void she left. A man can never replace a mom's role and a woman can never replace a dad's role. It takes both.

One eye opening evening a few months after Joy died, my older brother had the courage to bring some of this to my attention. He had an outside perspective and was experienced with kids. He pointed out that I'd told the kids various things throughout the evening, but they completely ignored my instructions. I didn't like hearing that. No parent wants to hear they're making mistakes with their own children. *But he was right.* I was training the kids to not take me serious. I wasn't giving them structure or discipline like I thought I was. In doing so, I was acting more like an undisciplined friend, than a loving father.

One big change I made over time with the kids was to stop saying 'yes' so often. I realized I was making a big mistake. Who's in charge, me or the kids? Giving into them prevents whining, but long term it's a recipe for disaster. It usually winds up with entitled kids, who turn into entitled adults. I knew I was being too easy on them and figured I'd change eventually, but remember, *someday* is a thief.

In the book, *The Warrior Poet Way,* John Lovell says it like this;

"As parents, we are responsible for providing structure for our kids so they have some direction in life and can learn to walk before they run. But we also want to give them enough freedom to fail and grow.....We are raising our own kids-not the state or a screen."

- John Lovell
The Warrior Poet Way, P. 212

It was hard, but I had to get real with myself and make changes that brought structure into our lives. As the 'artistic' night owl type, staying up late working and being loose with time was very normal, *but it wasn't working.* I needed to do the C word...*change.* Now, they have a bed time, wake up time, lunch time and quiet time. They have school time and play time. They have scheduled events during the week that also help their structure.

Another aspect I've improved is making sure they follow through with what I expect of them. In hindsight, when I was distracted by survival, my standards for them were too low. They're great kids and I needed to set a higher standard of what I expected from them. I also needed to inspect what I expected. Instead of telling them to do something and not checking on their follow-through, I worked at being present and aware of what was happening.

This may sound simple, but it was a game changer. At the suggestion of a special lady, I started telling the kids what I expected of them, *ahead of time.* For instance, before we went into a grocery store, I'd make eye contact with them and say something like;

"We're going to go into the store and stay focused on getting what we need. I expect you both to listen to me. You're going to stay put in the cart (or walk behind the cart as they got bigger). You're not going to grab things or ask for things. If you don't listen to me, we're going to turn around and leave. If we have to leave, that means we're not getting what we need for home. Do you understand?" They would both say yes.

There were a few times we stopped and left various places, but they eventually got it. Dad meant business, *finally*. I stopped giving them hollow threats of leaving places, we would just leave. I didn't care if it made a scene. I'm raising great kids, and discipline is a huge part of what's required to do so. The Bible says God disciplines those He loves. I love my children and I want them to be disciplined, productive and loving adults. These traits obviously start in childhood.

They don't run around the store anymore. They don't throw tantrums demanding things. I don't use treats to barter with them to get them to behave. They're continually getting better at listening. They know I mean business if I say we will leave if they misbehave. But it took them missing out on things by walking out, even if it cost money (movie theater, the fair, motocross event, restaurant).

I often see parents of young children making the same mistakes I made; bartering with kids to try to get them to listen and behave, or giving vain threats the child knows the parents won't follow through with. I hope these parents come to the same conclusion I did, and change. I'm grateful to have started making the necessary changes of setting a higher standard for my kids and helping them follow through. I'm learning to set good standards for them and they continue to rise to those healthy standards. It's actually enjoyable to go places with them now, when before it was chaotic and stressful.

I've learned to get down to their level and be present. Regardless of what I have going on. I've learned to stop and give them attention when I see they need it. I've learned to show interest in things they are interested in. God is a God of order and having order with them has been a huge blessing, for all of us. It's even freed up more time for me to work. It's hard to do our best when we're just trying to survive. Keep working through the survival stage and over time, a new normal will emerge. Be forgiving and gentle with yourself and with your children. Until they move out and get married, *you are the most important person in their lives.* They're looking to you for everything. Remember, you're on the same team, work as a team to have a loving and structured house. It takes time, but it is sooo worth it.

Chapter 8: What Now?

Most of our children's lives, they'll spend as an adult. Let's remember, as parents, we're not raising children. We're raising adults going through childhood. Let's help them grow to be disciplined, productive and loving men and women. Remember, we can't be hypocrites though. If we want them disciplined, it starts with us.

Lingering effects...

There were two things that haunted me for months after that fateful December morning; a sudden gunshot and the grotesque sight of Joy. As the saying goes; 'time heals all wounds.' Nearly four years later, it's rare that I think about the sights and sounds of that morning. Thankfully, when I do, they're much less vivid. If you saw something like I did, know that each day gets a little easier. There is coming a day when you don't even think about it.

The more lingering effect for me has been sudden loud sounds. In rural Montana, it's very common to hear people shooting guns. I think when done responsibly, it's great and is as normal as riding a bike. The problem was that I'd hear a gunshot and instantly think, "Oh no, someone just shot themself!" Then another gunshot; "They shot someone and then shot themself!" I know that's not a normal thought process, but that's where my mind would instantly go. Sudden loud sounds in a house would get me to jump and my heart to race. For instance, if a broom fell over, I'd quickly go check on everyone.

The part I noticed most was the couple times I went hunting after Joy died. On the first trip, my brother and I went elk hunting. Keep in mind, we've grown up hunting, it's second nature to us. I got a very clean 131 yard shot (very close), on my elk. It couldn't have been more textbook. The problem came next. Up to that point, I could process an animal without thinking about it. We're there to get meat for the freezer, but this time was different. It's not that I felt bad about it, because I didn't (and still don't, elk are delicious), it's that all I could picture was Joy, nearly a year before that moment. I forced myself to put on a good face, and I'm glad my Big Bro was there to help. I didn't let him know the inner struggle I was having.

A few weeks later, my brothers and I went antelope hunting. I've killed and processed more antelope than I can ever remember. They're probably my favorite wild game, we call them *speedgoats*. Again, I was blessed with a close shot. This time though, it was bedded down. All I could see was the antelope's head. The antelope died instantly. I walked up to her and that's when it happened again. My first observation was; "A hunting rifle didn't make as big of a mess as the pistol did a year earlier." Unlike the elk, I couldn't do it. I didn't want to tell my brothers, *but I couldn't.* I couldn't do the most basic part of hunting, something I grew up doing. How could I put meat in the freezer if I couldn't take it off the animal? Thankfully they jumped in and took care of it for me, without me even asking.

I've grown with the love of the heritage of this Country. The freedom of owning guns and hunting is part of the foundation of what being free means. I hope and believe to instill this heritage into my children. It's important that we pass along the mindset of freedom and what freedom means to the next generation, or they won't have it.

> "Freedom is never more than one generation away from extinction. We didn't pass it to our children in the bloodstream. It must be fought for, protected, and handed on for them to do the same, or one day we will spend our sunset years telling our children and our children's children what it was once like in the United States where men were free."[132]
>
> -Ronald Reagan
> 40th president of the United States

After that antelope, I determined I needed more time before I'm ready to go hunting again. I believe I'm better now than I was then, but I haven't hunted since to know for sure. I firmly believe by the time my kids are old enough, I'll be ready again to take them hunting; having wonderful bonding time with them while passing along age old wisdom.

The issues with loud sounds have progressively gotten easier. I bet they only startle me 10% as much as they used to. I still don't like random fireworks during the 4th of July season though. I don't do this anymore, but there were times I jumped and ran across my bedroom in a panic in the middle of the night before I realized it was just a neighbor's ill-timed large firework.

Your 'triggers' may not be the same as mine. They could be a knock at the door, a phone call, loud sirens, or a million other things. If you have certain triggers that bring you back to losing your loved one, from my experience, they decrease over time. Each day is a tiny bit easier. At the rate they've decreased for me, I anticipate not even thinking about them in the not too distant future.

Being out...

Suddenly being a single dad is a very unnatural and helpless feeling. It was very strange, being out and about with two little kids, responsible for everything. I don't know how I looked, but I felt very much out of place. I was changing diapers in a grocery store or the back seat of a car, planning meals, story times, cooking, cleaning, etc. I know you Moms are thinking; so what? Well, most of those things are very unnatural for men, especially when they're suddenly thrust upon us. They were all difficult moments, reminding me of just how difficult of a spot I was in. Things a mom wouldn't think twice about would leave me feeling completely inadequate. Those tasks made me feel a million miles from normal and how a family should be, *how we were*. I was certainly in tears at times...but what choice did I have? I had to keep going, two precious kids were depending on me.

I'd take the kids to the gym where they could play while I worked out. At gymnastics, my youngest required me to walk the courses with her. There I was, the only dad out there, surrounded by moms with their wee ones. It was the same thing for swim lessons, at parks, birthday parties, and most other venues. One dad, standing out like a sore thumb amongst a sea of moms with their little ones. I was careful to keep on a good face for my kids. I wanted them to be happy and feel normal. The last thing they needed from me was my frustration and struggles dumped on them.

People around have no idea the kind of pain and turmoil going on inside in those moments, especially for the first few months. Clawing for a sense of normalcy, when your world is upside down. Where normal feels like it's gone out the window. But I learned that isn't true. Much has changed, but the relationship between parent and child is still there, and that's the most important thing. It's the lifeline the children need.

It's said that the most important thing in life is to keep the important things, the important things. Work on keeping a good perspective and remembering the good things. If you have children, you have the biggest reason to overcome this season and persevere. I did, and I know you can too.

Anniversaries...

Christmas and our wedding anniversary were within two weeks of Joy's death. I'm very thankful I had friends and family invite me to do things and keep me busy during that time. We went to a Christmas party and I went to an 'escape room' for the first time.

Anniversaries of events have gotten easier. I used to think about an anniversary for weeks ahead of time, but nowadays I may not remember them at all. This is another aspect that gets easier over time. On the one year anniversary of Joy's death I certainly felt sad, but I wanted it to be something good for the kids. So the night before, I picked up cupcakes. The next morning, I told the kids it was a special day; "Mommy's been with Jesus for a year now." We ate cupcakes for breakfast on the living room floor while we talked about their mom.

Chapter 8: What Now?

We smiled and shared fun memories of her. We kept it positive, focusing on gratitude for a wonderful mommy. I told them how proud their mom was of them and how much she loves them. We built a positive memory together on that tough anniversary.

It was nearly two years before I realized I'd gone a whole day without thinking about Joy. This was a good thing, but it also made me feel a bit sad at the same time...I was getting over her and moving on.

Understandable concern...

After losing Joy the way I did and the demonic attack months later, I went through a short period of understandable concern. 'Could I do the same thing?' After the attack, I remember questioning if I should be alone. Even during the attack I had absolutely no desire to die. Afterward, it was strange. Like the calm after a storm, I was left wondering. But like we already discussed; focusing on what we don't want, is still focusing on what we don't want. It's like walking around afraid of being stepped on by an elephant. Why would I fear such a thing? Why would I fear something that's not an issue for me? I prayed about it, wanting clarity. Why would I be concerned about suicide when I don't have an issue with suicide?

I prayed for days, continually asking for clarity as to why I had even a slight fear of suicide, *when I knew I had no reason to.* By this time I'd closed the breach and would never do CBD again, so why would I have any lingering concern? As God often does with me, it was in the awakening moment one morning that I received the answer.

There have been about 4-5 times in my life where I know word-for-word what God said to me; "Be grateful.," was one, "What else would you expect?," was another. In those moments, it has always been something very direct and simple. (I think it's because I need it that way).

Most of the time though, for me, it's like He takes His statement, paraphrases and condenses it, then places it into my heart. It opens inside like a zip file. It's just there...*I know* the answer. It's always peaceful and calming. It's not a word-for-word instruction, I just understand the answer to my question.

'Her problem is not your problem,' was the understanding. You see, I had been fearing a problem that wasn't mine. She was the one with the problem, not me. I also realized there was a fear of my kids or someone else finding me the way I found Joy. In the understanding that He blessed me with, any concerns of suicide faded.

The thought of "Could I do that too?" was only fear talking. Of course not. I'm not suicidal and I don't have suicidal thoughts. I love my life and I'm incredibly blessed in so many ways. God freed me from depression and contemplations of suicide decades ago. Couple this simple revelation with what we already discussed about Jesus being tempted with suicide, and I was free again! He released my fear and my shame. He wasn't holding the fear and shame on me, I was. I let it go and it's been gone ever since.

Work balance...

'Conundrum' is my favorite word. Being able to work AND take care of two kids was just that...a conundrum. Like being stuck between a rock and a hard place. I'm sure single parents reading this can relate. Working hard is not an issue for me, *time* is the issue. I needed time to be able to work, but understandably the kids needed much of my time also. Balancing family and work time is very important. Since losing Joy, much of my time has been figuring out this important balance.

Most days are a mixture of meals, homeschooling, working, playing with kids, house chores and a little downtime. I'm not able to spend nearly as much time working as I'd like to, but at the same time, how do I define work? In the past, I'd say 'making music and books,' but what about everything else I just described? Isn't that

Chapter 8: What Now?

also work? The point I guess I'm trying to make is that my definition of work had to change drastically in the last few years. No longer am I able to be gone 10 hours from home 'working.' I've had to learn to be OK with only being able to 'work' in certain slots during the day. As I type this, everyone's asleep and the house is dark. I can complain about not being able to make music or books as much as I'd prefer (which would accomplish nothing), or I can simply do the best I can with a good attitude, trusting that God knows what He's doing. I choose the latter.

As a side note, I have a newfound respect for single parents, both moms and dads. If you're a single parent, my hat's off to you. For me, it has been difficult, but also very rewarding.

Hope and Keep on Hoping

> Love never gives up, never loses faith, is always hopeful, and endures through every circumstance.
>
> - 1 Corinthians 13:7(NLT)

Would you sell your legs for a million dollars? No? What about your eyesight or sense of hearing? No? How much money would it take to keep you bed ridden in a coma the rest of your life? Would you do it for ten million dollars? If a close friend came up to you and covered your nose and mouth, you may find it funny. What if they did it for ten seconds, would it still be funny? I bet after a minute you'd do everything in your power, including hurting them to get one more breath. How much would that breath be worth to you in that moment? How much would the people falling to their death from the bridge give to go back ten seconds?

My point is this...you, yes YOU! You have so much to be grateful for and live for. You're still alive and above the ground. You're still breathing. You can go out into this world and *choose* to see its beauty. This day can be the day you *choose* to have a smile on your face.

You can *choose* to look at the glass half full and know today is what YOU make of it.

Action. The opposite of success is not failure, the opposite of success is quitting. One guarantee in life is that we ALL fail. It's inevitable. What separates successful people from quitters is the ability to keep going. Those that have succeeded the most have also failed the most. Babe Ruth broke the record for the most home runs in a season in 1923, but that year he also struck out more times than any other player in Major League Baseball. He was willing to fail on his way to succeed. A quitter stops after they fail, a winner does not. *Choose to be a winner,* it's a choice only you can make.

This is why a cemetery is the richest place on earth. It contains books, songs, love, beauty and 'somedays.' The *fear of failure* keeps most people from ever trying, so their hopes and dreams are buried with them. Go ahead, take a swing! Risk getting struck out. Next time, it may be a base hit, a double, or even a home run. *Keep swinging... get up...try again.*

One of the saddest things to see is a capable person, lazily wasting their life away. No goals, no ambitions, no movement, no prospects, no new ideas. You live this life ONCE! You don't get a do-over. You're worth it. You're not an accident. You're not here by happenstance. You're not some random occurrence. *You matter! You have purpose!* You must believe it though. Our beliefs will dictate what our lives look like. If you have *stinkin' thinkin'* and have believed bad things about yourself, it's simple...acknowledge it, forgive yourself for treating YOU that way, then *change.* Replace A with B. Replace self deprecation with self love.

> Now faith is the substance of things
> hoped for, the evidence of things not seen.
>
> - Hebrews 11:1(KJV)

Believe the best and hope the best. Read 1 Corinthians chapter 13. Read it out loud every morning for a month. Can you do that?

Chapter 8: What Now?

I believe it would change your life if you did. If you want to take it to the next level, in verses 4-7, say your name instead of the word *'Love.'* It can be eye opening and help you know what you need to work on.

Many years ago I heard John Maxwell say;

"The man at the top of the mountain didn't fall there."

The analogy hit me hard. One of my favorite things to do at the time was to hike to mountain tops. On all of my hikes, it was rare to see anyone else. After all, you had to risk your life to a degree. The terrain or weather could be dangerous, not to mention there are animals on the journey that would be happy to eat you.

Meaningful achievements and accomplishments in life take calculated risk and hard work. When I was young I had a childish belief that somehow I was the exception. Good things would just fall in my lap, right? In hindsight, it's amazing how naive and prideful I was. You know what I learned? I found out I was not the exception. I was put in situations that humbled me and forced me to work hard, just to survive. I hated them at the time, but looking back, the hard things in life were necessary to form who I am today. I have news for you, you're not the exception either. *No one* is the exception. There's an old Chinese proverb that says;

"A journey of a thousand miles begins with a single step."

If you aren't where you want to be, focus on the one thing achievable in this moment. What is the 'single step' you can 100% accomplish, *right now* to begin the momentum. This could be something as simple as making your bed. Cleaning your room. Vacuuming the house. Or changing your diet,...even a little.

What have you been procrastinating? Is there a certain phone call you know you should make, but haven't? Do you need to de-clutter your house? Start with one room, or even just part of the room. From my experience, our living environment is a reflexion of our inner self. Do you want to have order and discipline? Then start by having an environment of order and discipline around you.

Having consistent times for waking up and going to bed is another great way to start having order in our lives. This is known as the circadian rhythm, our internal clock. When this clock is out of whack, it can make us feel out of control. This is one area I've had to work extra hard at over the years.

Another part of having order is the foods and drinks we put into our bodies. From my experience, it's amazing the swings we can feel from just what we eat. In Dr. Jordan Peterson's bestselling book *12 Rules for Life*, he had this to say;

> "Anxiety and depression cannot be easily treated if the sufferer has unpredictable daily routines. The systems that mediate negative emotion are tightly tied to the properly cyclical circadian rhythms.
>
> The next thing I ask about is breakfast. I counsel my clients to eat a fat and protein-heavy breakfast as soon as possible after they awaken...
>
> I have had many clients whose anxiety was reduced to subclinical levels merely because they started to sleep on a predictable schedule and eat breakfast."
>
> -Dr Jordan Peterson
> *12 Rules for Life*, P. 18

Your first step from where you're at now should be a very simple one. It should be 100% certain and achievable. After doing that, you're no longer where you were! Yes, it's not a lot different, but God does not see things the way we do...

> "Do not despise these small beginnings,
> for the Lord rejoices to see the work begin..."
> -Zechariah 4:10 (NLT)

It's essential that we don't minimize the importance of the little things. *Little things are not little, they're necessary.* We can't take 50 steps at once, no one can. One small step at a time in hope and faith is the only way to improve. After you do one, you have proven you can do 50, one at a time. You're worth it. Just take the first step and keep going. You have to do what you have to do, until you can do what you were meant to do.

Face your fears

I've heard it said that the greatest fear of man is the fear of change. Why do some people stay in abusive relationships, a terrible work environment, or keep toxic friendships? It's usually the fear of change. People are rut builders and sometimes the rut gets comfortable. A monotonous rut becomes familiar and less scary than the unknown, called *change*. The unfortunate thing about a rut is the longer you're in it, the deeper it gets.

Years ago, my friend Dale (one of the greatest men I've ever known) told me something profound; "Your comfort zone is your failure zone." I've never forgotten that. Growth is uncomfortable, but vital. Stretch your rubber band a little at a time. Go a little out of your comfort zone, regularly. You'll be amazed at the fears you push through and the ruts you crawl out of.

I encourage you to face the fears you have control over. The big fears you don't have control over, give those to God. Trust Him, He's greater than all our fears. If we don't push through fear, we can be controlled by it. Our choices will be made through fear. Our opportunities will be determined by fear. Our vision will be filtered through fear. Fear is a *huge* foothold for the enemy. It's #2, right behind *pride*.

Face your fears! It fits right into the small steps in the right direction. Some of those steps will likely involve getting over fears. It's OK and it's very normal. Many things in life can seem scary, but you'll get through it. You were meant for more than to pay bills and die. Face your fears.

Wonderful Additions

Since losing Joy, I kept hope that God would bless my kids and I with another wonderful woman. Being a widower with two young kids was a position I never imagined I'd be in. Through it all, I knew at some point, God would bring me another Godly helpmate. About a year and a half after losing Joy, God fulfilled what I hoped and knew He would.

I was heading home from getting the kids signed up for swim lessons when I realized I needed gas. I pulled up to a pump at a nearby station, got out and...*there she was!* I fumbled an awkward conversation with her and then we said a simple goodbye. After she drove off, I could feel it, I messed up big time. There was something very special about her, *and I blew it.* I didn't ask her name and I didn't get her number. Growing up with a dad as a mechanic, and working for years at a body shop, I was good with cars though. I called my brothers to see if they happened to know who she was from my description of her vehicle...they didn't. For weeks I kept an eye out for her car. I saw similar ones, but not hers. One day the skies parted and the angels sang...*I saw it!* It was parked along a side street in town. I left a simple note stating who I was, where we met, and left my number.

I knew it was a long shot. I figured I'd rather come across as a weirdo than not come across at all. Days went by, until one day...*a text!* We met for coffee a few days later. It was so great to see her again. We ended up talking and sipping on coffee for hours that day. You want to know something? *We've been together almost every day since.* Her name is KT and she's such a blessing to the three of us. She's a wonderful, Jesus loving woman that's been through more difficulties in life than most people I've ever met. Through all her hardships, she remained faithful. It was very evident from our first coffee together that God had orchestrated it.

One tragic thing both her and I share is the loss of a spouse to suicide. Years ago, she lost her husband to suicide and was left destitute with three young children. It's a terrible thing to have in common,

Chapter 8: What Now?

but at the same time, it's refreshing to be with someone that understands what I'm going through. My song, *The Joy of My Life* wouldn't be what it is today without her caring and patient input. She has a strong passion for music and has been a great sounding board for me.

Today, two of her kids are all grown up and moved away, but my kids are grateful to have a new big sister with her youngest. It's been a wonderful season of God joining two broken families together, bringing healing and restoration. After experiencing the depths of such a sudden and horrible loss, I can't picture my life without these two wonderful ladies. KT has patiently helped me understand how to be a better parent to my own kids. She was a teacher to younger kids for many years, pair that with raising three kids of her own (through massive difficulties as well), and I had someone who could speak clarity into my situation.

KT's had a lifelong dream to home school her kids, write and illustrate children's books and own her own business. God is good, because that's exactly what she's doing now. KT's first book, *Gideon the Goat Beats His Fears* was released on Amazon in 2023. It's a book for helping little kids learn to overcome their fears. It follows the basic storyline of Gideon in the Bible, but told in a fun way using a silly mountain goat. Like this book, it includes the audiobook (which she reads). It's our little girls favorite book.

Pet-Tonic Nose and Paw Balm came from KT seeing our dog with a dry nose and paws. It looked uncomfortable for him, so she set out to create a natural remedy. It worked so well that she started the *Pet-Tonic* brand and launched *Pet-Tonic Nose and Paw Balm*. Search "Pet-Tonic" on Amazon or visit her website KTHOPE.COM for more info. She has more products to follow. KT and I sincerely appreciate any support of her work.

A Common Question

I want to finish this book by addressing a common question. This is another section that could easily be an entire book, but I'll make it as brief as possible. Earlier I talked about going to a friend's funeral when I was a teenager. Another eye opening part of the experience that fateful day was a response I got to a particular question. After the service was over, I asked someone I thought would know the answer, an obvious question;

"Does he go to heaven or hell after killing himself?"

The response I received didn't satisfy me...at all;

"Some denominations believe he goes to hell,
but our denomination believes he goes to heaven."

Obviously, that didn't sit well with me. God's not going to have different rules for different 'denominations.' So...someone's wrong. But who? Which denomination? 'The other one, because it's not yours?'

If there's one thing I've learned in life, it's that there's beliefs held by groups of people that are purely out of tradition, and not Biblical. People repeating what they were told, not what's actually in God's Word, because most people don't even bother to read it. How does God view man's traditions? Listen to how Jesus talked to the most religious people of His day. The very ones that had Him killed;

> So the Pharisees and teachers of religious law asked him, "Why don't your disciples follow our age-old tradition? They eat without first performing the hand-washing ceremony."
>
> Jesus replied, "You hypocrites! Isaiah was right when he prophesied about you, for he wrote,
>
> 'These people honor me with their lips, but their hearts are far

from me. Their worship is a farce, for they teach man-made ideas as commands from God.'

For you ignore God's law and substitute your own tradition."

- Mark 7:5-8 (NLT)

Let's be careful not to follow tradition, for tradition's sake. Some people have a traditional belief that everyone who commits suicide goes to hell. I have a question; where does it say that in the Bible? Go ahead and look, I'll wait....*It doesn't say that.* Yet through tradition, some cling to that understanding. I get it, suicide is bad...really bad. It's murdering yourself, murder is sin. But it's *not* unforgivable, just like stealing is *not* unforgivable.

For the wages of sin is death, but the free gift of God is eternal life through Christ Jesus our Lord.

- Romans 6:23 (NLT)

In Leviticus, we get a look at how messy cleaning up sin is. Death is what pays for sin. God warned Adam and Eve what would happen if they didn't listen, eventually their poor choice changed all of human history. Man traded a perfect world for a fallen one. Even though it wasn't His fault, because of His great love, God provided substitutes as payment for man's sins.

Many people miss the part where the first animal killed was by God Himself, used to cover Adam and Eve, and the fallout of what *they* did. God allowed animals as a temporary payment for thousands of years. Remember, sin equals death. Sin requires a payment, and death is the only payment accepted. No amount of money or sweet talking can ever satisfy that debt.

Do I fully understand all of this? No. But I know God is perfect, fair and just. He created man and woman perfect, to be imperfect is to be opposite of God. You can read in the Old Testament the kinds of things man had to do, to even be near God when he was in the tabernacle.

It wasn't because God was bad, it's because He is perfect to a degree we do not understand, and we're not even close to that degree of perfection. But as mentioned earlier, even though man messed it all up, He provided us a way of escape from our imperfection to be made perfect again. The Bible says everything created was created by and through Jesus (Colossians 1:16 and elsewhere). Imagine this, The Creator came into His own creation; *to permanently pay the full debt* that no one else and no animal ever could. The moment before He died on the cross, Jesus said this; "It is finished!" The original word used there is *tetelestai*. It's only used twice in the New Testament and both times only by Jesus, right before His death. It's a Greek accounting term used during those times on legal documents when a debt was settled.[96] Jesus was stating what had been prophesied for thousands of years beforehand. He was, is and always will be the *only* permanent payment for man's sins.

Imagine being sick in the hospital your whole life and eventually getting discharged. As you check out at the front counter they tell you the total you owe them is a billion dollars! You are dumbfounded as it's a debt that you could never possibly pay and will certainly destroy you. At that terrible moment, a man walks up and says; "I'll pay that for you, will you accept my payment?"

Each one of us has a choice to make, do we humble ourselves and let *Him* pay our astronomical debt, or do we choose to retain the debts we have accrued during our lifetime? Remember, death is the only form of payment. Every single person sins nearly every day, including you. The only question is, who pays for it? Mankind views things on a sliding scale. We judge ourselves by our intentions and everyone else by their actions. We are terrible judges, full of hypocrisy and double standards. God is not. He's perfect. Sin is sin. Someone murdering themselves is sin, just like stealing is sin, just like having a wrongful desire for a neighbor's property is sin, etc.

So, how does this relate to the question I asked at my friend's funeral service? ("Does he go to heaven or hell after killing himself?") Who is Jesus to that person? That's the answer.

Chapter 8: What Now?

There's also the subjects of headship and the age of accountability. In many places in scripture, it says "You and your household will be saved." Here is one example;

> And they said, "Believe in the Lord Jesus, and you will be saved, you and your household."
>
> - Acts 16:31 (ESV)

If a believer is in a household of unbelievers, their headship over them is of vital importance. I don't believe sex, age or relationship has anything to do with this. Who's in your household? In your heart of hearts, who have you accepted into your household? As the head of my house, subject to Jesus, my entire house is made clean. By house, I don't just mean those within these four walls. This doesn't mean they will never have a decision to make, because they certainly do, eventually. Most people think in terms of bare minimums; saved or unsaved. Let's stop thinking about what's minimally required and instead focus on being useful and productive.

> For the unbelieving husband is made holy because of his wife, and the unbelieving wife is made holy because of her husband. Otherwise your children would be unclean, but as it is, they are holy.
>
> - 1 Corinthians 7:14 (ESV)

Lastly, can a child be held accountable for suicide? From all the Biblical examples I see, children are covered by age and headship. I want to keep this simple; one example was when the Israelites were unbelieving fools in the wilderness. The people that paid for it were ages 20 and up (Numbers 32). The 'kids' 19 and under didn't pay for their participation. Also, 20 was considered the fighting age. There are other examples, but age 20 has a significant implication for becoming accountable for things. Having said that, we see some 20 year olds are mature like they're 40, and other 20 year olds are still as immature as four year olds. Fear not, God knows the difference. (1 Samuel 16:7)

Is God subject to time like we are? No. What Jesus did 2000 years ago pays for our yesterdays, today and tomorrows. If you are a parent of a child who died by suicide, I believe who you are to Jesus and claiming your child in your house covers them. Also, remember John 20:23 from earlier.

I also believe most people's understandings of heaven and hell are very skewed, mostly based on traditions and fictitious Hollywood movies. I don't want to divert the focus of this book, but people that want to understand heaven and hell better need to set aside any religious or worldly bias and instead open a Bible and get things into context.

I was hesitant to have this part in the book, but I
believe it will help bring clarity to what I'm describing:

After Joy died, the kids and I went back to Montana for a while. During our time away, my pastor, my cousin and some others volunteered to get the kids playroom looking back to normal. This was very important to me, so that when we returned to Washington, their playroom would look completely normal.

Everything in the room was hauled out. The carpet needed removed, part of the sub floor needed replaced, various items needed thrown out or replaced, new carpet installed and then everything put back the way it was. I'm so grateful they were able to work together and accomplish this important task.

Early in the process, my pastor stopped by to get some measurements, while his wife waited in the car. *This is the part that will likely poke against your understanding*...while kneeling down and measuring for the replacement piece of sub-floor, he suddenly felt Joy's presence in the room, *right behind him*. He said it was very strong, like a sense of urgency. She was trying to get his attention or communicate something.

He quickly finished what he was doing and headed toward the front door. He didn't even want to turn around. Knowing if he did, he'd see her and he wasn't prepared for that, it was too much. The sense decreased as he walked down the hall. Once outside, he asked out loud, "Lord, what was that?!"

He was instantly reminded of the morning she died. The very moment that I asked him to pray with me over her, but were prevented from doing so by the police. My pastor knew I'd forgiven and released Joy of all her actions, but in the daily to-do of things, he hadn't...and in that moment, he was reminded he hadn't.

"I agree with Chad. Joy Taylor, you are forgiven. I loose you and release you of this act." He said it was like a bubble instantly burst. Just like that, the strange sense of Joy's presence went away completely. Once he got back to the car, his wife asked what happened, because she sensed something was going on.

Headship is so little known and understood. Both my pastor and I were in positions of headship over her. For whatever reason, both of us were required to release and forgive (Matthew 18:18).

Do I fully understand all of this? No.

Do I understand what was happening spiritually? No.

Do I believe she was a ghost, stuck in the house? No.

Contrary to what tradition and Hollyweird depict, the Bible says we sleep *in* Christ after death. To me, it's like Joy was having a restless sleep and God allowed her the gift of reconciling with our pastor, an ambassador of Christ. Once that happened, I believe she's back asleep *in* Jesus. Again, do I fully understand all of this? No. *But I believe it!* Through and through (Proverbs 3:5-8). I certainly miss her, but I'm at peace knowing I'll see Joy again. I live every day in the present, surrounded by people I love.

For the Lord himself will come down from heaven with a commanding shout, with the voice of the archangel, and with the trumpet call of God. First, the believers who have died will rise from their graves. Then, together with them, we who are still alive and remain on the earth will be caught up in the clouds to meet the Lord in the air. Then we will be with the Lord forever.

- 1 Thessalonians 4:16-17 (NLT)

In Conclusion

Congratulations on making it all the way through this book! Even though I'm sure there were parts you disagreed with or were foreign to you, you kept going. Great job, I'm proud of you. My hope is that this book has helped bring you peace and a deeper understanding.

Grace. Have grace. On yourself. On your spouse. On your children. On your current situation. On your life. On those around you. On your living environment. Lean on God and enjoy life...even when it's really hard. You're worth it. Forget yesterday, don't worry about tomorrow. Live life, and that abundantly, today.

More Resources:

Years ago, I started reading one chapter of the Bible each morning. I'm not a fan of reading programs where you try to get through the Bible in a year. To me, that's a different goal; quantity over quality. We're after the spirit IN the words, not the quantity OF words.

I encourage you to keep it simple. Start at Matthew chapter one. Once you get to the end, start back over at Genesis chapter one. Then, repeat. Personally, over the years I've used the KJV, NKJV, NIV, and ESV versions, but the last few years, my favorite has been the NLT. I've found it to be a good balance between being easy to read, yet retaining the details for context. When I get to sections I want clarity on, I compare it with other versions (the Bible app or a parallel Bible helps for this).

Just one chapter in the morning, that's it. It doesn't matter how long it takes, remember, this isn't a speed reading plan. It's planting good seeds each morning. Also, I encourage you to read it out loud (with your significant other if you have one too). It's important to hear the words;

"So then faith comes by **hearing**, and **hearing** by the word of God."

- Romans 10:17 (NKJV)

More Resources Continued:

My pastor has very insightful teachings on dozens of subjects like spiritual warfare, brokenness, fear and many others. They have been very helpful to me for years now. They are all free to listen to at: **thevoiceoftruth.net** or by scanning this code;

After the Bible, there have been a handful of other books that have helped me over the years. These are my favorites, in no particular order (the QR codes are affiliate links);

Victory Over the Darkness by Neil T. Anderson ....

A More Excellent Way by Dr. Henry W. Wright ....

How to Win Friends and Influence People by Dale Carnegie

Being Happy by Andrew Matthews

Wild at Heart by John Eldredge (Especially for men)

Be Set Free From Shame, Guilt and Condemnation by Victor Chatellier

The Warrior Poet Way by John Lovell (Especially for men) ...

The Tipping Point by Malcolm Gladwell

The 360 Degree Leader by John Maxwell ....
(Or any of his other books for that matter)

Rich Dad Poor Dad by Robert Kiyosaki ....

The 5 Love Languages by Gary Chapman ....

The Slight Edge by Jeff Olson

Conclusion and Resources

Links to things mentioned in the book:

KT Hope's *Pet-Tonic*
Nose and Paw Balm:
(affiliate link)

KT Hope's book,
Gideon the Goat Beats His Fears:
(affiliate link)

The Protocol That Kills:
A TRUE CRIME STORY (affiliate link)
About my friend Rob's unexpected and horrific death.

An example video about 'The Great Reset':

An example video about
"local news stations say the same thing."

Dr. Naomi Wolf's journalism talk:

The docudrama, *Gender Transformation*
gendertransformation.com

The documentary; *What is a Woman?*
dailywire.com/videos/what-is-a-woman

About the "It's All One" Curriculum from CSE
comprehensivesexualityeducation.org

The "Died Suddenly" documentary (2022)

What you can do to help:

1. If this book was helpful, please leave a review on Amazon. Reviews are very helpful in getting this book in the hands of others like yourself. Simply go to the book on Amazon, look at the review section and add yours. Thank you in advance!

2. Consider loaning or giving a copy of this book to someone else. There's only so much I can do myself, but if everyone passed along a copy to someone that needs it, imagine the positive impact it could make. (I keep copies in my car and give them out regularly).

3. Subscribe to my YouTube channel and follow me on Instagram:

   My YouTube Channel:  My Instagram:
   @ChadTaylorMusic   #chad_taylor.music

4. I'm strongly considering starting a non-profit for helping struggling suicide survivors who lost their spouse, especially those with children. My vision would be to help them focus on the early important things by helping with their bills for the first few months. From experience, there's so much to deal with early on (especially with children), that helping with the initial financial burden is a monumental way to help while they get back on their feet.

   I am trying to get an idea if people would support this charity before starting it. If this is something you'd consider supporting, please leave me a message at **chadtaylor.com** (code at bottom). I will send any updates about it to the email list.

5. Check out my website and let me know how this book has helped you. God deserves all of the credit for this book and the good fruit that comes from it. I'd love to hear how He helped you through this book. You can leave me a message at **chadtaylor.com** and also subscribe to my email list.

ChadTaylor.com:

References:

#1. https://www.cdc.gov/injury/wisqars/animated-leading-causes.html
#2. https://save.org/wp-content/uploads/2022/01/2020datapgsv1a-3.pdf
#3. https://www.cdc.gov/suicide/suicide-data-statistics.html
#4. https://www.samhsa.gov/data/sites/default/files/reports/rpt35325/NSDUHFFRPDFWHTMLFiles2020/2020NSDUHFFR1PDFW102121.pdf
#5. https://ourworldindata.org/suicide
#6. https://web.archive.org/web/20061108171731/http://www.newyorker.com/fact/content/articles/031013fa_fact
#7. https://www.forkidsandcountry.org/get-educated-about-sexxx-ed-toolkit/#none
#8. https://www.comprehensivesexualityeducation.org/
#9. https://en.wikipedia.org/wiki/Th2022/01StateNumberOfSui1990to2020TABLE.pdf
#14. https://nbcmontana.com/news/local/youth-suicides-in-kalispell-continue-to-grow-community-takes-a-stance
#15. https://news.yahoo.com/kalispell-schools-offer-counseling-resources-130800987.html
#16. https://dailyinterlake.com/news/2021/sep/19/families-students-left-reeling-after-several-death/
#17. https://en.wikipedia.org/wiki/First_they_came_...
#18. https://www.pacer.org/bullying/info/stats.asp
#19. https://news.yale.edu/2008/07/16/bullying-suicide-link-explored-new-study-researchers-yale
#20. https://www.health.harvard.edu/blog/what-parents-should-know-and-do-about-young-children-and-mobile-devices-2017102412619
#21. https://www.history.com/news/8-reasons-why-rome-fell
#22. https://www.foxnews.com/politics/oregon-allowing-15-year-olds-to-get-state-subsidized-sex-change-operations
#23. https://www.ncbi.nlm.nih.gov/pmc/articles/PMC6583682/
#24. https://save.org/about-suicide/suicide-statistics/
#25. https://www.nimh.nih.gov/health/statistics/major-depression
#26. https://en.wikipedia.org/wiki/Spotlight_effect
#27. U.S. Department of Veterans Affairs, Office of Mental Health and Suicide Prevention. 2022 National Veteran Suicide Prevention Annual Report. 2022. Retrieved 4/12/23 from https://www.mentalhealth.va.gov/suicide_prevention/data.asp.
#28. https://americanaddictioncenters.org/veterans/suicide-among-veterans
#29. https://www.psychologytoday.com/us/blog/the-well-lived-life/202103/covid-19-and-how-it-affects-our-children
#30. https://www.medicalnewstoday.com/articles/solitary-confinement-effects#mental-health-effects
#31. https://en.wikipedia.org/wiki/Suicides_at_the_Golden_Gate_Bridge
#32. https://mynorthwest.com/2666243/doc-washington-correctional-center-women-men-transfer/
#33. https://nypost.com/2022/04/14/edna-mahan-womens-prisoners-pregnant-after-sex-with-transgender-inmate/

#34. https://nypost.com/2022/04/04/swimmer-who-tied-lia-thomas-taken-aback-in-trophy-handling/
#35. https://www.comprehensivesexualityeducation.org/
#36. https://www.washingtonexaminer.com/news/father-jailed-defy-court-order-discuss-gender-transition
#37. https://www.huffpost.com/entry/margaret-sanger-eugenics-birth-control-planned-parenthood_n_5f1f2a40c5b638cfec4893a8
#38. https://www.lifenews.com/2020/09/23/planned-parenthood-puts-86-of-its-abortion-facilities-in-minority-neighborhoods/
#39. From the documentary Connect. https://connectmovie.com/
#40. https://www.bmj.com/content/347/bmj.f5239
#41. https://pubmed.ncbi.nlm.nih.gov/1932152/
#42. https://store.samhsa.gov/sites/default/files/d7/priv/sma16-4935.pdf
#43. https://www.hhs.gov/about/news/2023/01/04/samhsa-announces-national-survey-drug-use-health-results-detailing-mental-illness-substance-use-levels-2021.html
#44. https://www.oxfordlearnersdictionaries.com/us/definition/english/pharmacy
#45. https://www.etymonline.com/word/pharmacy
#46. https://www.dictionary.com/browse/pharmacy
#47. https://strongsconcordance.org/results.html?k=5332
#48. https://biblehub.com/greek/5331.htm
#49. https://strongsconcordance.org/results.html?k=5331
#50. https://hpi.georgetown.edu/rxdrugs/#
#51. https://www.singlecare.com/blog/news/prescription-drug-statistics/
#52. https://drugabusestatistics.org/prescription-drug-abuse-statistics/
#53. https://www.ncbi.nlm.nih.gov/books/NBK430763/
#54. https://www.propublica.org/article/we-found-over-700-doctors-who-were-paid-more-than-a-million-dollars-by-drug-and-medical-device-companies
#55. https://www.forbes.com/sites/roberthart/2023/02/07/heres-why-big-pharma-spends-more-on-ads-pushing-lower-benefit-drugs-study-suggests/?sh=32416834711b
#56. https://www.statista.com/statistics/184914/prescription-drug-expenditures-in-the-us-since-1960/
#57. https://www.britannica.com/science/Milgram-experiment
#58. https://progressreport.cancer.gov/after/economic_burden
#59. https://pubmed.ncbi.nlm.nih.gov/25355584/
#60. https://blogs.bmj.com/bmj/2016/06/16/peter-c-gotzsche-prescription-drugs-are-the-third-leading-cause-of-death/
#61. https://www.cdc.gov/injury/features/prescription-drug-overdose/index.html
#62. https://www.webmd.com/a-to-z-guides/ss/slideshow-medical-mistakes
#63. https://www.findlaw.com/healthcare/patient-rights/can-i-sue-vaccine-manufacturers-.html
#64. https://www.cnbc.com/2020/12/16/covid-vaccine-side-effects-compensation-lawsuit.html
#65. https://www.menshealth.com/health/a19520982/3-meds-with-the-craziest-side-effects-ever/
#66. https://nymag.com/news/features/43892/

References

#67. https://www.reuters.com/article/us-smoking-drug-idUKTRE7A181220111102
#68. https://iea.org.uk/publications/did-lockdowns-work-the-verdict-on-covid-restrictions/#
#69. https://www.reuters.com/business/healthcare-pharmaceuticals/pfizer-recalls-all-lots-anti-smoking-drug-over-carcinogen-presence-2021-09-16/
#70. https://www.nationalgeographic.com/science/article/chantix-suicide-and-the-point-of-prescription-drug-warnings
#71. https://www.fda.gov/drugs/postmarket-drug-safety-information-patients-and-providers/suicidality-children-and-adolescents-being-treated-antidepressant-medications
#72. https://www.justice.gov/civil/vicp
#73. https://vaers.hhs.gov/about.html
#74. https://www.imdb.com/title/tt23810972/
#75. https://nypost.com/2023/02/06/911-dispatch-reveals-lindsay-clancy-suffered-neck-lacerations/
#76. https://nypost.com/2023/02/06/mass-mom-lindsay-clancy-to-be-arraigned-from-hospital-bed-on-charges-of-murdering-her-children/
#77. https://news.yahoo.com/unsealed-court-documents-reveal-dozens-100925404.html
#78. https://www.patriotledger.com/story/news/2023/02/07/lindsay-clancy-judge-plymouth-court-deaths-cora-dawson-callan-army-of-love/69878042007/
#79. https://ourworldindata.org/water-access#access-to-safe-drinking-water
#80. https://www.ala.org/aboutala/intellectual-freedom-quotes
#81. https://dictionary.cambridge.org/us/dictionary/english/divide-and-conquer
#82. https://www.mpe.mpg.de/ir/lucifer
#83. https://www.youtube.com/watch?v=GuB6wavzcww&t=33s
#84. https://www.health.harvard.edu/a_to_z/phobia-a-to-z
#85. https://www.ncbi.nlm.nih.gov/pmc/articles/PMC10027312/
#86. https://www.thegatewaypundit.com/2023/03/we-were-wrong-evidence-shows-puberty-blockers-are-neither-safe-nor-reversible-says-canadian-doctor-who-helped-pioneered-puberty-blocker-drugs/
#87. https://www.youtube.com/watch?v=4RrLPn3h5dQ
#88. https://nypost.com/2023/04/29/transabled-people-choosing-to-identify-as-handicapped/
#89. https://en.wikipedia.org/wiki/Hippocratic_Oath
#90. https://www.pbs.org/wgbh/nova/article/hippocratic-oath-today/
#91. https://www.msn.com/en-us/news/us/trans-athlete-sparks-outrage-after-toppling-womens-powerlifting-world-record-completely-unfair/ar-AA1fwTQk
#92. https://nypost.com/2023/06/24/drag-marchers-spark-outrage-with-chant-at-nyc-pride-event-were-here-were-queer-and-were-coming-for-your-children/
#93. https://www.dailywire.com/videos/what-is-a-woman
#94. https://gendertransformation.com/
#95. https://www.reuters.com/article/uk-factcheck-lincoln-quote-fake/fact-check-false-quote-attributed-to-abraham-lincoln-is-distortion-of-an-1838-speech-idUSKBN29V2HH
#96. https://bible.org/question/what-does-greek-word-tetelestai-mean

#97. https://www.youtube.com/watch?v=doaHPFWEa7E
#98. https://www.youtube.com/watch?v=NcAO4-o_4Ug
#99. https://williamsinstitute.law.ucla.edu/wp-content/uploads/LGBT-Youth-US-Pop-Sep-2020.pdf
#100. https://en.wikipedia.org/wiki/Alexander_Fraser_Tytler%2C_Lord_Woodhouselee
#101. https://pubmed.ncbi.nlm.nih.gov/21364939/
#102. https://journals.plos.org/plosone/article?id=10.1371/journal.pone.0016885
#103. https://theconversation.com/factcheck-qanda-was-lyle-shelton-right-about-transgender-people-and-a-higher-suicide-risk-after-surgery-55573
#104. https://thehill.com/homenews/education/3975959-one-in-four-high-school-students-identify-as-lgbtq/
#105. https://en.wikipedia.org/wiki/Illusory_truth_effect
#106. https://thehill.com/homenews/wire/3514357-dallas-drag-queen-event-for-kids-sparks-outrage-defense/
#107. https://www.ala.org/advocacy/libraries-respond-drag-queen-story-hour
#108. https://nypost.com/2022/06/11/over-200k-being-spent-on-drag-queen-shows-at-nyc-schools/
#109. https://www.christianpost.com/news/texas-church-location-hosts-family-friendly-drag-show.html
#110. https://www.foxnews.com/us/masked-antifa-protesters-show-brandishing-weapons-texas-drag-bunch-kids
#111. https://www.dailymail.co.uk/news/article-12213579/How-schools-allowing-kids-identify-cats-horses-dinosaurs.html
#112. https://thefederalist.com/2023/03/24/youve-probably-never-been-woman-of-the-year-but-these-9-men-have/
#113. https://www.youtube.com/watch?v=6fcyZE3B7yc
#114. https://www.newsweek.com/boycott-tampax-trends-company-slammed-trans-sponsors-1761556
#115. https://www.fox43.com/article/life/food/hershey-womens-history-month-ad-campaign-transgender/521-ce85cf83-2399-4d6d-b352-e4639ffb5c69
#116. https://www.goodreads.com/quotes/34152-the-most-terrifying-words-in-the-english-language-are-i-m
#117. https://www.usnews.com/news/politics/articles/2023-03-14/sanders-signs-arkansas-trans-care-malpractice-bill-into-law
#118. https://nypost.com/2022/03/30/disney-is-boasting-about-pushing-gender-theory-to-kids/
#119. https://www.nationalreview.com/corner/merriam-webster-changes-the-definition-of-female/
#120. https://www.cnn.com/2020/11/09/world/woman-definition-revised-oxford-dictionary-trnd/index.html
#121. https://www.deseret.com/2022/12/27/23516893/definition-of-woman-dictionary-gender-recognition-certificate
#122. https://www.breitbart.com/europe/2022/08/12/disgraced-trans-tavistock-child-clinic-faces-lawsuits-from-1000-families/
#123. https://www.cnn.com/2023/07/31/entertainment/kris-tyson-mrbeast-hormone-replacement-therapy-cec/index.html

References

#124. https://www.californiafamily.org/2022/09/gov-newsom-signs-bill-to-strip-children-from-parents-to-medically-transgender-them/
#125. https://www.californiafamily.org/2023/09/ca-legislators-pass-bill-to-take-children-from-parent-who-doesnt-affirm-kids-gender-identity/
#126. https://globalnews.ca/news/6399468/bc-gender-change-court/
#127. https://www.independent.co.uk/news/uk/home-news/church-of-england-god-gender-neutral-b2277911.html
#128. https://www.washingtonexaminer.com/news/military-transgender-surgery-free
#129. https://www.military.com/daily-news/2021/06/18/heres-how-much-pentagon-has-spent-so-far-treat-transgender-troops.html
#130. https://www.newsweek.com/johns-hopkins-accused-trying-erase-women-its-lesbian-term-1806134
#131. https://www.christianpost.com/news/four-companies-facing-backlash-for-pushing-transgenderism.html?page=5
#132. https://www.goodreads.com/quotes/13915-freedom-is-never-more-than-one-generation-away-from-extinction
#133. https://www.dictionary.com/browse/outlet
#134. https://www.merriam-webster.com/dictionary/outlet
#135. https://www.dictionary.com/browse/narcissistic
#136. https://www.dictionary.com/browse/illicit
#137. https://www.merriam-webster.com/dictionary/illicit
#138. https://www.dictionary.com/browse/amplify
#139. https://www.dictionary.com/browse/complacency
#140. https://www.merriam-webster.com/dictionary/complacency
#141. https://www.dictionary.com/browse/inception
#142. https://www.merriam-webster.com/dictionary/inception
#143. https://www.dictionary.com/browse/Divide
#144. https://www.dictionary.com/browse/Conquer
#145. https://www.merriam-webster.com/dictionary/conquer
#146. https://www.dictionary.com/browse/artificial
#147. https://www.dictionary.com/browse/scarcity
#148. https://www.dictionary.com/browse/propaganda
#149. https://www.dictionary.com/browse/phobia
#150. https://www.dictionary.com/browse/affirm
#151. https://www.merriam-webster.com/dictionary/affirm
#152. https://www.dictionary.com/browse/grace
#153. https://www.merriam-webster.com/dictionary/grace
#154. https://www.azquotes.com/author/5626-Joseph_Goebbels
#155. https://www.bbc.com/news/stories-55854145
#156. https://www.cbsnews.com/pictures/blowing-smoke-vintage-ads-of-doctors-endorsing-tobacco/
#157. https://bigthink.com/health/milk-transfusion/
#158. https://science.howstuffworks.com/life/biology-fields/10-bizarre-treatments.htm
#159. https://www.cbsnews.com/pictures/15-most-bizarre-medical-treatments-ever/4/

TIME STOOD STILL

About the Author:

Chad Taylor is a music composer, author, public speaker and entrepreneur. Suicide has been an unexpected, yet integral part of his life. His hope is to inspire others to live an incredibly fulfilling life, free of the bondage of suicide. He's been through the minefield of this dark and misunderstood subject and shares what he learned with others.

Chad grew up in Northwest Montana with a love for music, adventure and the great outdoors. Due to his success in business and as an author, he has been invited to speak across the country to thousands of people. He is incredibly grateful for all of the opportunities he has been blessed with and all the wonderful people he's met along the way. He and his family moved from the mountains of Montana and now call Texas home.

Stay up to date with Chad:

ChadTaylor.com

Chad on Instagram

Chad's YouTube Channel

Emergency Suicide Number, call or text 988

**National Suicide Prevention Hotline
1-800-273-8255**

Milton Keynes UK
Ingram Content Group UK Ltd.
UKHW020927051124
450766UK00014B/1138